KU-792-181

F.E. STRAND
1991

Lazar Trifunović

YUGOSLAVIA
MONUMENTS OF ART

from prehistory
to the present day

YUGOSLAVIA

from prehistory to the present day

General editor:
RADOJKO MRLJEŠ

Consultant:
Dr. SRETEN PETKOVIĆ

Editor:
TATJANA STANOJEVIĆ

Translated by:
VESELIN KOSTIĆ

Art and Technical Editor:
BOLE MILORADOVIĆ

lazar trifunović
MONUMENTS OF ART

jugoslovenska knjiga, belgrade, 1988.

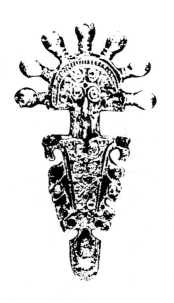

THE WORD ABOUT THIS BOOK

During the long and frequent walks along the left bank of the Sava, my friend Bole Miloradović and I had many talks. Of the many projects that were conceived during these conversations, some floated down the Sava and some have been carried into practice. This book of Professor Lazar Trifunović on the monuments of culture in Yugoslavia is one of the latter ones.

It is a sad thought that Professor Trifunović is no longer among the living and cannot see his work published in his mother tongue, but this book on the monuments of culture in Yugoslavia will remain an enduring contribution to Yugoslav cultural heritage.

There have been various ideas as to how this text should be presented to the reader. The present form, with colour illustrations, has been chosen because it seemed to us that it presents the rich artistic heritage of Yugoslavia in the most suitable way.

Profesor Sreten Petković, a historian of art and a close friend of Professor Trifunovć, has given us invaluable help in the preparation of the press. He has selected the illustrations, revised the text and updated some entries.

In presenting this book to the readers we hope that they will find it a helpful and reliable guide to the cultural heritage of Yugoslavia and that it will make their travels in Yugoslavia more exciting and meaningful.

Radojko Mrlješ

Belgrade, summer 1987

The Socialist Federative Republic of Yugoslavia consists of six republics (The Socialist Republics of Bosnia and Herzegovina, Croatia, Montenegro, Macedonia, Serbia and Slovenia) and two autonomous provinces (The Federal Autonomous Provinces of Vojvodina and Kosovo) which are a part of the Socialist Republic of Serbia. The nations and nationalities which form the present-day Yugoslavia were united for the first time in 1918 and attained their full national recognition only in 1945, after the end of the People's Liberation War and the revolution. Previously, their historical developments had been independent and diverse, and that is clearly reflected in their monuments of culture. There are so many of them in Yugoslavia that they have not been fully inventoried yet,

although much work has been done in this respect by all the republican institutions for the preservation of the monuments of art. Therefore I have been compelled to make a rigorous selection of monuments in this book. In doing this, I have tried to include the most representative examples from all epochs.

In the writing of this book I have benefited by the advice of numerous colleagues, but I should like to express my particular thanks to Dr. Emilijan Cevac, Prof. Sreten Petković, Dr. Gojko Subotić, Prof. Miodrag Jovanović, Prof. Dragoslav Srejović, Dr. Andrija Andrejević, and Mr. Dušan Tasić. I am also very grateful to Dr. Vojislav Matić for his help in the preparation of the drawings and maps.

L. T.

The territory of modern Yugoslavia is bounded by the Adriatic Sea, the Pannonian plain, the foothills of the Alps, the Carpathians, the Balkan and the Rhodopes. This region, cut through by large rivers and consisting of fertile plains and woody mountains, enjoys a pleasant Mediterranean or mild continental climate and has been from times immemorial a favourable ambience for the development and sustenance of human communities. Three major European communication lines passed through it: one led along the Danube, the Morava and the Vardar rivers to the Aegean Sea, the second ran from Asia Minor to the Pannonian plain and on to Central Europe, and the third led through the Ljubljana pass, connecting the Bay of Trieste and the Mediterranean with the Baltic. The historical development and evolution of art did not have an even and peaceful course along these routes. This region saw great migrations of peoples; various cultures and civilizations replaced one another; powerful states emerged and mighty empires fell; people were afflicted by wars, disastrous, earthquakes and devastating epidemics, so that many towns were several times razed or burnt to the ground. In spite of all this, man fought against the adverse forces of destiny by building edifices, making sculptures and painting pictures, and thus saved from oblivion the human values of his time. These monuments of art have been preserved, sometimes as remains only, to the present day, and it is with them that this book is concerned.

PREHISTORY AND CLASSICAL
ANTIQUITY

In the territory of Yugoslavia, as in other regions, life is older than art. The first traces of habitation in this region are still insufficiently known and hidden in the darkness of early prehistory. The earliest anthropological remains and fragments of primitive stone implements were found in the caves of Risovača, Kutina, Makljenovac and Crvena Stijena, and belong to the Moustérian period. We do not know the course of evolution from these earliest communities of Ice Age hunters to the early pre-pottery Neolithic, but we do know that as early as the 6th millennium B. C. a mature and unique culture appeared at Lepenski Vir. Its houses, with the ground plan in the form of a trapeze and a decorated hearth, and its monumental sculptures with fishlike human heads are almost without parallel in the proto-Neolithic cultures of Europe. The art of Lepenski Vir, which developed in the wild and rugged region of the Iron Gates, on the very bank of the Danube, illustrates excellently the transition from a hunting-gathering economy to farming. An architecture based on strict proportions, naturalistic representation of man in sculpture and a complex ornamental system in relief carvings represent the external attributes of a culture in which magic taboos and rituals were the basic means through which man communicated with nature and the universe.

The art of Neolithic farmers has left deeper traces in the cultural history of the Yugoslav territory. From the 4th millennium B. C. onward it spread almost all over this region and its main centres were Starčevo and Vinča, Kakanj and Butmir, Vučedol and Bijelo Polje, Ljubljansko Barje and Drulovka, Predionica and Demir Kapija. These were settlements with pile-dwellings, wattle-and-daub houses and sunk dwellings in which the polishing of stone for the production of implements and weapons was perfected and the art of pottery--making was discovered. The Neolithic art was decorative and functional, because it was a combined response to man's intellectual and material needs. The ornaments were geometric and abstract, made by engraving, painting or scratching. There seems to be no geometric design which the Neolithic potter did not use for the decoration of his vessels: horizontal, vertical and zig-zag lines, triangles, rhombs, spirals and meanders. We do not know the symbolical significance of these motifs, but some meaning they must have had, for these ornaments were in such frequent, everyday use that it is quite likely that they stood for some archetypal images which dominated the spiritual life of the Neolithic man. As opposed to the expressive naturalism of Lepenski Vir, the Neolithic artist subjected the human and animal figures to severe stylization. This change in the mode of artistic expression was caused by a new way of life, by the psychology of the farmer and his different attitude to nature and the world around him. The Palaeolithic hunter depended on his own ability and skill to catch the quarry, and his magic ritual aimed at the engagement of the psychic energy in his identification with the animal. The existence of the Neolithic farmer was conditioned by the fertility of the soil, the climate, the weather conditions — in other words, by divine powers which he was not able to explain or identify with. He had to serve them, to worship them and to propitiate them. Magic was replaced by the cult of the soil, and therefore an important and common product of the Neolithic culture was the earthenware female figure representing Mother Goddess, the supreme divinity of the farmers. These are stylized figurines, without naturalistic details, with scratched lines and coloured bands, which testify to a very refined sense of abstract and symbolic expression.

The Neolithic tribal and communal organization disintegrated with the discovery of metal and its use. The social differentiation and separation of smaller groups within the larger community, the appearance of ownership and of wealthy families, the division of labour and the differences between occupations resulted in a new structure of society, which found its artistic expression in new techniques and new forms. Belts and masks, bronze ear-rings, bracelets and fibulae, knives, swords and helmets, vessels, votive sculptures and representations of deities were decorated with copious and various ornaments. Numerous centres and large settlements, with good workshops for the production of metal vessels, weapons, jewelry, ritual and decorative objects, such as Vatin, Žuto Brdo, Ptuj, Vrebac, Glasinac, Vače, developed in the territory of Yugoslavia in the Metal Age. Towards the middle of the 2nd millennium the geometric style of the Bronze Age reached its climax (the *Chariot from Dupljaja,* the *Idol from Kličevac*), after which it declined, undergoing a crisis towards the end of the millennium, which lasted two centuries. About the 8th century, in the period of transition from the Bronze Age to the Iron Age, the ancient Balkan populations already included the Illyrians, who were distributed, in several tribal communities, throughout the central part of this territory. The tribes of the Thracians, also of Indo-European origin, settled in the eastern and southern regions. Applied arts began to flourish among the Illyrians and the Thracians, and the geometric style was revived at the end of the 6th century B. C. The graves of Illyrian princes, with rich silver and gold grave goods consisting not only of Illyrian products, but also of objects of the Greek archaic culture, show that the autochthonous populations had a complex social organization, with a tribal aristocracy at its head. From the 4th century B. C. new social, ethnical and cultural processes began: the Celts penetrated from the north along the Danube, bringing the superior La Tène culture, while a strong Greek influence spread in Macedonia and along the Adriatic coast. Pressed from two sides, the Illyrians withdrew into the central parts of this territory, where they preserved the vital forms of their autochthonous art for a long time.

In the Hellenistic age the Greek cultural tradition continued to expand in the old homeland of the Illyrians and the Thracians. Greek colonies were founded in the Adriatic as early as the 4th and 3rd centuries B. C. They included Vis, Hvar, Korčula, Trogir and Budva, where strong urban centres developed and in which a cultural symbiosis of the Greek and Illyrian populations was gradually achieved. The same developments took place in the towns in Macedonia (Stobi, Ohrid, Heraclea). In addition to the products of local schools and workshops, in which native traditions were fostered, numerous Greek imports were to be found in these towns and colonies. All sorts of products, were imported: copies of the works of famous sculptors (Lisyppus, Praxiteles, Phidias), steles, gold and silver jewelry, terracotta figurines from Beotia, vases from Attica and Sicily, pottery from Pergamon, bronze figures from Alexandria.

After the Roman conquests the situation in the Illyricum changed considerably. As early as the 2nd century the Romans crushed the resistance of the Illyrians, took Macedonia and incorporated the earlier Greek colonies into their state. At the beginning of the 1st century A. D. they increased pressure from the north and, having suppressed a great Illyrian rebellion, the so-called "bellum Batonianum", they finally subjugated the entire territory of present-day Yugoslavia. This territory was divided into several administrative provinces — Noricum, Pannonia, Dalmatia, Moesia Superior, Thrace, Dacia, Macedonia. It defended the Roman Empire from the inroads of the barbarians, and its wealth in minerals and timber was exploited to the greatest possible extent. Therefore it made fast progress: good roads were constructed, the northern frontier towards Dacia (the *limes*) was fortified with towers and military stations, and large and rich towns, in which several Roman emperors were born, were founded. The skilful Roman builders constructed a number of striking monuments: the amphitheatre in Pula, the road through the Djerdap gorge, the bridge across the Danube near Kladovo and a masterpiece of Roman architecture — Diocletian's palace in Split. Well-ordered towns with good amenities, such as Solin, Sirmium, Naissus, Stobi, Caričin Grad or Heraclea, had theatres, baths, public buildings with mosaics and tombs with frescoes. Mosaic was the favourite technique, although Roman artists were very good at sculptured ornaments, too. Roman sculpture is not of so noble proportions as the Greek sculpture, but it does have a powerful expressiveness and it is more life-like. In other techniques, too, the Romans proved themselves skilful artists and good craftsmen: in the minting of coins and medals, in the working of precious stones, in the production of earthenware and glass vessels, in the casting of bronze and in gold-working.

After the division of the Roman Empire, some Roman provinces in this territory passed under the dominion of Byzantium, and this led to a renewed, but brief development of towns. The spreading of Christianity, the establishment of episcopal centres, the building of churches and the reconstruction of towns led to increasingly complex forms of life and art. However, the penetration of the Goths and the invasion of the Huns, and, later, the arrival of the Slavs and Avars into the Danubian basin marked the beginning of the end of the classical world in the Balkans. The great communication routes were severed and the towns were either devastated by the Slavs and the Avars, who began their incursions across the Danube at the end of the 6th and the beginning of the 7th century, or destroyed in earthquakes. Out of this obscure period of struggles between Byzantium, the Avars and the Franks, which lasted two whole centuries, there emerged the vital Slav element. During the 7th, 8th and 9th centuries the Slavs made various tribal alliances, which were not always lasting or firmly organized. As early as the 7th century the Slavs in Macedonia had tribal leagues headed by princes, against which Byzantium moved ruthlessly on several occasions. In the west, the independent principality of Karantania established itself after the collapse of the great alliance of the Slav tribes under the leadership of Prince Sam, and it succeeded in preserving its independence until the first decades of the 10th century, in spite of the constant onslaughts of the Langobards, the Franks and the Avars. Dalmatian Croatia, founded on the slopes of Velebit, was the nucleus of the future state, and when Prince Ljudevit in the Sava region of Croatia raised a major rebellion against the Franks (819—822), he was supported by the Slovenes from Karantania and Pannonia and by the tribe of the Timočani, who came from the east. This period also saw the formation of tribal alliances of the Serbs in the regions of Zahumlje, Travunia, Doclea and Rascia. With the coming and spreading of Christianity (Cyrilus and Methodius and their disciples Clement and Naum) substantial changes took place in the cultural development of the Slavs: the first Slav alphabet was created, manuscripts were copied, churches were constructed and foundations were laid for firmly organized states.

PRE-ROMANESQUE
AND ROMANESQUE ART

In the towns on the Adriatic coast the Middle
Ages began when they were incorporated into
the Dalmatian thema and the Ravenna exarchate, i. e. when Byzantium established its administrative and political domination in the
Adriatic basin. Its influence in this territory is
most clearly seen in the basilica at Poreč and in
its representative mosaics from the Justinianian
epoch, but it is also noticeable in the later,
Romanesque architecture and frescoes. The developments in this area in the early Middle
Ages are not sufficiently known since the scant
historical evidence concerns mainly the struggle
against the Avars and the Franks, which complicated even more the complex relations of the
Dalmatian towns with the neighbouring states.
Two processes were, however, of special historical importance: the Slavization of the native
population in the towns, which was sometimes
fiercely resisted by the Hellenized and Romanized Illyrian element, and, somewhat later, the
conversion of the Slav population to Christianity. These processes were speeded up after the
termination of the war against the Franks and
after the conclusion of the Aachen peace in 812
A. D., when Istria was incorporated into the
Frankish Empire and Byzantium re-organized,
administratively and economically, the towns in
the Dalmatian thema. It was then that pre-Romanesque style began to spread on the islands
and in small settlements in the mountainous
hinterland, where the nucleus of the early
Croatian state was forming round popular
leaders. As early as 862 A. D. Croatia had
a prince, Trpimir, whose seat was at Nin.
At the end of the century a bishopric was
founded in that place, and the church service

in it was held in the vernacular. At the beginning of the 10th century Croatia attained considerable power: it had a strong army and navy,
and under King Tomislav (910—930) it extended its territory into the Pannonian plain as far
as the Drava river. It was during this period
of expansion and administrative stability that
many churches were built. These were small and
simple buildings with autochthonous forms and
spatial arrangement, which did not depend on
Eastern or Western models, but were based on
the native carving and building traditions. They
are usually built of broken or roughly hewn
stone, and their facades are enlivened by lesenes, shallow niches and blind arcades. Their
ground plans are very varied and original, even
strikingly imaginative in the organization of
space. In addition to the usual single-nave
church (St Peter at Priko, St Michael at Ston)
and the basilica with the nave and two aisles
(St Barbara at Trogir), there appear buildings
with a central circular design in several variants:
the pure rotunda (St Donatus in Zadar), the
trefoil plan (the Church of the Holy Cross in
Nin), the ground plan with six semicurcular
niches (St Trinity in Split) and even the plan
with eight semicircular niches, as in the church
at Ošalj near Ston.

These buildings had sculptured decoration
on the portals, round the windows, and on
church furniture (altarpieces, ciboria, baptismal
fonts). Carved in shallow relief, strongly linear
and usually in the form of a geometric design
formed by three interlaced bands, this decoration also represents a valuable historical
source, for it contains inscriptions with the
names of early Croatian princes. This has made
it possible to date these reliefs into the period
between the 9th and the 11th century. We find
inscriptions on the baptismal font of Prince
Višeslav in Nin, on the altar screen from Riž-
nice near Klis with the name of Prince Trpimir, on the altar screen from Gornji Muć,
which mentions Prince Branimir, and on the
gable of the Church of St Luke at Uzdolje near
Knin, which refers to Prince Mutimir. The
early examples of these plaitwork reliefs do not

show the human figure. It appears only later, in the 11th century, as on a panel from the Split baptistry, on the stonework from the destroyed Church of St Domenica in Zadar, or on the *pluteus* from the Church of St Lawrence in Zadar. These are representative examples of pre-Romanesque figural reliefs in which the human figure is treated with geometric linearity, although the *pluteus* from St Lawrence already shows a tendency towards modelling and fully sculpturesque forms. However, carved decoration with the three interlaced bands as the dominant motif did not develop only in central Dalmatia and on the islands; it was the style of the epoch and it spread southward (Ulcinj, Bar, Kotor) and inland, into the Bosnian hinterland (Zavala, Glamoč).

At the end of the 11th and the beginning of the 12th century the entire artistic activity on the Adriatic coast was dominated by Romanesque style. The urban communities attained a remarkable level of economic, political and cultural development. Life in them was considerably more complex than earlier; their needs became more varied, urban amenities were improved, public buildings, palaces and dwelling houses were constructed (Trogir) and a number of towns from Kotor, Dubrovnik and Zadar to Poreč and Piran were encircled with strong fortifications. Romanesque style was introduced into Dalmatia by the Benedictines from Monte Cassino, who began to restore the ruined and neglected churches and to found new monasteries in the favourable political atmosphere under Krešimir IV and Zvonimir (the first king to rule the entire territory of the Byzantine thema of Dalmatia). In addition to monastic churches and small domed single-nave buildings (St Luke and the Church of the Virgin in Kotor), which show strong traces of Byzantine influence, large cathedral churches were built in many towns on the Adriatic coast during the Romanesque epoch (Kotor, Dubrovnik, Zadar, Trogir, Rab). These are basilicas with the nave and two aisles, furnished with elaborate portals, rosettes, niches, blind arcades and galleries. Adjoining them were frequently high bell-towers, some of which are real masterpieces of Romanesque architecture, such as the campanile of the Church of the Virgin in Zadar or the belfries of the cathedrals of Rab and Split.

Romanesque style was not confined to the coastal region; we find it in other territories, too — in Bosnia, Serbia (Studenica, Dečani) and northern Croatia (Bapska, Rudine). It attained its most elaborate form in Slovenia, which it reached together with the Benedictines, whose monastery at Gornji Grad was founded by Dietbald de Chager, a nobleman, in 1140. The church of this monastery, a basilica with a nave, two aisles and three semicircular apses, was finished already at the end of the 12th century. Members of two other monastic orders also built their churches in Romanesque style — the Cistercians at Stična and the Carthusians at Žiča. In Slovenia, however, there developed three types of small-size Romanesque single--nave basilicas: with a semicircular apse (St Martin at Zgornja Draga); with a square presbytery (St Primož above Kamnik); and with a bell-tower on the eastern side (St Vitus at Dravograd). Small town chapels, such as that in Mali Grad at Kamnik and very rare rotundas (Selo in Prekomurje and the Baptistry in Koper) complete this typology of churches.

Romanesque sculpture is very rare in Slovenia. The carved decoration on the portals in Mali Grad at Kamnik and in Špitalič is very modest, but the wooden sculpture of the Virgin with Christ from Velesovo (beginning of the 13th century) is very valuable indeed. The Adriatic coast, on the other hand, saw a vigorous development of Romanesque sculpture in the 13th century. It emancipated itself completely from pre-Romanesque linearism and, turning to the classical traditions, it abandoned the anonymous, collective expression of the geometric ornament. In 1214 master Andrija Buvina finished the carving on the great door of the Split cathedral. The twenty-eight panels, framed with floral ornaments, illustrate Christ's life with the Passion in terms of Byzantine iconography. A similar representation appears somewhat later on two wooden backs of the choir stalls in the Split cathedral. They combine very skilfully and boldly ornamental designs with human figures, fantastic animals and scenes from everyday life. In addition to these works, which testify to the existence of good wood-carving workshops, there developed sculpture in stone, in which Romanesque style attained its full maturity. Master Radovan completed the monumental portal of the Trogir cathedral in 1240. He represented the Nativity in the lunette and a series of scenes from everyday life in the archivolts and on the colonnettes. He even made use of ordinary human pursuits and activities when he carved the allegory of the twelve months. He favoured realistic treatment and combined a narrative gift with an exceptional feeling for the expressive treatment of volumes. Radovan's style was adopted by many carving workshops in the middle of the 13th century; it is evidenced also in two reliefs (the Annunciation and the Nativity) which are incorporated into the bell--tower of the Split cathedral.

In the southern parts of the Adriatic coast, in Dubrovnik and Kotor, the principal monuments of Romanesque art date from the middle of the 14th century. It was then that Mihoje Brajkov, a master from Bar, built the cloister in the Franciscan monastery in Dubrovnik. The slender octagonal columns, forming six-light windows, have richly decorated bases and capitals, with typically Romanesque fantastic animals and bizarre human heads. The ciborium in the Kotor cathedral, the last remarkable work in late Romanesque style, dates from about the same time. One of its most striking parts is the frieze, which extends on three sides of the architrave and illustrates the legend of St Triphones, the patron-saint of Kotor. It is a rudimentary and sharply carved relief, concise in form and rich in contrasts of light and shade. The other carved ornaments of the ciborium already exhibit elements of the transitional style and herald the Gothic art, which reached the southern Adriatic in the latter half of the 14th century.

Romanesque paintings have not been preserved in large ensembles, so that we can hardly form an adequate idea of their real value and function in old religious buildings. Their arrangement, iconographic content and formal elements are associated with the West European Romanesque tradition. The surface treatment of the forms, the emphasized drawing, the linear representation of the clothes, the red circles on the faces and bright colours are the basic features of this art. The earliest examples date from the end of the 11th century, and the most representative works are the frescoes in the Church of St Michael at Ston, which include a splendid founder's portrait. Attention should also be drawn to the frescoes in the bell-tower of the Church of the Virgin and in the Church of St Peter in Zadar, as well as to the frescoes of St Chrysogonus (Sveti Krševan), Zadar and in Donji Humac on Brač, which combine Byzantine and Romanesque elements. The monuments in Istria represent a separate group: St Michael in Limska draga, St Agatha near Kanfanar, St Fosca at Peroj and St Martin in Sveti Lovreč. Although they are based on the artistic conceptions of the Benedictines, we can also discern in them some iconographic patterns typical of the 12th century Aquileia.

MEDIEVAL ART IN MACEDONIA AND SERBIA

After the conversion to Christianity in the second half of the 9th century, and especially during the episcopate of Methodius's disciple Clement, the position of the Slav population in the Byzantine empire (and particularly in the territory of Macedonia) improved considerably. The first medieval architectural monuments also date from that time. They were built on the shores of lakes Prespa and Ohrid (St Panteleimon, the Church of the Holy Archangels) and they were the centres of Slav culture. As such, they played an important role in the cultural history of the Slavs living in the southern regions of the Balkan Peninsula. After the rapid decline of Byzantium and the fall of the Bulgarian empire, an insurrection flared up in Macedonia which led to the establishment of an independent Macedonian state under Emperor Samuilo (976—1014). His capital was Prespa, and two churches were built in it: St Achilius and St Germanus. However, when the ambitious Basil II came to the throne in Constantinople, Byzantium began to expand northward again. Samuilo's empire was the first to be attacked. After the battle at Belasica (1014) the Byzantines crushed the resistance of Samuilo's successors and penetrated as far as the Sava and the Danube, which became the northern boundaries of the empire from 1018 onwards. The economic and administrative activities in the Byzantine provinces were reorganized in the first half of the 11th century, and this led to the renewed use of old communications and a revival of urban life. The Ohrid archbishopric, which was given ecclesiastical autonomy in the subjugated territory from Ohrid to the Danube, was also reorganized at that time.

From the middle of the 11th to the end of the 12th century the building and artistic activity in the territory of the Ohrid archbishopric was very intensive, and some monuments from that epoch rank among the most outstanding works of Byzantine art. The most important of them is the cathedral church of St Sophia in Ohrid. It was constructed and adorned with frescoes in the middle of the 11th century, during the incumbency of Archbishop Leon, and it gave full expression to the artistic conceptions of the high clergy of Byzantium. Hard outlines, lively movements and expressive austere physiognomies impart to these frescoes a monumental quality which was never to re-appear in this form in the Byzantine world. Several other important Byzantine churches were built in the second half of the 11th century: Veljusa and Vodoča in the vicinity of Strumica, the lower part of the basilica in Staro Nagoričano, the Church of St Nicholas in the village of Manastir. The forms of these buildings had not become standardized yet (basilica, quatrefoil, inscribed cross), although some basic features of Byzantine architecture, such as the dome, building with brick, and polychromatic facades, were always present. In the 12th century, in the time of the Comnenes, the type of the church with the ground plan in the form of an inscribed cross established itself and the vivid treatment of the facades was further elaborated. This was the time of the stabilization of Byzantine art, when a new style in painting was being evolved and when frescoes got a stock iconographic content and symbolic meaning. Two masterpieces of Comnene style have been preserved in Macedonia: St Panteleimon at Nerezi (1164) and St George at Kurbinovo (1191). Nerezi, the foundation of the Byzantine prince Alexius Angelos, is based on the court conception of art. Its frescoes are characterized by restrained sensibility, ceremonious aristocratism in the attitude and movements of the figures, bright colours and a certain graphic quality resulting from a combination of coloured lines — a feature which can be noticed, in a somewhat more rudimentary form, in the frescoes at Kurbinovo. The art in Macedonia reached such heights only once more — at the end of the 13th century (1295) in the frescoes of the Virgin the Peribleptos in Ohrid. They precede the narrative style and learned classicism of the Palaeologues, and their masters Mihailo and Evtihije founded a school of painting which continued to be active for the next twenty years. Their artistic conceptions found a very full expression in the remarkable series of icons painted in Ohrid at the end of the 13th and the beginning of the 14th century.

North of Macedonia lay old Raška, the centre of the Serbian medieval art. The development of its art was based on the ideological and aesthetic conceptions of Byzantine culture. At the time of Stefan Nemanja, in the 1170s, when Raška was an independent state, several remarkable churches were built: St Nicholas at Kuršumlija, the Church of the Virgin at Toplica and Djurdjevi Stupovi near Novi Pazar, a representative monument of Comnene art, which was, unfortunately, badly damaged in the two world wars. The last foundation of Nemanja, the large Church of the Virgin at Studenica, was built of white marble at the end of the 12th century, and it represents a splendid synthesis of architecture, sculpture and painting. Its frescoes date from 1290, they bear Serbian inscriptions and show elements of an independent style. This is not surprising, because Byzantine political and cultural influence began to wane rapidly after the fall of Constantinople in 1204 and the establishment of the Latin Empire, and this facilitated the development of national schools in Serbia, Russia and Bulgaria. When the papal legate crowned Stefan the First-Crowned in 1217 and when Sava Nemanjić obtained an independent archbishopric from the emperor and patriarch of Nikea in 1219, thus emancipating his Church from the domination of the high clergy of Ohrid, the Serbian state became fully consolidated as a stable feudal and political organization. It had its language and alphabet, its church, laws, trade and a strong army. During the following two centuries the frontiers of Serbia continually expanded under Nemanja's successors: westward towards Bosnia, south--west towards the Adriatic, southward towards Byzantium and Salonica and northward, towards Belgrade. The warlike Serbian kings and nobles were also active founders of churches and other buildings. They raised towns and military fortifications, built churches and foundations, commissioned frescoes and icons, promoted the copying of books and illumination of manuscripts.

Several stylistic currents and schoola evolved during this period of lively activity in the field of art. The so-called Raška School flourished in the 13th century, and its style survived on representative church buildings of the 14th century, too. Studenica is the most representative example of that group of monuments and it comprises almost all the elements which appear in later churches. The churches belonging to this group are domed single-nave buildings with lateral chapels and a spacious apse, built of costly materials, either stone or marble. The rhythm and proportions of their forms, the decoration of their facades and the stonework on their portals and windows show traces of Romanesque influence which had reached this region via the Adriatic. An important feature of the great royal mausolea, such as Studenica, Banjska, Dečani and the Holy Archangels near Prizren, is the sculptured decoration, which was not popular elsewhere in Byzantine Orthodox world. This sculpture uses the entire range of religous fantastic beings combined with the typical floral ornaments. If the rulers of the Nemanjić family engaged architects and masons from the coastal region of the Adriatic for the building of their churches, they brought painters of frescoes from Greece, and primarily from Constantinople and Salonica. There is some evidence that Archbishop Sava negotiated with the imperial masters from the monastery of

St Andrew in Constantinople during his stay in that town. The entire Serbian painting of the 13th century is characterized by a certain representative quality and monumentality. In the long series of monuments, from Studenica, Mileševa (c. 1225), the Church of Holy Apostles at Peć (c. 1250) and Morača (c. 1260), to Sopoćani (1264) and Arilje (1296) a unique style of fresco painting, based on classical proportions and classical ideals of beauty, was perfected. Neatly conceived compositions with life-size figures are usually shown on a golden background imitating mosaics. Their iconography is simple, reduced to what was deemed ideologically and theologically essential. As opposed to that, the relations of colours are very complex and rich. This style culminated in the frescoes of Sopoćani. In these paintings everything is harmoniously blended and integrated — light and colour, drawing and form, the internal and the external. Everything is subordinated to the cheif aim, which is to represent the idea of divine harmony in terms conceivable to man. In its essence, this style is an expression of the classical conception of art, and represents a specific revival such as was unknown in the Byzantine world either before or after it.

At the end of the 13th century the development of Serbian art began to stagnate (Gradac, Arilje) for the great achievements of Mileševa and Sopoćani began to disappear gradually. The new revival symbolically coincided with the great conquests of King Milutin in the southern regions, in Macedonia. A new style, based on the artistic conceptions of the Constantinopolitan "Palaeologue Revival", is evidenced in the churches built by this ruler, who was the greatest founder in medieval Serbia. This style reached Serbia via Macedonia and during the first two decades of the 14th century it became established as the official court style. Its chief artists were Mihailo and Evtihije, whom we meet first in the Church of the Virgin the Perilebtos at Ohrid in 1295. These painters, their assistants and disciples painted the frescoes in the Church of the

Mother of God Ljeviška (Bogorodica Ljeviška, 1307), the Church of St Nicholas (Sveti Nikita, 1310), the King's Church at Studenica (1314) and Staro Nagoričano (1317). The main features of their works are a markedly narrative character, an increased number of compositions and cycles, lavish illustration of apocryphal texts, church dramas and poems, the introduction of learned elements and a tendency towards didacticism. The emphasis on narration led to the diminishing of the human figure and the deepening of space, which became filled with architectural scenery. The language of painting also changed: the earlier warm harmonies of colours typical of the 13th century were replaced by cold plastic modelling achieved by means of contrasts of light and shade. These frescoes were painted in buildings designed in a different architectural style. The Romanesque traditions of the Raška School had been completely abandoned: the interiors of the majority of King Milutin's churches are crowded with pillars and they are poorly lit. The new edifices adopted the Byzantine architectural pattern: their ground plan is in the form of an inscribed cross, they have one or five domes, and their facades are built of alternate courses of stone and brick and are enlivened by polychromatic brickwork in the form of chessboard designs, meanders, zig-zag lines, crosses, etc. What is lost in the interior space is sometimes compensated, as in Gračanica, in the lively rhythm of the external volumes.

The southward expansion of the Serbian state continued after the death of King Milutin, and this led to the rapid growth of the power of the feudal lords and the ecclesiastical circles. The monastic complex at Peć was enlarged by new buildings (St Demetrius, the Church of the Virgin Hodeghetria and St Nicholas) and an aristocratic art began to develop in Macedonia (Ljuboten, Lesnovo). The situation changed considerably about the middle of the 14th century. Local movements and provincial schools of art emerged in Dušan's extensive empire; outstanding among them were those of Ohrid, Prilep and Kotor.

However, their representatives were craftsmen rather than artists, and their frescoes exhibit a tendency towards encyclopaedic narration rather than firmly grasped ideological and theological concepts. This is best seen in the church at Dečani, in which Greek masters from the coastal district reproduced almost the entire Byzantine iconography of the 14th century, but without genuine artistic power. In the latter half of the 14th century, the chief founders were nobles and provincial feudal lords, who had become virtually independent of the royal authority. Their foundations were not particularly important or representative, but they were sometimes adorned with exquisite frescoes, as Marko's Monastery or Andreaš (1380—1390).

In the 1370s, after the penetration of the Turks into the Balkan Peninsula, the centre of the state was transferred to the north, to the valley of the Morava river. A new art developed in the state of Prince Lazar and his son Despot Stefan in spite of the chaotic political circumstances. Remarkable buildings, sculptures and paintings have been preserved from this period. The edifices of the Morava School — Ravanica, Lazarica, Kalenić and Ljubostinja, to mention just a few — are trefoil in plan and have articulated facades, rich polychromatic ornaments and sculptured decoration. They belong to a new type of the church, unknown in the Balkans up to that time, in which decorative sculpture is given a very prominent place. It adorns portals, windows, rosettes and archivolts, and it consists of plaitwork, fantastic animals and even human figures carved in shallow relief. The great tradition of Byzantine painting had its last and brilliant flowering in the frescoes of the Morava School. The compositions are monumental and spacious, as in the 13th century, but the drawing is softer, the modelling is more tender, and the colours are more poetic and refined. This art has aristocratic elegance and combines elevated spirituality with restrained realism. It displays a type of human sensibility which is more akin to the Italian Renaissance than to Byzantine

Orthodoxy. The Morava School achieved a complete synthesis of architecture, painting and sculpture. Its monuments were permeated with a specific creative spirit and view of the world, which disappeared from the historical scene with the fall of Smederevo in 1459 and the final collapse of the Serbian state.

THE GOTHIC
AND THE RENAISSANCE

The Gothic reached the Yugoslav territory comparatively late, only at the end of the 13th century, since the conditions for its appearance matured slowly. Its most vital centres were in the small feudal estates in the territory of present-day Slovenia, then a part of the Habsburg Empire. They were, naturally, strongly influenced by the developments in Germany and Austria. The rapid rise of the Celj lords to the rank of princes enjoying extensive possessions and the support of Hungary, made these provinces economically strong and independent. King Sigismund of Hungary conferred the title of prince to Herman II of Celj, granted him the right to coin his own money and to levy taxes on mines. He also gave him the town of Varaždin and estates in Hrvatsko Zagorje and in Medjumurje. With the death of Ulrich II in 1456 the dynasty of the lords of Celj became extinct and their possessions reverted to the Habsburgs. It was in these complicated legal and economic relations between the small feudal holdings and mighty empires that the national indentity of the Slovenes was forged. A new type of founder, belonging to the ranks of ordinary citizens and peasants, appeared on the historical scene. As a result of this lively artistic activity and the appearance of new patrons of art there emerged a specific variant of Gothic style in Slovenia. Its expansion was promoted particularly by the Cistercites, the Franciscans and the Dominicans, so that schools and workshops fostering the new building skills sprang up in the vicinity of their monasteries at Ptuj and Kostanjevica. Among the building centres especially important were those at Ptuj and Gornja

Radgona, in which the eminent painter and architect Johannes Aquila was active towards the end of the 14th century. Two of his masterpieces, the church at Hajdina and the church at Ptujska Gora, already contain all the elements which were to become common in later architecture: the hall-type design (the nave and the aisles of equal height), stellar vaulting, brackets with masks and a prominent presbytery. The further development of Gothic style was based on these elements, and it culminated in the 15th century. The factors contributing to this development were the influence of Parler's style, the broader cultural interests of the urban populations and the increased need for parish churches (the churches at Radovljica and Škofja Loka, the Church of St Primus above Kamnik).

Sculpture in Slovenia developed on a very modest scale in the Romanesque period, and attaind full growth only in the Gothic age. The early examples (the Virgin from Solčava) show traces of the influence of the "broken style" *(Zackenstil)* from the second half of the 13th century, or of the 14th century French Gothic (the Virgin with Christ from Šempeter). Besides, the sculptured decoration of the churches at Hajdina and Ptujska Gora incorporates elements of the "soft style" and of Parler's circle, while the two altars from Ptujska Gora rank among the supreme achievements of the 15th century. One of them features a relief of great iconographic enterest, which shows the Virgin covering with her cloak eighty figures. Many local workshops for the production of coloured wooden statues were active in Slovenia in the 15th century, for there was a rapid growth of interest in richly furnished church interiors.

In Slovenia and Istria Gothic style found its fullest expression in painting. Several tendencies succeeded one another in the 14th century — the "flat style" (the northern aisle at Crngrob), the style of the Furlanian masters (Udine), the "soft style" (Gosteče), and the style of Johannes Aquila (Martijanci, Turnišče) — until the Gothic reached its full stylistic and iconographic maturity at the beginning of the 15th century. It was then that a specific iconographic programme, known in the history of art as the "painted Kranj presbytery" established itself. As the term itself shows, the emphasis is on the presbytery, in which the arrangement of the subjects of frescoes is adjusted to the stellar vaulting: Maiestas Domini with the symbols of the four Evangelists is painted in the central panel, while the other panels show angels playing music and singing. In the lower zone of the walls are the Apostles, and above them are scenes from the lives of Christ and the Virgin or an illustration of the legend of the saint to whom the church is dedicated. The Annunciation and Cain and Abel offering sacrifice are represented on the triumphal arch, and St George with the dragon is depicted on the inner side of the arch. This carefully planned iconographic programme is continued on the walls of the nave: the Adoration of the Magi (in Istria also the *Danse Macabre*) is shown on the northern wall, scenes from the life of the Virgin or of the patron saint are depicted on the southern wall, and the Last Judgment is shown on the western wall. St Christopher, the patron saint of travellers and the protector from accidental death, was frequently painted on the facade. Fine examples of the complete programme can be seen in the Church of St John (Sv. Janez) at Bohinj and in Suha near Škofja Loka. The stabilization of the iconographic scheme in the 15th century was accompanied by the maturing of the style, which continued to develop in two basic directions: one was based on the conceptions of the Furlanian masters (Suha, Bodešče), and the other had its origin in Koruška, in the paintings of Friedrich from Beljak, who based himself on the traditions of the "soft style". This style was adopted by his son Janez Ljubljanski, who became the most distinguished Gothic painter by the middle of the century (Visoko pod Kureščkom, Muljava). Tendencies towards lyricism and idealism persisted throughout the second half of the century (Mače) and are also evident in the paintings of Wolfgang, who was active at Crngrob.

Realism was introduced into the Gothic fresco painting only at the beginning of the 16th century, when stylistic elements of the Renaissance also appeared. In Istria, one influence came from Venetian painters, and another emanated from the north (Pazin). The native school was based on this latter style and its most important representatives were Vincenco and Ivan from Kastav. Their frescoes are in the church at Škriline near Beram and at Hrastovlje.

Very few Gothic monuments have survived in the inland parts of Croatia, because most of them perished in wars and earthquakes, or were subsequently remodelled so thoroughly that they have lost their original appearance. This is the case, for example, with the Zagreb Cathedral, which was built between 1263 and 1287 in pure Gothic style, but was subsequently damaged and reconstructed several times. An early Gothic chapel dedicated to St Stephen and containing 14th century frescoes has been preserved within the Bishop's Palace in Zagreb. Subsequent reconstructions have also damaged the Church of St Mark in Zagreb, which still has the original southern portal, with sculptures inspired by Peter Parler and his Prague circle. Small village and parish churches were built at this time in Slavonia (Slavonska Požega, Vočin, Vinkovci), but they were products of local workshops and their architectural value is not great.

The situation was different in Dalmatia, where the carving tradition persisted in the 14th, 15th and 16th centuries. It was a period of lively artistic activity in maritime towns. Old fortifications were reconstructed and new ones erected, town cores were urbanized, public buildings, monastic complexes and parish churches were constructed, palaces (the Ćipiko palace at Trogir) and luxurious summer residences (the Sorkočević villa on Lapad) were built. In addition to native masters, foreigners were also active in this region. They were mostly Italians, such as Bonino from Milan, Onofrio della Cava, Michelozzo Michelozzi and others. They spread Italian influences, and the strongest among them were those emanating from Apulia, Ancona and Venice. Here, as in Slovenia, the penetration of the Gothic was promoted by the monastic churches of the Franciscans and the Dominicans. However, Dalmatia had a peculiar development: the early Gothic developed in it for a fairly long period in a symbiosis with the Renaissance, so that we commonly find two transitional styles, Romanesque-Gothic and Gothic-Renaissance. The mature Gothic found its most complete expression in the work of Juraj Dalmatinac, a sculptor from Zadar who was trained in Venice. It is owing to the work of Juraj and his numerous collaborators and disciples that the florid Gothic spread in many stone-working workshops along the Adriatic coast (Split, Korčula, Dubrovnik). Master Juraj united in his work architecture and sculpture and his most important achievement, the cathedral in Šibenik, was a veritable fountain of Gothic ideas. He also adorned the Chapel of St Anastasius in the Split Cathedral, which contains his strikingly expressive Whipping of Christ. He also worked in Dubrovnik (fortification walls, the Rector's Palace) and in Ancona. Andrija Aleši, Juraj's collaborator for many years in the Šibenik Cathedral, developed further his art and translated it into Renaissance terms. Aleši's works include the exquisite baptismal font in the Trogir Cathedral, which has pointed Gothic arches faced with Renaissance coffers.

The merging of the Gothic and the Renaissance is most clearly evident in the monuments of Dubrovnik: in the reconstructed fortification walls and bastions, in the Dominican cloister, in the Restor's Palace and in the Sponza. These monuments are the work of various Italian and native masters but the blending of styles manifest in them was not a result of the mixture of masters with different training; it was primarily an expression of the taste of a society which had its own views of artistic values. Thus we find a natural combination of a Gothic and a Renaissance zone on the facade of a Dubrovnik building; Gothic arches can be seen incorporated into Renaissance arcading, and Gothic threelight windows are sometimes coupled with Renaissance arches. The Renaissance, in its pure form, made its appearance at the end of the 15th century in the works of Nikola Firentinac. He assisted Aleši in his work on the Trogir baptistry, but his first independent work, the Chapel of Blessed John at Trogir (1468), has purely Renaissance features, both as regards its spatial arrangement and its sculptured ornaments. Since the construction of this monument lasted very long, some of its statues were carved by Andrea Aleši, and two statues are the work of Ivan Duknović, on outstanding Renaissance master who worked mostly in Italy. The major achievement of Nikola Firentinac is the Šibenik Cathedral, where he completed the work begun by master Juraj. He added the vaulting above the longitudinal aisles and the transept, built the entire roof structure, completed the front facade and raised the dome, a masterpiece of Renaissance architecture in Dalmatia. The architectural conceptions of Nikola Firentinac influenced a number of native masters working at the end of the 15th and the beginning of the 16th century — especially Marko Andrijić, Paskoje Miličević and Petar Andrijić, who built the Dubrovnik Church of St Saviour in pure Renaissance style in 1520.

In addition to these imposing buildings in the rich maritime towns, the Gothic and Renaissance spread, in a somewhat more modest form, inland, into Bosnia and Montenegro. The Gothic was introduced into Bosnia by the Franciscans, as is testified by their churches at Zvornik and Srebrenica and by the Gothic churches which were subsequently converted into mosques (Bihać). The bogumils, who fostered folk art, presented the greatest obstacle to the penetration of Western architectural ideas. Therefore the Gothic was confined to the circle of the great feudal lords. The royal castle at Jajce, built by Dalmatian masters, is an example of their undertakings. The capitals of the old monastery at Cetinje, founded by Ivan Crnojević in 1485, after he had transferred the capital of Montenegro to that town and established the new seat of the Zeta Metropolitanate, represent a unique synthesis of Renaissance style and the architecture of the Orthodox Church.

While Gothic painting developed in Istria and Slovenia in the frescoes of parish and monastic churches, in Dalmatia it appeared only on altarpieces and altar covers. Of decisive importance for its development was the influence of the late Venetian Gothic brought by Carlo and Vittorio Crivelli during their short stay in Dalmatia, the import of numerous Italian 15th and 16th century paintings, and the surviving Byzantine tradition in the southern part of the Adriatic region.

The native school of painting, represented by Dujmo Vušković and Lovro Dobričević, became independent concurrently with the establishment of a large centre of painting in Dubrovnik. The period of the most fertile activity of this centre was the end of the 15th and the beginning of the 16th century, when the Renaissance conception of painting took root in it. Three masters played a decisive role in this development: Vicko Lovrin, Nikola Božidarović and Mihailo Hamzić. They combined successfully the discoveries of the Venetian Quattrocento with the native tradition and thus left a specific imprint on the entire Dubrovnik school of painting. After their death in the 1520s, this school began to decline, for it received no new and vital stimuli.

At the time when the art in the western parts of present-day Yugoslavia was characterized by Gothic and Renaissance elements, the central region, the territory of the old Bosnian state, saw the rise of an autochthonous and original art of sepulchral monuments, the *stećci* as they are popularly called. Their inscriptions show that they originally marked the graves of the members of feudal families, although this form of burial became quite common later. Cemeteries with *stećci* can be also found outside Bosnia and Herzegovina — in Dalmatia, Montenegro, Lika, Slavonia and western Serbia. This wide geographical distribution is reflected both in the typology and in the sculptured decoration of *stećci*. Although there are four basic forms — tablet, chest, sarcophagus and cross — there are numerous variants in various regions, where local workshops also introduced their specific ornamental and figural motifs. The decoration of the *stećci* is very rich and includes figural compositions with hunting scenes and jousts (Kupres), or with monumental human figures holding a raised hand (Radimlja), geometric and floral motifs, heraldic emblems and other symbols. This complex and enigmatic decorative system, based largely on traditions of folk art, old cults and burial rites, has been associated, without sufficient grounds, with the ideology and religion of Bosnian bogumils. This hypothesis may or may not be confirmed by future research, but the *stećci* definitely remain an exceptional expression of spontaneous and unsophisticated popular art.

THE PENETRATION OF THE TURKS
AND ISLAMIC ART

In their drive towards the north and the west, the Turks first conquered Macedonia, then Serbia (1459) and finally Bosnia (1463), so that by the end of the 15th century almost the entire territory of the Balkan Peninsula was incorporated into the Ottoman Empire. In spite of persistent attempts, the Turks did not succeed in capturing the towns on the Adriatic coast, in which Venice established its rule at the beginning of the 15th century, or the Dubrovnik Republic, which managed to preserve its independence for a long time. In the inland regions of Croatia and in Slovenia a defensive zone, the so-called military frontier, was formed from Christian refugees, primarily Serbs, who were settled there to defend the Habsburg monarchy from the penetration of the Turks towards Vienna. In the occupied territories the Turks established their administrative, legal and economic institutions, and this marked the beginning of the Islamization of the Slavonic population in the towns. In pursuing their administrative and religious policy, the Turks did not completely abolish the freedom of the Christian Church. The building of new churches was prohibited by law, but the Christian population was almost completely free to restore, rebuild or reconstruct the existing churches. This enabled Christian art to survive in the new circumstances. The rich founders from the ranks of the feudal aristocracy were succeeded by monastic communities, groups of craftsmen or ecclesiastical dignitaries. As new buildings were raised only rarely, artistic activity was reduced to the painting of frescoes, icons and miniatures or the making of church furniture. High quality work was sometimes done in the field of applied arts, especially wood-carving, as the objects from monasteries Slepče and Treskavac show.

In the period between 1459 and 1557 frescoes continued to be painted in the southern parts of Serbia (Poganovo), in Macedonia (Treskavac, Sveti Nikita) and in the monasteries north of the Sava and the Danube (Krušedol). After the restoration of the Patriarchate of Peć in 1557 there began a fertile period of artistic activity under the auspices of the enterprising Patriarch Makarije Sokolović. It was then that the frescoes in the nartheces of Peć, Mileševa, Studenica and Gračanica were painted or restored. The new painting seeks to uphold the great medieval tradition by copying the old style and using the old iconographic patterns. As a result, some splendid works were produced, as the frescoes in Studenica and Gračanica show. Important artistic workshops were active in the major monastic centres, such as Peć and Dečani. One of them (that in Peć) produced the greatest 16th century painter of icons, monk Longin, who has left several exceptionally fine works at Lomnica, Piva and Dečani. In the time of patriarch Pajsije (after 1612) several very competent masters began to work in Montenegro and Serbia. The most important of them was Georgije Mitrofanović, a monk from Chilandar, who based himself on the traditions of the Cretan schools of painting (Morača, Zavala, Dobrićevo). In the second half of the 17th century another good artist appeared. It was Radul, who was predominantly active in Montenegro. The artistic activity of the Orthodox Church ceased almost completely at the end of the 17th century, when the increased oppression of the Turks and the Austrian-Turkish war led to a great northward migration of the Serbs under Patriarch Arsenije Čarnojević in 1690. New forms of life and new art began to develop in the homeland of the Serbs, north of the Sava and the Danube, in the territory of Austria.

Following the Islamization of the Slavonic population and the imposition of the Turkish military and administrative rule, Islamic art, essentially different from the traditions of Christian culture, took root in the Balkan region. In accordance with its basic religious tenets, the Islam concentrated on Oriental ornaments and picturesque details. This is evidenced in the production of books and in the working of metal, wood, leather and textile, in which Islamic craftsmen displayed great technical skill and imagination. Islamic art fostered a decorative quality not based on meaningless ornaments, but on a specific system of symbolical motifs which constituted the idiom of the Near Eastern culture. Among the main adornments in mosques were the moral sayings from the Koran, while objects for everyday use were frequently decorated with the tree of life, the celestial dome, the triangle, the square cypress or series of geometric, floral and zoomorphic ornaments carrying a specific symbolical meaning. The finest achievements of Islamic art were in the field of architecture. The Turkish house introduced new structural elements and a new functionality into the secular architecture of the Balkans. Besides, the needs of the urban population led to the introduction of new types of buildings — covered markets, baths, caravanserais — which testify to the skill of the Turkish architects in the construction of domes and vaults. As a state with a strong military organizaciton, Turkey devoted special attention to the building of fortifications. The Turks built new fortresses (Travnik, Ram on the Danube) and reconstructed many medieval strongholds, adapting them for canon warfare.

The main type of Byzantine churches, featuring a large dome, such as St Sophia in Constantinople, influenced the structural form of the Turkish mosque. However, the imposing vertical line of the minaret — a harmonious counter-balance to the arched line of the dome — and the conception of the interior as a unified and tranquil space differ from the Byzantine symbolism of the sacred space. The mosque has three basic parts: the porch, the area for worship and the minaret. It also has a yard, in which there are usually richly decorated fountains and funeral monuments. In the territory of present-day Yugoslavia they originated parallel with the advance of the Islamic civilization: the earliest ones were built in Macedonia and Kosovo in the 15th century, and the later ones were constructed in the Belgrade pashalik and date from the 16th century. Although some mosques were designed by native masters, they were usually the work of architects from Constantinople, and were built by local masons and craftsmen, many of whom were from the Adriatic coast. All three major styles — the Brusa style, the early Constantinopolitan style and the classical style — were represented in this territory. The Brusa style adopted the Byzantine technique of building in alternate courses of brick and stone, and it favoured very simple interior decoration. Two mosques in Skopje — the Sultan Murat Mosque (1436) and the Isak Bey Mosque (1438), were built in this style. The former has the interior in the form of a basilica, with a nave and two aisles, and the latter has several interior spaces covered with vaulting and a dome. The early Constantinopolitan style, which developed at the end of the 15th and the beginning of the 16th century, perfected the building with stone and brick, introduced the semidome, and favoured a longitudinal space for worship with two equal domes. The Sultan Mohammed Fatih Mosque in Priština (1461), the Mustapha Pasha Mosque in Skopje (1492) and the Multi-Coloured Mosque in Tetovo (1495) belong to this style. The activity of the imperial architects, mimar Hayredin and his successor mimar Sinan contributed to the development, in the 16th century, of the classical style, in which the structure of the mosque was further perfected. The space for worship was constructed in the form of a single cube covered with a broad dome, exhibiting a refined relationship between the width and the height. The interior decoration is rich, and the minber, mihrab and mahvil frequently have lavish carved ornaments. Such mosques were built predominantly in Bosnia in the 16th century: the Aladža at Foča (1550), the Ali

Pasha Mosque in Sarajevo (1561), the Sinan Bey Mosque at Čajniče (1570) and others. The Gazi Husrev Bey Mosque in Sarajevo (1530) also belongs to this style, although its structure is somewhat more complex since it has a semidome as well as a dome.

Some monumental buildings were built in the 18th century, too, but they were less numerous and less original. Later on, at the end of the 18th and the beginning of the 19th century, the Ottoman Empire was faced with a grave economic and political crisis, and its art began to stagnate and decay.

In the 17th and 18th centuries, after a long cultural stagnation, the regions not subjugated by the Turks witnessed a revival of art and a renewal of building activity. The narrow, semi-circular zone consisting of Dalmatia, inland Croatia, Slovenia and southern Hungary, which was surrounded on three sides by the northern part of the Ottoman Empire, received Baroque impulses from two directions: from Venice, and from Vienna and Graz. These two influences merged in this territory and stimulated the development of local schools. However, the Baroque did not develop with the same intensity everywhere. It attained its fullest development in Slovenia. Ljubljana was an important centre, with architects, sculptors, painters and numerous workshops for the production of church furniture and equipment. Two factors contributed to the spreading of the Baroque in Slovenia: a period of comparatively peaceful historical and cultural development after the battle of Sisak (1593), when the Turks were routed out and had to abandon their military pretensions to the westernmost parts of present--day Yugoslavia, and the foundation of the *Accademia Operosorum* in Ljubljana in 1693, which mobilized patriotic, ambitious and educated artists, who, in their turn, enlisted the support of new patrons of art: local feudal lords, well-to-do citizens and members of the clergy. The Jesuit order contributed most to the spreading of the Baroque. The earliest Baroque building, the Ljubljana Cathedral, was designed by Andrea Pozzo, the most eminent Jesuit architect. The other major monuments of Ljubljana dating from this early period were also built by foreigners: the church of the German order of knights was designed by Domenico Rossi, the Church of St Peter by Fusconi, the Ursuline Church by an anonymous master from the school of Venice. Giulio Quaglio, who painted the frescoes on the vaults of the cathedral, set the model of Baroque illusionism, which was to be followed by other painters. The native masters were merely collaborators and assistants at the beginning, but later, in the 18th century, when the Baroque reached its culmination, all the major undertakings were entrusted to them and they determined the character of the architecture in Ljubljana and in Slovenia generally. The most outstanding among them was Gregor Maček, who combined Italian models with the native traditions. Other eminent masters were M. Perski, L. Prager, D. Gruber and others, In their work the Baroque was transferred from sacred to secular architecture: to town-halls, aristocratic residences, chateaux, villas, palaces, theological schools and libraries. Their influence is also felt in the layout of the towns reconstructed in this period. The Baroque influence coming from Vienna and Graz established itself in Štajerska, in which it found its fullest expression in luxurious castles and palaces (Štatemberg, Dornava). In church buildings, picturesque facades were happily combined with the illusionism of the interiors. The church at Slatka Gora is the best example of such a synthesis.

As a style of grand synthesis and unity of all artistic techniques, the Baroque gave a strong impetus to the development of painting and sculpture. After Quaglia, the Slovenian type of illusionism was further developed by Franc Jelovšek, and he was assisted by Valentin Metcinger, Fortunat Bergant and Anton Cebej. They painted mainly religious pictures on Baroque altars, but there were also other paintings among their works, including representative portraits. The greatest Baroque sculptor was Francesco Robba. He was trained in Venice, but he settled in Ljubljana in the 1720s, where he joined the workshop of Luka Mislej, which he took over after his master's death. Robba was a master of fountains (the Fountain of the Kranjska Rivers in Ljubljana) and marble altars (the altar in the Ursuline Church), and he introduced Baroque sculpture into Zagreb in the middle of the century (the altar in the Church of St Catherine) and thus exercised a strong influence on the artists in Croatia. In addition to Mislej's and Robba's studio, there existed in Ljubljana several other workshops because of the great demand for marble statues and altars.

The Baroque reached the inland parts of Croatia at the end of the 17th century, and it was brought there, too, by the Jesuits. Their Church of St Catherine in Zagreb was modelled on the church Il Gesù in Rome — a domed nave flanked by lateral chapels. This became a very common form of church building and the same design was reproduced in the Baroque churches in Varaždin, Samobor and Krapina. Bernardo Bobić, the first Croatian early Baroque painter, began his activity at about the same time. His major works are in the Zagreb Cathedral. In the 18th century, when the Baroque became fully established and when the influence of the Ljubljana centre became stronger, the Franciscans and the Paulines (the Order of St Paul the Hermit) began to play an active role in the development of art. They reconstructed Gothic churches in Baroque style (the Pauline church in Lepoglava) and introduced new spatial arrangements and new types of ground plans (the church at Belec). In some churches a dome was added above the sanctuary (the Church of the Virgin in Zagreb). The front part of urban churches was considerably modified, and it was now dominated by one (Petrinja, Bjelovar) or two bell-towers (Osijek). In addition to the work on monasteries, parish and pilgrimage churches, some urban centres were reconstructed along Baroque lines, so that entire new Baroque complexes, with public monuments, administrative buildings and palaces were formed. Some of them, such as the Baroque part of Varaždin, have been preserved to the present day.

Painting and sculpture were influenced by Slovenian masters, who furnished many churches in Croatia with altar icons. F. Jelovšek and his son Andrija worked for the Church of St Catherine in Zagreb, V. Metcinger painted icons for Zagreb, Samobor and Karlovac, F. Bergant for Lika and the coastal region, and A. Cebej worked for the Church of the Virgin in Zagreb. The Pauline monastery at Lepoglava had a flourishing school of painting, headed by Ivan Ranger, a great master of illusionism. Although the Paulines had good sculptors and skilful makers of church furnishings in their order, the most important Baroque works in Croatia are those by Francesco Robba, who spent the last years of his life in Zagreb (he died in 1757).

Baroque did not attain particularly rich forms on the Adriatic coast and in Istria because of the specific economic and political circumstances prevailing there. The greatest concentration of Baroque monuments is in the south, in Dubrovnik, where there was intense building activity after the disastrous earthquake in 1667. There are three Baroque churches and all three were built by Italian architects: A. Bufalini designed the Dubrovnik Cathedral, M. Gropelli the Church of St Blaise, and A. Pozzo built the Jesuit church, which is approached by a striking and monumental stairway designed by Padalacqua. The Baroque monuments in Kotor, Perast and Dobrota, dating from the end of the 17th and the beginning of the 18th century, were also the works of Venetian masters (Fonte, Riviera). Italian imports dominated in painting and sculpture, too. At this time, however, there also appeared a native artist, Tripo Kokolja (1661—1713), whose masterpiece was painted for the Church of Our Lady of the Rocks (Gospa od Škrpjela) at Perast.

In southern Hungary, present-day Vojvodina, Baroque style had quite a different character. After the great migration of the Serbs in 1690 and their settlement in the territory between the Sava and the Danube, West European culture began to spread gradually in this region. This process was accompanied by the strengthening of the middle classes. The wall paintings in the earlier churches, such as Bodjani and Krušedol, show a combination of Byzantine traditions and Baroque elements, while the later buildings, dating from the middle of the 18th century onwards, are completely dominated by Baroque conceptions. Although it was the art of the Catholic Counter-Reformation, the Baroque influenced the art of the Orthodox Church because the Serbian communities in this territory looked to the Western and Central European centres. In Vojvodina, Baroque elements are particularly evident on iconostases. They consist of large wooden partitions, richly carved and filled with icons arranged according to a fixed pattern. The first native Baroque painters — Teodor Kračun, Teodor Ilić-Češljar, Georgije Tenecki and Jakov Orfelin — painted predominantly religious pictures, but they also introduced the portrait into Serbian art, because it was the type of painting that suited the new middle classes.

In the 19th century the entire territory from the Soča river to Djevdjelija was a scene of major historical upheavals. The fall of Venice (1797), Napoleon's brief invasion and the annexation of Dalmatian towns by the Austrian Empire at the beginning of the 19th century changed completely the economic and political position of the Slavonic peoples. The construction of railways, industrial development, the growth of capitalism and the expansion of organized urban life contributed to the strengthening of the middle classes and the growth of their economic prosperity. Parallel with this, there was a general revival in literature and science. There was also a growing sense of national identity, which became increasingly associated with the idea of the common fate of all the South Slavonic peoples. In the regions under Turkey, the disintegration of the Ottoman Empire was accompanied by rebellions and ruthless reprisals in Macedonia and by large-scale insurrections which led to the establishment of the first free states in Serbia and Montenegro. The development of art was very dynamic in this historical situation. The towns were reconstructed on more modern lines, so that they expanded over and beyond the old town walls and fortifications, in harmony with the new economic, political and cultural requirements of town life. Building activity was very intensive, because of the increased need for new types of public buildings (theatres, libraries, shops, schools, hospitals, exhibition halls) and for private dwellings, both patrician palaces and ordinary middle-class houses. The first half of the 19th century saw the spreading of classical architectural style, elaborated by Bartol Felbinger in Croatia and Jozef Šempra in Ljubljana. In the second half of the century and later, until the beginning of the First World War, the architecture in Belgrade, Zagreb and Ljubljana was dominated by historicity. Many monumental edifices and even some private buildings were designed in neo-Gothic, neo-Baroque, neo-Renaissance style or in the spirit of the Secession. The first wave of historicity was very strong because it had its great theoreticians, such as Hermann Bollè in Zagreb, but it began to decline gradually on the eve of the First World war, when there appeared three young architects, Jože Plečnik, Maks Fabiani and Viktor Kovačić, whose work marks the beginning of modern architecture in this territory. They introduced a new conception of space out of which present-day architecture was to develop.

The 19th century painting passed through stylistic phases which were also typical of West European art: classicism, Biedermeier, romanticism and realism. These styles were represented not only in religious paintings, but also in portraits, landscapes and representations of still life. Since these works are for the most part in museums and galleries, they have not been discussed in this book. This also applies to sculpture, which began to flourish in the Yugoslav territory at the end of the 19th century. The development of painting and sculpture in the 20th century presents a similar picture. They display a great variety of tendencies, but they are mainly intended for indoor display, and therefore do not fall within the scope of this book, which is limited to what we regard as monuments of art. Special attention has been paid here to Ivan Meštrović only, for some of his monumental works represent a complete fusion of architecture and sculpture and thus bring a long tradition to its logical conclusion.

ARANĐELOVAC, OLD EDIFICE

ARANDJELOVAC [H, 4]
The Old Edifice (Staro zdanje)

The building was designed by Kosta Šreplović and it was constructed in 1868—1872. It was originally intended for the summer residence of Prince Mihailo, but after his death it was converted into a hotel for visitors to the spa. The facades are designed in the spirit of pure Romanticism. The structure and finish are strongly influenced by Jan Nevola and by the architectural features of Kapetan Miša's Foundation in Belgrade.

ARILJE [G, 5]
The Church of St Achilius

The church was built at the end of the 13th century, and its frescoes date from 1296, as an inscription in the dome testifies. It was founded by King Dragutin. It is a single-nave building (26 metres long) with a semicircular apse and a low transept. The prothesis and the diaconicon are covered with the same roof as the choir spaces. The dome is hexagonal, which is exceptional in Serbian medieval architecture. The church is built of stone and plastered on the outside, and the facades are enlivened with lesenes and a frieze of small arcades below the roof cornice. The outer narthex was added later. The frescoes follow those of Sopoćani as regarded their arrangement and iconography: the scenes of the Eucharist are in the sanctuary, illustrations of the Old

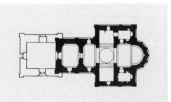

ARILJE, ST ACHILIUS'S, FRESCO, KING DRAGUTIN

Testament are in the narthex, while the Great Feasts, the Passion and the life of the Virgin are shown in the nave. There are also some impressive scenes among the other paintings: the procession of the Nemanjić family, the procession of Serbian archbishops, and the founders' composition, which shows King Milutin, King Dragutin and his wife Katelina.

AVALA [H, 3]
The Tomb of the Unknown Hero

AVALA, TOMB OF THE UNKNOWN HERO

Avala is a mountain in the vicinity of Belgrade. The tomb of the unknown hero, designed by sculptor Ivan Meštrović, was built on the site of the medieval town of Žrnov in 1934. Two long paths (oriented east-west) lead to the two entrances to the monument. The mausoleum is made of black granite and it is in the form of a magnified sarcophagus. Four caryatides in the form of women in national costumes are placed on each side of the entrances.

BAČ [F, 2]
The Medieval Fortress

The fortress was built betw~en 1338 and 1342 on a little island formed by a canal and the river Mostong. It was held by the Turks between 1529 and 1687, and during Rákószy's rebellion at the beginning of the 18th century the fortress was burnt down and partly demolished. It has never been restored. The ground plan of the fortifications is in the form of an irregular quadrangle. Three round and a four-sided tower are at its corners. They had a defensive balcony supported on brackets. A tower with a draw-bridge stood in front of the entrance to the fortress.

BADIJA [D, 6]
The Franciscan Monastery

The monastery is located on a small island near Korčula. It was founded by Franciscan friars from Bosnia, who had settled there at the end of the 14th century. The church was built after 1420 and is in the form of a single-nave basilica with a rich portal. Especially remarkable is the cloister, which was completed in 1477. Its architectural form and sculptured decoration are typical of the Dalmatian art in the period of transition from the Gothic to the Renaissance.

BANJA NEAR PRIBOJ [G, 5]
The Church of St Nicholas

This place was the centre of the Archbishopric of Dabar in the time of St Sava of Serbia and therefore the church used to be called St Nicholas of Dabar. The present church was built by King Stefan Dečanski on the site of an earlier building in 1329. Its ground plan is in the form of an inscribed cross, and it has a dome supported on four pillars. At the eastern end are three semicircular niches (the middle one is wider, longer and three-sided without), and at the western end is a narthex which was originally surmounted by a blind dome. In front of the narthex is an open porch. The whole church has recently been plastered and whitewashed. The frescoes have been preserved in the nave and the narthex. Only some of them date from the 1330s (the figures of bishops in the sanctuary, the life of the Virgin in the diaconicon, the standing figures on the northern wall of the nave). They owe much to the tradition of the court school of art of King Milutin, but they also display certain features which were to attain their fullest expression in the paintings in Dečani (1337—1350). The frescoes in the nave were painted over the 14th century paintings in about 1572 and

BANJA NEAR PRIBOJ, ST NICHOLAS'

reproduce the old iconography and style in every detail. Especially interesting is the founders' composition on the southern wall, which shows King Stefan Dečanski, his son Dušan and the Archbishop of Dabar Nikola. The author of these paintings went further than any of his contemporaries in the imitation and copying of old frescoes. The paintings in the narthex were done at the same time by another artist, who did not seek to imitate the old style. Although his frescoes lack precise drawing and refined colours, they introduce some iconographic novelties — e. g. the illustration of the legend of the Holy Cross, which includes an interesting composition showing the victory of Constantine the Great over Maxentius. The scenes from the legend of St Nicholas, the patron of the church, are also full of lively details.

BANJA LUKA, FERHAD PASHA MOSQUE

BANJA LUKA [D, 3]
The Ferhad Pasha Mosque

The mosque was built in 1579 by the first Beglerbey of Bosnia Ferhad Pasha Sokolović. It is popularly called the Ferhadija. Although built in classical style, it has an unusual structure. The central space (12.10 × 12.60 metres) is extended laterally by two narrow aisles covered with tunnel vaulting. In the axis is a domed space, half-square in plan. The main dome is placed on a tall drum, and the height from the floor to the top of the dome is 17.5 metres. The minaret springs from the lateral mass of the wall and is 41.5 metres high, with a sherefa supported on brackets made of stalactite work. In front of the mosque is a porch, the roof of which rests on four stone pillars connected with pointed arches. The porch has three small domes, the middle one being a little higher than the other two. The minbar, mihrab and mahvil have rich carved decoration. The walls are ornamented with calligraphic quotations from the Kuran written in Arabic letters. A fountain and three turbehs are in the courtyard. The founder of the mosque is buried in one of the turbehs.

BANJSKA [H, 6]
The Church of St Stephen

The Church of St Stephen is located at the foot of mountain Rogozna, north-west of Titova Mitrovica. It was built between 1313 and 1315 as the mausoleum of King Milutin on the foundations of an earlier edifice. It is modelled after Studenica

BANJSKA, CHURCH OF ST STEPHEN

windows and on the western portal. A well preserved statue of the Virgin with Christ, with rusticated Romanesque-Gothic stylistic features, originally in the church, is now in the village of Sokolica. The monastery and the church were short-lived. As early as the beginning of the 16th century the church was converted into a mosque, and the other buildings were pulled down. In 1940 they were partly restored. Remains of a tower and of a representative refectory have been discovered west of the church.

and Archbishop Danilo II supervised its construction. The church is in the form of a single-nave building (36 metres long) with a transept and a semicircular apse at the eastern end. The western bay has groin vaulting. Two lateral parekkleseions, on the northern and southern sides, are entered from the narthex, while the main entrance to the church was flanked by two high towers. The facades are made of polished blocks of bluish, pale red and white marble. Rich carved decoration existed originally above the brackets supporting the frieze of blind arcades below the roof cornice, on the

BAR [F, 7]
The Mediaeval Town

The town is five kilometres distant from the shore. It is first mentioned in the 10th century by Constantine Porphyrogenitus. In the 11th and 12th centuries it was in the possession of the rulers of Zeta, who transferred the seat of their archbishopric to it. Stefan Nemanja annexed it to the Serbian state in 1183 and from that time onward the town recognized the

BAR, MEDIEVAL TOWN

sovreignty of the Nemanjić rulers, and, subsequently, of the Balšić family and of Despot Stefan Lazarević. It was under the Venetian domination from 1443 until 1571, when it was captured by the Turks. It was liberated by the Montenegrins only in 1878. The remains of mediaeval Bar include parts of the town walls and of the town gate dating from the 11th century. The best preserved parts in the upper fortress, which is girdled with massive walls and round towers, are those constructed in the time of Venetian rule. The old settlement was deserted after 1878, and a number of buildings was damaged by gunpowder explosions. They included the Cathedral of St George, which was in the form of a two-aisled basilica (13th century) and the Late Romanesque Church of St Nicholas, which stands by the old gate. Both were converted into mosques under the Turks. Some remains of secular buildings — the bishop's palace, the aqueduct and Turkish baths — can also be seen in the town.

BEGUNJE [B, 1]
The Church of St Peter

The church was built at the beginning of the 16th century in late Gothic style as a hall-church of the Gorenje type. It is a building with two naves and a five-sided apse. Two octogonal pillars in the centre of the church support stellar vaulting. The bell-tower is on the western side. The presbytery was made in the Baroque period. The frescoes were painted by master Jernej from Loka between 1530 and 1540. The cycle of the Passion is on the northern wall of the nave and the legend of St Peter is illustrated in the presbytery.

BELEC [B, 1]
The Church of Our Lady of the Snows (Sv. Marija Snežna)

The earlier 17th century edifice, founded by the widow of Juraj Erdödy, was reconstructed between 1739 and 1741. It is a single-nave building with a polygonal sanctuary on its eastern end and a high bell-tower on its western side. Two lateral chapels were added on its northern and southern sides. The interior of the curch is lavishly decorated in mature Baroque style. The wall paintings were painted by Ivan Ranger (the legend of Our Lady of the Snows is depicted on the vault), and the pulpit, the main altar (1743) and the two lateral altars (1746), which herald Rococo style, have rich carved decoration.

BELGRADE [H, 3]
The Fortress on Kalemegdan

A settlement called Singidunum existed at the junction of the Sava and the Danube as early as the Celtic times. In the time of the Romans the Fourth Flavian Legion was stationed at this place, and

BELGRADE, KALEMEGDAN, ZINDAN GATE

afterwards it became a municipium and a colony. The foundations of the Roman *castrum* have been preserved in Gornji grad (the Upper Town). In the 5th century the town was ravaged by the Huns. After its restoration it was long ruled by the Byzantines and the Hungarians. After the arrival of the Slavs in this region the old name Singidunum disappeared and from the 9th century onward the Slavic name Beograd was already in use. The town belonged for some time to King Dragutin of Serbia, and at the beginning of the 15th century it was incorporated into the state of Despot Stefan Lazarević, who transferred his court to it. In the Middle Ages the town had already a large suburb girdled with walls and strong towers. After several unsuccessful sieges it was finally captured by the Turks in 1521. When it was taken by the Austrians for a brief period (1717—1739), it was reconstructed as a modern fortress adapted for cannon warfare. In 1867 it was incorporated into the Serbian state. The entire complex of the fortress is divided into two parts: Gornji grad (the Upper Town) and Donji grad (the Lower Town). Gornji grad is built on the foundations of the Roman *castrum*. The mediaeval

remains include the Zindan kapija (Zindan Gate) with the notorious prisons in its towers. It was subsequently reconstructed several times. Behind it is Dizdareva kapija (Dizdar's Gate), built in the early years of the 15th century, at the time when the town was ruled by Despot Stefan. The Turks also fortified the town several times, and the Sahat kapija (the Clock Gate) is a building dating from that phase (17th century). Donji grad and the port had separate fortifications with towers. Kula Nebojša (the Nebojša Tower) was built before the 15th century, but its upper section was pulled down and rebuilt in the 18th century, when it was

KALEMEGDAN, NEBOJŠA TOWER

BELGRADE, CHURCH OF ST MICHAEL

reconstructed to be made suitable for cannon warfare. It has three storeys and it protected the old port, which is silted up today. The remains of the 18th century Austrian constructions include massive walls built of brick and Karlova kapija (Carlo's Gate), decorated in a typically Baroque manner.

BELGRADE [H, 3]
The Church of Archangel Michael

The cathedral church of Belgrade. It was built between 1836 and 1841 on the orders of Prince Miloš on the site of an earlier church. Metropolitan Petar and Toma Vučić Perišić were in charge of its construction. The facades are in classical style, and the bell-tower is Baroque. The church was built by Franc Janke, a civil engineer in the Ministry of the Interior. Especially noteworthy is the wooden iconostasis carved by Dimitrije Petrović in 1841. The icons on it were painted in classical style by Dimitrije Avramović between 1841 and 1845.

BELGRADE [H, 3]
The Residence of Princess Ljubica (Konak kneginje Ljubice)

The house was built from 1829 to 1831 on the orders of Prince Miloš as the residence of his wife Princess Ljubica and their children Milan and Mihailo. The building was designed by Hadži Nikola Živković, and the master builders were Bogdan and Stojiljko. It is an example of Balkan architecture, with some traces of Western influence. It was the first house in Belgrade to be built of durable material. It consists of the ground floor and an upper storey, with an oriel window above the entrance. In the middle of the building is an enclosed porch with a *divanhana* on the upper floor. After it ceased to be used as a residence, it housed the Belgrade High School and, after that, the Court of Cassation. Between the two wars it was used for a time by the Institute for Deaf

BELGRADE. RESIDENCE OF PRINCESS LJUBICA

and Dumb Children and the Museum of Contemporary Art. After the Second World War the Institute for the Protection of Cultural Monuments was located in it. Now the building houses a permanent exhibition of 19th century applied arts.

BELGRADE [H, 3]
Captain Miša's Palace — The University (Kapetan-Mišino zdanje)

The building was constructed in 1863 by Miša Anastasijević, a rich merchant, who donated it to the state to be used as the High School. At the beginning it housed, in addition to the High School, the National Library, the National Museum, the Grammar School and the Ministry of Education. It was designed by Jan Nevola, a Check civil engineer,

who was the chief architect of the Ministry of the Interior of Serbia for nearly twenty years. Another architect, Kosta Šreplović, also took part in its planning. The building has the ground floor and two upper storeys and is designed as a closed palace with an interior courtyard. It is a clear example of Romantic architecture and its facades are inspired by mediaeval buildings. Today it houses the central administrative offices of the Belgrade University.

BELGRADE [H, 3]
The Old Royal Palace (Stari dvor)

The edifice was constructed in 1882 as the residence of Prince Milan, who abdicated in the great hall of this building in 1889. It was designed by Aleksandar Bugarski and it belongs to the type of the closed palace with a conservatory in the middle. It has a basement, ground floor and an upper storey. The facades are in classical style, with pillars, tympanums and caryatides flanking the windows. It was damaged in the Second World War and when it was repaired the two domes above the lateral projections were removed. Today the building is the seat of the Municipal Assembly of Belgrade.

BELGRADE [H, 3]
The House of Aleksa Krsmanović

The house was built in Neo-Baroque style in 1885 for Aleksa Krsmanović, a rich Belgrade merchant. It was designed by Jovan Ilkić. It has a

spacious ground floor and lavishly decorated chambers on the upper storey. It was in this house that the unification of the Serbs, the Croats and the Slovenes was formally proclaimed in 1918.

BELGRADE [H, 3]
*The Old Lottery Building
(Stara klasna lutrija)*

The buildings was designed by Milan Kapetanović in an eclectic style (Renaissance, Baroque, Classicism) and constructed in 1896. The ground floor has a rusticated finish, and special attention is devoted to the truncated corner frontage, which is surmounted by a quadrangular dome. The building houses the Civic Record Office of Belgrade.

BELGRADE, OLD ROYAL PALACE

BELGRADE [H, 3]
The Old Ministry of Justice

The edifice was built in early Renaissance style in 1893. It was designed by Svetozar Ivačković. The ground floor has a rusticated finish, and the upper storey is covered with red ceramic tiles and has five decorative windows.

BELGRADE [H, 3]
The Building of the Federal People's Assembly

This building was designed by Jovan Ilkić and its construction began in 1906, but it was not completed, owing to the wars and political friction, until 1936. Pavle Ilkić made some changes in the original design. It is a typical example of eclecticism, with a mixture of historical styles (Renaissance, Baroque, Classicism). The two monumental sculptures flanking the entrance stairway, which illustrate the folklore theme of the "frolicsome black horses", were sculptured by Toma Rosandić.

BELGRADE [H, 3]
Nikola Spasić's Foundation (Zadužbina Nikole Spasića)

The building was constructed in 1889 for Nikola Spasić, a rich merchant. The house was designed by Konstantin A. Jovanović in

BELGRADE, BUILDING OF THE FEDERAL PEOPLE'S ASSEMBLY

BELGRADE
1. Fortress on Kalemegdan
2. Nebojša Tower
3. Church of Archangel Michael
4. Old Secondary School
5. Residence of Princess Ljubica
6. Captain Miša's Palace (University)
7. Old Royal Palace
8. House of Aleksa Krsmanović
9. Old Lottery Building
10. Old Ministry of Justice

11. Building of the Federal People's Assembly
12. Nikola Spasić's Foundation
13. Hotel Moskva
14. National Bank
15. Officers' Co-operative Society
16. Funds Board Building (The National Museum)
17. Third Begrade Grammar School
18. Officers' Club

BELGRADE, HOTEL "MOSKVA"

neo-Baroque style. In has the ground floor and two upper storeys. The structure of the roof includes three richly decorated square cupolas. It was restored in the 1960s.

BELGRADE [H, 3]
Hotel Moskva

The building was constructed for the "Russia" Insurance Company in 1906. It was designed by Jovan Ilkić, but when the design was sent to Peterburgh for approval, its facade was altered to incorporate some Secession features. It has the ground floor, three upper storeys and an attic floor. The facade is faced with Sweedish granite, yellow ceramic tiles and green ornaments made of faience. The building has been restored several times, but it has retained its original appearance.

BELGRADE [H, 3]
The Officers's Co-operative Society

The building was designed by Svetozar Jovanović with the assistance of Danilo Vladisavljević and Vladimir Popović in Secession style and constructed in 1908. It was one of the first buildings in Belgrade to use reinforced concrete. Especially remarkable is the functional interior space, which houses a department store today.

BELGRADE [H, 3]
The National Bank

The older part of the building, the corner between the 7 July and Car Lazar streets, was constructed in 1889, and the later part was built

BELGRADE, NATIONAL MUSEUM

in 1922. The building was designed by Konstantin A. Jovanović. It is modelled after the closed Renaissance palaces. It has the ground floor, two upper storeys and an attic floor. The stairways, the vestibule and the galleries are especially richly decorated.

BELGRADE [H, 3]
The Funds Board Building, The National Museum

The building was designed by Andra Stevanović and Nikola Nestorović for the Funds Board. It was constructed on the site of the old restaurant "Dardaneli" in 1903. It is in the form of a four-sided closed palace with a roofed atrium in the middle. The facades are in Renaissance style and are divided into three zones. The front part has three domes above the projections.

The building was enlarged in 1930 and it was heavily damaged during the bombing of Belgrade in 1944. After the Second World War it was adapted and converted into the National Museum.

BELGRADE [H, 3]
The Third Belgrade Grammar School (Treća beogradska gimnazija)

The building was designed by Dragutin Djordjević and Dušan Živanović, and its construction was completed in 1906. It displays a combination of academic and Secession stylistic features. The bronze busts on the facade — representing Vuk Karadžić, Dositej Obradović and Josip Pančić — were made by Petar Ubavkić. The school was originally named after Josip Pančić, but was later re-named Treća muška gimnazija, and today it is the Osma beogradska gimnazija.

BELGRADE [H, 3]
The Officers' Club

The building was designed by
Jovan Ilkić and Milan Ruvidić and
built as the Officers' Club in 1895.
It is an example of belated Romantic
architecture inspired by Renaissance
and Baroque elements. It has the
ground floor and an upper storey.
The front facade, which connects
the two lateral wings, is in the form
of a domed tower. In the late 1960s
it was adapted to house the Culture
Centre of Belgrade Students.

BELGRADE [H, 3]
The Building of the Smederevo Bank

The building was designed by
Milorad Ruvidić in pure Secession
style and constructed in 1910.
It has the ground floor, two upper
storeys and an attic floor. The
facade is articulated and finished
with decorative elements. As the
frontage is narrow, the building
extends in depth, projecting into the
courtyard.

BERAM, FRESCO, ENTRY INTO JERUSALEM

BERAM [A, 3]
The Church of the Virgin at Škriline

The church was built in the 15th century. It is a single-nave building with a rectangular sanctuary. Extensive alterations were made in the 18th century: the Gothic vaults were pulled down and replaced with a flat ceiling, a porch was added and a stone altar was made. The frescoes date from 1474 and were painted by Vincent from Kastav with his assistants, as is testified by an inscription on the southern wall. Forty-six paintings depicting the lives of Christ and the Virgin have been preserved. Especially striking, as regards their iconography, artistic skill and size, are the Danse Macabre and the Adoration of the Kings.

BIGORSKI [H, 7]
The monastery of St John near Rastuša

The monastery was built by monk Ilarion on the foundations of some earlier church. The church was consecrated in 1800, and the monastic residences and the refectory date from 1812 and 1825 respectively. Local masters took part

BERAM, FRESCO, DANSE MACABRE

BIGORSKI MONASTERY

in its construction, and they incorporated some elements of native architecture into the residential buildings. A splendid iconostasis, carved in wood by masters Petar Filipović and Makarije Frčkovski between 1830 and 1840, has been preserved in the church.

BIHAĆ [C, 3]
The Captain's Tower

According to historical evidence, the old fortress was built in 1205. It was in the form of a quadrangle with towers at the corners. Subsequently it was added to and reconstructed several times. The Austrians pulled it down in 1890/91. The only surviving part is the so-called Captain's Tower (Kapetanova kula), dating from the beginning of the 16th century. It has the ground floor and three upper storeys, and its walls become narrower in the upper part. A Franciscan Gothic church (pointed arches, rosette) with massive Romanesque walls was built towards the end of the 16th century within the now ruined walls of the old fortress. The church was turned into a mosque in 1592.

BIJELA [F, 6]
The Church of the Virgin (Crkva Rize Bogorodice)

The church is in the vicinity of Hercegnovi. A semicircular apse

BIHAĆ, FATIH MOSQUE

BIHAĆ, CAPTAIN'S TOWER

surviving from an earlier, 12th century church, leans on to the more recent, early 19th century church. Frescoes dating from the late 12th and early 13th century have been preserved in the apse. The Virgin with Christ in her arms and two angels are shown in the semidome, and the Hetimasia with six figures of church fathers is represented below them. An iconographic rarity is the portrait of Bishop Danilo, the founder of the church, in the niche above the episcopal throne. All the inscriptions are in Greek.

BIJELO POLJE [G, 6]
The Church of St Peter

The church was built at the end of the 12th century, some time before 1195, and its founder was Prince Miroslav of Hum, a brother of Stefan Nemanja. This is testified by an inscription carved in stone on the northern portal. It was the cathedral church of the bishops of Hum. It was damaged by the Bulgarians in the latter half of the 13th century. It is a single-nave building (14.5 metres long) with a transverse tunnel vault. The semicircular altar apse is integrated into the cubic mass of the wall. The narthex, to which two high bell-towers were added in the second half of the 14th century (only one has been preserved), is on the western side. A porch and a chapel were added subsequently. The frescoes date from c. 1320. Portraits of Serbian archbishops and bishops, the founder's portrait and scenes from the cycle of the Great Feasts have been partly preserved. The cycle of the Great Feasts includes an Ascension which has unusual iconographic features: angels carry Christ in the mandorla and bring him to the Ancient of the Days.

BIJELO POLJE, CHURCH OF ST PETER

During the Turkish rule the church was converted into a mosque and the frescoes were covered with whitewash. They were cleaned between 1955 and 1960.

BILEĆA [F, 6]
Cemetery with medieval tombstones
(stećci)

The typology of the tombstones in this cemetery is typical of the Herzegovina school. The graves are commonly in the form of a high casket. The ornaments consist of shallow arcades. Figural decoration is very rare. The graves date from the 15th and 16th centuries.

BITOLJ [I, 8]
Heraclea Lyncestis

Heraclea Lyncestis was a classical town founded by Philip II of Macedon in the middle of the 4th century B.C. on the site of a previous native settlement. After the Romans captured it in the middle of the 2nd century B.C. the town continued to develop because it lay at the crossing of the Via Egnatia and the road leading from the north, from Skopje and Stobi. In the imperial times it enjoyed the status of a colony (Septimia Aurelia Heraclea), and in the Christian times it became an episcopal seat. During the migration period and the invasion of the Slavs its major buildings were laid waste, and the town lost its economic importance. Important sculptures of Heracles (now in the Classical Museum in Constantinople), a copy of Phidias' Athena Parthenos (in the National Museum of Belgrade), and a bust of the rhetorician Aeschines (in the British Museum in London) had been found on this site before systematic explorations were initiated. The outstanding architectural monuments of the town include baths, a theatre and a court-house porch, built at the end of the 1st or the beginning of the 2nd century A.D. The porch has a rectangular ground plan (17.45 × 7.45 metres), a colonnade of columns and honorary and votive monuments. They include a monument to goddess Nemesis and a life-size statue of Titus Flavius Orestus, a distinguished citizen and high priest. The statue belongs to the usual type of honorary monuments, but it is superior in quality to the ordinary products of provincial workshops and it has stylistic features typical of the early 2nd century. The small basilica was built towards the end of the 5th century, probably after an incursion of the Goths. It is a building with a nave, two aisles, a semicircular apse, a floor made of marble, a colonnade separating the nave from the aisles and small columns which formed the altar screen. A mosaic floor, consisting

BITOLJ, HERACLEA LYNCESTIS

BITOLJ, HERACLEA LYNCESTIS, MOSAIC

BITOLJ, HERACLEA LYNCESTIS, MOSAIC

of two rectangular compositions with geometric ornaments and with the representations of fruit and marsh fowl is extant in the outer narthex. Fifth century mosaics have been preserved in all parts of the large basilica (36 metres long). The mosaic floor in the narthex represents a masterpiece of late classical and early Byzantine art. A unified composition covers an area of more than 100 square metres: an oval medallion showing a kantharos with vine and two roebucks is in the centre; on either side is a frieze with wild animals and trees full of fruit. Marsh fowl, dolphins, fish, squids and octopuses are represented in the panels along the edges.

BLAGAJ ON THE BUNA RIVER [E, 5]
Šćepan grad

Šćepan grad is located on the hill of Hum near Mostar. It was originally an Illyrian settlement, in which

the Romans built a castrum and to which a medieval fortress was added. The fortress is mentioned by Constantine Porphyrogenitus in the 10th century. In the 15th century the Bosnian feudal lords of the Kosača family converted it into a castle, and Dukes Sandalj Hranić and Stjepan Vukčić had their seat in it. The ground plan of the fortress is of an irregular oval shape, and the walls are up to 15 metres high, crenellated and fortified with towers at the entrance.

BLED [A, 1]
The Bled Castle

An early medieval settlement existed on the shores of Lake Bled, as testified by a cemetery which yielded rich jewelry and other grave goods dating from the 7th—10th centuries. The fortified castle was built at the end of the 10th century, and it is first cited in historical sources in 1011, when it was presented to the Brixen

BLED, BLED CASTLE

BODJANI

BODJANI [F, 2]
The Church of the Presentation to the Temple

bishopric. It remained in the possession of its dignitaries until 1803. It is situated on a cliff above the lake. It has round defensive towers and walls with a corridor. The building technique is typical of the Middle Ages. A 16th century chapel with early Baroque paintings dating from about 1700, and several dwelling houses have been preserved within the castle. After the Second World War the castle was restored, converted into a museum and made open to the public.

The monastery was founded as early as the 15th century, and the old church was demolished and restored several times during the 16th and 17th centuries. The present building dates from 1722. It is in the form of a domed trefoil. The narthex is on the western side and above it is a bell-tower which has a window on each side. Baroque pediments with volutes surmount the lateral spaces. The frescoes in the church were painted in 1731 by Hristifor Žefarović, who had come to southern Hungary from Macedonia. They exhibit a mixture of Byzantine and Baroque elements. The arrangement is traditional: the Divine Liturgy and the archbishops are shown in the sanctuary, scenes from Christ's life and the Great Feasts are represented in the nave, while illustrations of the Old Testament are depicted on the intrados of the arches. The bottom zone contains the standing figures of male and female saints (the latter

BODJANI, WALL PAINTING, ADULTERESS

are particularly numerous in the narthex). A large composition of the Coronation of the Virgin is in the vault of the narthex.

BOHINJ [A, 1]
The lake of Bohinj
The Church of St John the Baptist

The present single-nave building with a presbytery and a bell-tower

on the eastern side was built in several phases. The foundations of the nave date from the Romanesque age, from about 1300. At the beginning of the 15th century the earlier semicircular apse was replaced by a presbytery with a three-sided termination. About 1430 it was painted with frescoes, arranged according to the typical iconographic pattern of the "painted Kranj presbytery". They are the work of an unknown but industrious painter, a disciple of the "Furlanian masters", who also painted several other churches. He has been named, after these frescoes, the "St John's Presbytery Master". In the 1520s new stellar vaulting was added. The frescoes on the triumphal arch are in early Renaissance style and date from about 1525. The frescoes on the facade and in the lower part of the presbytery were painted by Jernej from Loka around 1530. The sacristy was added in the 17th century, and the Baroque bell-tower with a lantern was built at the beginning of the 18th century. Valuable furniture has been preserved in the church. It includes the main altar (1688), a fine example of early Baroque "golden" altars in Slovenia.

BOHINJ, CHURCH OF ST JOHN THE BAPTIST

BUDISAVCI [G, 6]
The Church of the Transfiguration

The church was built in the 15th century, but its founder is not known. The ground plan is in the form of a cross-in-square with an altar apse. The facades are harmoniously designed and built in alternate courses of stone and brick. The church was restored 1568.

BUDVA [F, 7]
The Medieval Fortifications

The old Illyrian settlement existing on this site was transformed into the Greek colony Buthoe in the 4th century B.C. The Romans captured it in the 2nd century B.C. (Butua), and in the Middle Ages it was a part of the Byzantine thema Dalmatia. It was then that the town became an episcopal seat. The Saracens devastated it twice — in 841 and 867. It was granted autonomy and a civic statute under the Nemanjić rulers. In the second half of the 14th century it was in the possession of the Balšić family, and it was captured by Herzog Sandalj Hranić at the beginning of the 15th century. From 1442 to 1797 Budva was under Venetian rule, and then it passed into the hands of the Russians, the French and, finally, the Austrians (1814—1918). The building of the town fortifications began in the early 15th century and it was completed during Venetian rule, when the corner citadel was constructed. Major repairs were made at the beginning of the 17th century. Several old churches were situated within the fortifications: the Benedictine Church of the Virgin from 840 (in the foundations of the present Church S. Maria in Punta), the old cathedral of St John the Baptist and the Church of St Sabas of Jerusalem. The new cathedral was designed by Filippo Perutti and it was built in 1418. All these churches underwent reconstructions in the 18th and 19th centuries, so that they have lost their original appearance. After the 1979 earthquake extensive conservation work was undertaken, so that the original appearance was restored to some churches.

BOHINJ, ST JOHN'S, ICONOSTASIS

BOHINJ, ST JOHN'S, FRESCO

BUDVA, MEDIEVAL FORTIFICATIONS

CAVTAT [E, 6]
The Mausoleum of the Račić Family

The mausoleum was built as a family tomb in the Cavtat cemetery in 1923. It was designed by Ivan Meštrović, who also made the sculptures. It is built of white Brač stone. It is octagonal and has a melon dome, surmounted by a lantern with the figure of an angel. A porch with two caryatides in the form of angels with folded wings is at the

CAVTAT, MAUSOLEUM

entrance. The vaults are covered with stylized reliefs. A sculpture of the Virgin with Christ is on the altar, and a relief representing the Lamentation is below it. The figure of St Roch with the dog stands out as the most impressive in the entire ensemble of sculptures.

CELJE [C 1]
The Church of St Daniel

In about 1379 the original edifice consisting of a nave and two aisles was extensively reconstructed: the long choir on the eastern side was added, the entire interior was covered with Gothic vaulting and a bell-tower was added on the western side. At the end of the 14th century the Chapel of Our Lady of the Sorrows, one of the most beautiful Gothic chambers in Slovenia, was added north of the choir. Its vaults were painted between 1410 and 1420. These frescoes show the Throne of Grace, the symbols of the Evangelists, angels and the Church Fathers. Rich stonework

CELJE, OLD CITADEL

has been preserved in the chapel, including reliquaries, stalls, brackets below the canopy and the Pietà, an early 15th century Gothic sculpture resembling the Salzburg statues dating from about 1400. The church was restored after the Second World War.

CELJE [C, 1]
The Old Citadel

CELJE, CHURCH OF ST DANIEL

The citadel is located on a hill south-east of Celje. It was built in the time of Friedrich I of Celje in the latter half of the 14th century and it attained its greatest prosperity under the Celje feudal lords. With the extinction of the Celje family the town began to decay. Some repairs were made in the 16th century, but the fortress was definitely abandoned in the 18th century. The fortress is rectangular in plan and it is divided by an internal trench into the town core proper and a suburb, but the entire complex is encompassed by massive walls with ten towers. The core consists of the keep with rooms for dwelling (several Gothic windows have been preserved) and an inner courtyard with corridors. An outstanding feature of the suburb is Friedrich's Tower, 23 metres high, dating from about 1400. Conservation works were initiated in the middle of the 19th century and were subsequently resumed on several occasions, the last being in 1951.

CELJE [C, 1]
The Old County Hall

The construction of this edifice began in Renaissance style in 1580, and it was completed, with Baroque elements, in 1660. It was built in imitation of Italian models and had originally two symmetrical wings. In the middle of the 17th century the entrance stairway, the corridors with arcading on the ground floor and the first storey were added. On the first floor is a representative hall with a balcony and a ceiling painted around 1600. It is with these paintings that Baroque illusionism was introduced into Slovenia. A large composition with painted architecture is in the centre. A complete illusion of height is created by means of columns, balustrades, balconies and human figures represented among architectural elements. Four titans are shown in the corners round this painting, and the four seasons and two battle scenes are depicted on the sides. Models by A. Pempesta and C. Cornelisz, based on the engravings of H. Goluns, were used for these compositions. The author of the paintings is not known, but he is supposed to have come from northern Italy and to have been trained in Venice.

CETINJE [F, 6]
The Monastery

The monastery was built in 1484, in the time of Ivan Crnojević, as the residence of the Metropolitan of Zeta, since the seat of the Metropolitanate had been transferred

CELJE, CHURCH OF ST DANIEL, PIETA

from Vranjina to Cetinje because of the inroads of the Turks. It is inferred, on the basis of a woodcut from the Obod Octoechos, that the monastic church, consecrated to the Virgin, was a domed basilica with a nave and two aisles and that it had a rosette on its western side. The monastery was destroyed by a devastating explosion in 1692.

The only remains are an inscription of Ivan Crnojević and some Renaissance capitals, used secondarily to support the present-day arcading in the porch. The new monastery was built by Bishop Danilo in 1701, but it, too, was heavily damaged (in 1714 and 1785) so that it underwent several reconstructions. Petar Petrović Njegoš, the famous Montenegrian poet, built the bell-tower. The monastery was restored for the last time after the First World War, when its original appearance was altered.

CETINJE [F, 6]
Biljarda

Biljarda was built in 1838 to serve as the residence of the bishop and poet Petar Petrović Njegoš. It is built of stone and harmonized with the surrounding landscape. It belongs to the type of the fortified palace, with a surrounding wall and corner towers. After the Second World War the building was restored and converted into a museum.

CETINJE [F, 6]
The Palace

The Palace was built to serve as the residence of King Nikola of

CETINJE, MONASTERY

CETINJE, PALACE

Montenegro. Its design is neo-Classic, and it was built from 1863 to 1871. It was reconstructed several times, the last time in the late 1960s. Today it houses a museum.

CRNGROB [B, 2]
The Church of the Virgin

A pilgrim church in the vicinity of Škofja Loka. It was built in several stages. The original small

CRNGROB, FRESCO, ST CHRISTOPHER

Romanesque chapel was remodelled in the first half of the 15th century as a Gothic basilica with a nave, two aisles and a flat ceiling. Cross ribbed vaulting was added about the middle of the 15th century. The two-aisled late Gothic presbytery and the bell-tower on the southern side were built at the beginning of the 16th century (1521—1530). This reconstruction was made by master Jurko Maurer from Škofja Loka. The pillared porch in pseudo-Gothic style was added in 1858. The frescoes have been preserved in the northern aisle and on the facade and were painted in several stages. The earliest date from the beginning of the 14th century and are on the northern wall of the northern aisle. They depict the cycle of the Virgin. Scenes from the Passion above them were painted in the latter half of the 14th century. Master Wolfgangus painted the Nativity and several saints on the eastern side of the same aisle in 1453. A group of Furlanian painters painted, around 1400, the frescoes on the facade illustrating the Passion. The influence of Giotto's art is especially apparent in the Last Supper. A fresco of St Dominica, with numerous details from everyday life is also on the facade. It was painted by a disciple of Janez Ljubljanski c. 1460. The figure of St Christopher (1464) was painted by an artist from the circle of masters who worked at Mače. Rich Baroque furniture has been preserved in the church: "golden altars" from the 17th century and a large "golden altar" from 1652, the work of master Georg Skarnos from Ljubljana.

of the mosque. In front of the mosque is a porch supported on four pillars and covered with three small domes. Near the mosque are two turbehs with cupolas, which belong to the founder and his wife, the sister of Mehmed Pasha Sokolović.

ČAJNIČE [F, 5]
The Sinan Bey Mosque

ČURUG [G, 2]
The Church of the Ascension

The mosque was built in 1570 on the orders of the Sanjak-Bey of Herzegovina Sinan Bey Boljanić, who founded a number of buildings in this place (the mecteb, the caravanserai, etc.). It is designed in classical style and it has a square ground plan surmounted by a large dome. A minaret, with a decorated sherefa, adjoins the wall

The church was built in 1860. The marble iconostasis was designed by Mihailo Valtorović, who, inspired by the ideals of historicism, sought to revive the medieval tradition by introducing elements of Byzantine altar screens into its structure. The icons were painted by Djordje Krstić and set in place in 1897.

CRNGROB, CHURCH OF THE VIRGIN

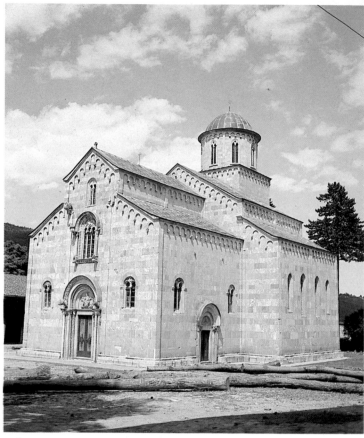

DEČANI. CHURCH OF CHRIST THE PANTOCRATOR

DEČANI [H, 6]
The Church of Christ the Pantocrator

The church was built between 1327 and 1335 as the royal mausoleum. The founders were King Stefan III and Emperor Dušan, and the architect was Vita, a friar from Kotor, as shown by an inscription carved above the southern portal. The building is in the form of a domed five-aisled basilica 36.5 metres long. A tripartite sanctuary is in the east, and a triple-nave narthex with four pillars is in the west. All the bays in the nave and the narthex have cross vaulting strengthened by ribs. Byzantine, Romanesque and Gothic elements are combined in the design and decoration of the church. The facades are built of alternate layers of yellowish and mauve marble and are enlivened by lesenes and a frieze of small blind arcades running on brackets below the roof cornice. Elongated Gothic windows are pierced in the lateral walls. Especially rich is the stone decoration of the portals, windows, capitals

DEČANI, STONE LION

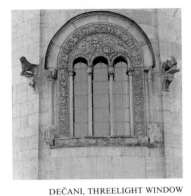

DEČANI, THREELIGHT WINDOW

DEČANI, FRESCO, ST PAUL ON THE ROAD TO DAMASCUS

and brackets. Representations in deep relief of the Last Judgment and the Baptism are in the tympanum of the western portal and the southern portal respectively. The threelight window in the altar apse, modelled on that of Studenica, is richly decorated with tendrils and fantastic animals, while a representation of St George rescuing the Emperor's daughter from

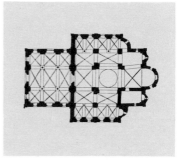

the dragon is in the tympanum of the threelight window on the western facade. The sculpture shows typical features of Romanesque style, and the high quality of its workmanship is particularly apparent in the execution of individual details, such as the lion on the portal between the narthex and the nave. The frescoes were completed in the time of Emperor Dušan, c. 1350, and represent the largest ensemble of wall paintings in medieval Serbia. They are of an encyclopaedic character and represent a veritable treasury of Byzantine iconography. In addition to twenty major cycles, some rare themes are illustrated, such as the cycle of the Genesis, the Wisdom of Solomon and the Acts of the Apostles. Special attention was devoted to the portraits of rulers. A monumental Nemanjić family tree is represented, together with a Calender consisting of 365 scenes,

DEČANI, EASTERN WALL OF THE NARTHEX

in the narthex. The frescoes were painted by several masters, but only one name has come down to us — that of Srdj the Sinful. It is supposed that some of the painters who worked in Dečani had come from the coastal region. The old iconostasis is preserved in the church. Its icons date from the middle of the 14th century, and the most notable among them are the Virgin (164.5 × 56 cm) and St John (164.5 × 56 cm). The wooden sarcophagus of King Stefan Dečanski, a singular example of old wood-carving, also dates from the

DEČANI, ICON, THE VIRGIN

14th century. Its decoration is in the form of intertwined twigs with foliage and flowers. The relief was painted and the frames were covered with silver plaques. The church furniture includes the stone throne of Emperor Dušan and a large bronze polycandilion (choros), decorated with reliefs of two-headed eagles and gryphons, which was presented to the church by Princess Milica.

The monastic treasury is very rich and contains a large number of objects of applied arts and over 150 manuscript books.

DEČANI, NARTHEX, FRESCO, THE NEMANJIĆ FAMILY TREE

DJERDAP, TABULA TRAIANA

DJERDAP [I, 3]
The Roman Road

A Roman road was built along the entire stretch of the Upper Gorge in Djerdap (the Iron Gates). A large part of it was cut into the rock, and where the required width of seven Roman feet could not be obtained, the road was widened by means of wooden galleries. Its construction began c. 30 A. D. and it was completed in 100 A. D. The road ended at modern Kostol, where the imperial architect Apollodorus of Damascus built, in 103 A. D., a bridge across the Danube, over 1000 metres long and supported on twenty strong pillars. The road was of great strategic importance: it enabled the Romans to penetrate into Dacia and contributed to the security of the northern frontier of the Empire. Four stone tablets refer to various stages of its construction and repair: Tiberian (34 A. D.), Claudian (43 A. D.), Domitianian (93 A. D.) and the Tabula Traiana (100 A. D.). With the rising of the level of the Danube after the building of the hydro-electric power plant, the greatest part of the road was submerged.

DJERDAP [I, 3]
Tabula Traiana

An architectural and sculptural structure carved in the rock above the Roman road leading through the Iron Gates gorge in the time of Emperor Traian. The size is 3.60 × 1.75 metres. An inscription commemorating the construction of the road along the Danube is in the centre, two genii are below it, and above it is a ledge in the form of a coffered gable surmounted by an eagle. The inscription reads IMP(ERATOR) CAESAR DIVI NERVAE F(ILIUS) NERVA TRAIANUS AUG(USTUS) GERM(ANICUS) PONTIF(EX) MAXIMUS TRIB(UNICIA) POT(ESTATE) III PATER PATRIAE CO(N)S(UL) III MONTIBUS EXCISI(S)ANCO(NI)BUS SUBLAT(I)S VIA (MR)E (FECIT). After the rising of the level of the Danube the entire structure was cut out and removed to a new place, seventeen metres higher.

DOBOJ [E, 3]
The Fortress

This fortress is first mentioned in historical sources at the beginning of the 15th century, in the time of the internal struggles among the Bosnian feudal lords, in which the Turks and the Hungarians intervened The Turks captured it in 1503 and kept a garrison in it until 1851. It came twice under the rule of the Austrians (in the 17th and at the beginning of the 18th century), who partly demolished it and set fire to it. It is in the form of an elongated triangle, with massive walls of roughly hewn stone and three large towers. A low wall leading to the town, which grew up a little later, runs down the slope. Conservation work was carried out in 1950 and 1951.

DORNAVA [B, 1]
The Baroque Palace

The edifice was built for the Steiermark family Attems, and the construction was completed about 1740. The architect is not known, but he is supposed to have belonged to the Viennese school of architecture. The palace range consists of three pavilions, the two-storeyed main building, and two courtyards. The inner courtyard was converted into a French park modelled on Versailles, with a fountain and sculptures. The interior was richly furnished, and the ceiling of the main hall is painted with illusionistic representations of mythological subjects. It is the finest late Baroque palace with a park in Slovenia.

DRAVOGRAD [B, 1]
The Church of St Vitus

The church was built in the latter half of the 12th century and it is first mentioned in historical sources in 1177. It is an outstanding example of a peculiar type of Romanesque churches in Slovenia: the rectangular nave is extended on the eastern side by a bell-tower and a rectangular choir. The total length is 27 metres. The nave had originally a flat ceiling, and the bell-tower and the choir have tunnel vaulting. The church is built of stone and covered with plaster. The narrow windows have semicircular tops.

DORNAVA, BAROQUE PALACE

DUBROVNIK

DUBROVNIK [E, 6]
The Town Walls

The town was founded in the first half of the 7th century by the refugees from Epidaurus (modern Cavtat), which had been devastated by the Avars and the Slavs. It was under the protection of Byzantium, and later, in the time of the crusades, it recognized the sovereignty of Venice. From 1358 it was incorporated into the Hungarian-Croatian kingdom, to which it paid tribute, but it achieved complete self-governement.

The period of its greatest prosperity as an independent state was the 15th and 16th centuries, when it developed intense commerce with East and West and built a powerful merchant and war navy. During the catastrophic earthquake in 1667 the town was heavily damaged and a great number of buildings within the town walls was ruined. Napoleon's marshal Marmont abolished the Dubrovnik Republic in 1808, and from 1815 to 1918 the town was under Austrian rule. Dubrovnik was fortified in several stages from the 12th to the 17th century. The town walls are 1490 metres long, 4 to 6 metres thick on the mainland side and 1.5 to 3 metres thick on the seaward side. At places the walls are 25 metres high and are reinforced with three round and twelve quadrangular towers, five bastions and the large fortress of St John.

A low outer wall, with one large and nine small semicircular bastions and the casemated fortress of Bokar, runs in front of the main wall on the mainland side. The town had four gates: two on the mainland side and two on the harbour side. The most monumental tower is the Minčeta in the north-western corner of the walls. It was built in 1319 as a quadrangular tower, but it was reconstructed in the second half of the 15th century as a round tower with two platforms, so as to be able to withstand cannon fire.

The reconstruction was designed by Michelozzo Michelozzi and Juraj Dalmatinac. Outside the city walls are two separate fortresses: Revelin on the eastern side, designed by Ferramolin (1539—1551), and Lovrijenac on the western side.

According to old chronicles, the latter fortress was built as early as the 11th century, but it was subsequently added to and reconstructed several times (in the 15th, 16th and 17th centuries). The architects who worked on the town fortifications included, in addition to foreigners, many native masters, such as J. Dalmatinac, N. Ranjina and M. Hranjac.

DUBROVNIK [E, 6]
The Dominican Monastery

DUBROVNIK, MINČETA TOWER

The construction of the church and the monastery began in 1315. The first architects were Nikola and Juraj, sons of Master Lovro from Zadar. The sacristy was built by Paskoje Miličević in 1485. The construction of the bell-tower began at the end of the 14th and was completed by the end of the 15th century. The church was frequently altered and reconstructed, especially after the earthquake and after the French occupation, so that it has lost much of its original appearance. The cloister, designed in Gothic-Renaissance style by Maso di Bartolomeo of Florence and built in the 1450s, is a part of the old building. Local masters (Utišenović, Grubačević, Vlatković and others) altered the original design in many details. The quadrangular courtyard is surrounded by a porch with cross vaults. The Renaissance semicircular arches supported on pilasters contain Gothic windows with tripartite tops. Above the porch are terraces with a balustrade. A number of works of art has been preserved in the church. Especially noteworthy is the triptych of the Lukarević family, painted by Mihajlo Hamzić in 1512.

DUBROVNIK, DOMINICAN MONASTER

DUBROVNIK, CHURCH OF ST BLAISE

DUBROVNIK [E, 6]
The Church of St Blaise
(Crkva sv. Vlaha)

The first Church of St Blaise was built in 1348 on the site on which the present church stands, but it was burnt down in 1706. The new

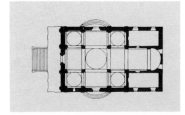

church was designed by Marino Gropelli in the style of the Venetian Baroque and built between 1706 and 1715. Its ground plan is an inscribed cross and it has a dome supported on four free-standing pillars. Four blind and low domes are at the corners and a bay ending in a semicircular apse is on the eastern side. The lateral walls are heavy, enlivened by lesenes, while the front facade is richly ornamented. Four Corinthian columns divide the facade into three zones, the left and right ones being pierced by windows. A broad stairway with a terrace leads to the front entrance. The portal is flanked by Corinthian columns which support a broken gable. The frontage becomes narrower above the richly carved attic and ends in a semicircle

DUBROVNIK, ONOFRIJE'S BIG FOUNTAIN

surmounted by a statue of St Blaise. Another statue of St Blaise, holding the model of the church — an exquisite work of medieval craftsmanship — is on the main altar. It was made of gilt silver in the 15th century and belonged to the original church.

DUBROVNIK [E, 6]
Onofrije's Big Fountain

It was built as a reservoir for the town water supply system. It was designed by Onofrio di Giordano della Cava, a Neapolitan architect, and its construction lasted from 1438 to 1444. It is a sixteen-sided structure, with small columns with capitals at the edges. Between them are sculptured masks from which the water spouts. The upper part is surmounted by a dome built by Pietro di Marino from Milan. The fountain was damaged in the earthquake of 1667, but it was restored later.

DUBROVNIK [E, 6]
The Rector's Palace (Knežev dvor)

The old Rector's Palace, which was in the form of a fortified castle, was destroyed by a gun-powder explosion and a great fire in 1435. The new building was designed

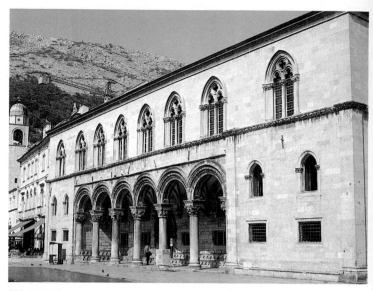

DUBROVNIK. RECTOR'S PALACE

in the style of the South Italian Gothic by Onofrio di Giordano della Cava and constructed between 1435 and 1442. He was assisted, among other masters, by Ratko Ivančić, a mason from Korčula. In another gun-powder explosion in 1463 the greatest damage was done to the western front with the porch. A design for a reconstruction in Renaissance style was proposed by M. Michelozzi, a Florentine architect, but it was not accepted because it was considered too expensive. After his departure from Dubrovnik, the work was entrusted to other masters, who seem to have retained some ideas

DUBROVNIK, RECTOR'S PALACE, COURTYARD

CAPITAL

DUBROVNIK, SPONZA

from his design. The restoration was made by Salvi di Michiele from Florence and by local masters. Two styles are combined on the facade: the Renaissance style on the ground floor (with six arches) and the Gothic style on the upper storey, with eight twolight windows. The entire vaulting is of the cross vault type reinforced with ribs, and the capitals have rich carved decoration. Some of them are ascribed to Pietro of Milan. The inner courtyard is rectangular and surrounded by wide arcades on the ground floor and narrower ones on the upper storey. It was built by Petar Andrijić in 1520, and it was repaired after the 1667 earthquake by Jerolim Škarpa, a master from Korčula. An exquisite picture of the Baptism, painted by Mihajlo Hamzić in 1509, is in the hall of the Great Council. During the Austrian occupation the Rector's Palace was reconstructed several times, and after the Second World War extensive restoration work was carried out. Today it houses the

Municipal Museum, the Scholars' Library and the Conservation Institute. Concerts and recitals are held in its courtyard during the Dubrovnik Arts Festival.

DUBROVNIK [E, 6]
Sponza (Divona)

The building used to be a customs-house, mint and the office for the measurement and valuation of commodities. The upper storeys were used as armories and grain stores. It was built between 1516 and 1522 according to the designs and model made by Paskoje Miličević. The chief masons were brothers Nikola and Josip Andrijić. A Renaissance porch with five round arches is on the ground floor, three Gothic windows are on the first floor and four Renaissance windows are on the second storey. This combination of the Gothic and the

DUBROVNIK, SPONZA, WINDOW

FRANCISCAN MONASTERY

Renaissance, popular among the Dalmatian architects, appears for the first time in the Rector's Palace. In the centre of the building is a courtyard surrounded by a porch, which has arcades with round arches on the ground floor and with pointed arches on the upper storey. The entire porch has cross vaulting. The building was designed and built so solidly that it was not damaged in the great earthquake. In the courtyard is a loggia with the inscription FALLERE NOSTRA VETANT ET FALLI PONDERA — MEQUE PONDERO DUM MERCES, PONDERAT IPSE DEUS (We are prohibited to cheat and make false weights, and while I measure merchandize God himself measures with me). The building houses today the Museum of the People's Liberation War and the Dubrovnik Archives.

DUBROVNIK [E, 6]
The Franciscan Monastery

At the beginning of the 14th century the Franciscans abandoned their old monastery, which was outside the town walls, because of frequent wars, and began to build a new church in 1317. It was completed in 1343. Further work was carried out on several later occasions. The bell-tower was constructed in 1424, and after the 1667 earthquake the church was reconstructed, so that the original appearance of the building was altered. The oldest part of the monastery is the cloister, a masterpiece of the transitional Romanesque-Gothic style in Dalmatia. It was made by master

DUBROVNIK, FRANCISCAN MONASTERY, CLOISTER

Mihoje Brajkov from Bar. It is square in plan (27 × 27 metres) and has the form of a porch which surrounds the inner yard on all four sides. The small and light arcades, resting on paired slender colonnettes, are grouped in sixlight windows separated by massive pilasters. The ornaments carved on the capitals include foliage, human heads and fantastic animals. After the death of master Mihoje in 1348 his work was carried on by Miljen Radimislić and Leonard Stjepanov from Florence, who added the Gothic cross vaulting. The fountain in the centre of the courtyard was installed in the 15th century. A well-preserved element on the facade of the church is the southern portal, carved in late Gothic style by Leonardo and Petar Petrović in 1499. In the lunette is the Pietà with St Jerome and St John the Baptist to the left and right of it,

and God the Father on the top. The church has a rich treasury and an old pharmacy with complete equipment.

DUBROVNIK [E, 6]
The Church of the Holy Saviour

The church was built in 1520 in fulfilment of a vow by the citizens of Dubrovnik after a disastrous earthquake and other misfortunes which befell the city. It was designed by Petar Andrijić, an architect from Korčula. It exhibits a combination of the Gothic (the windows and the frieze of blind arcades on the lateral sides) and the Renaissance,

CHURCH OF THE HOLY SAVIOUR

which is most evident on the front facade. The upper portion, above the cordon cornice, is modelled on the Šibenik Cathedral.

DUBROVNIK [E, 6]
The Cathedral

A new church, designed in the style of Roman Baroque, was built on the site of the old Romanesque cathedral which was destroyed in the 1667 earthquake. The construction lasted from 1672 to 1713. Andrea Buffallini of Urbino was the author of the design and the model, and the master builders were Paolo Andreoti and Tomaso Napoli. The finishing works were supervised by Ilija Katičić, a local master. The church is in the form of a domed basilica with the nave, two aisles and a transept. The front facade is divided into two parts by a large attic. The lower part is

broader and has five vertical zones. The main portal is higher than the two lateral ones. The upper portion is narrower. It has a window with two pilasters in the middle and a gable. A number of important works of art is preserved in the church. The Ascension of the Virgin, attributed to Titian, is on the main altar. The rich treasury contains more than a hundred reliquaries made of silver and gold.

DUBROVNIK [E, 6]
The Church of St Ignatius

The church of the Jesuit order in Dubrovnik was built between 1699 and 1725 and its architect was Andrea Pozzo. His models were the Jesuit churches in Rome. It is in the form of a vaulted basilica with a nave and two aisles. The front facade is divided into two parts by a strongly emphasized attic. A portal flanked by two Corinthian columns and surmounted by a gable decorated with cartouches and figures of angels is in the lower part. On the lateral sides are two niches with triangular gables. The upper part is narrower, and emphasizes the verticality of the building. The ornate window is flanked by two Ionian columns. In front of the church is a monumental Baroque stairway, built by Padalacqua, a Roman architect, in 1738. The Baroque interior is especially ornate in the sanctuary. In the conch of the apse are the frescoes painted by Gaetano Garcia in the style of the South Italian Baroque in 1737/38.

DUBROVNIK [E, 6]
The Church of Our Lady of Danče (Crkva sv. Marije na Dančama)

DUBROVNIK [E, 6]
The Summer Residence of the Sorkočević Family

The church is located on the Danče peninsula in front of Dubrovnik. It is a small votive church consecrated to the Virgin and built in 1457. It contains two masterpieces of the Dubrovnik school of painting: the polyptych of Lovro Dobričević on the main altar, dating from 1465 and painted in the transitional Gothic-Renaissance style, and Nikola Božidarević's triptych from 1517.

The palace was built for the well-known Sorkočević family in 1521. It belongs to the type of the Renaissance villa, with terraces, a large garden, a basin and a high surrounding wall. The facade exhibits a combination of the Renaissance (arcades in the porch) and the Gothic (windows on the upper storey), which was very popular in Dubrovnik at the beginning of the 16th century.

DUBROVNIK, CHURCH OF OUR LADY OF DANČE, TRIPTYCH

FOČA, ALADŽA MOSQUE

FOČA [F, 5]
The Aladža Mosque

The mosque was built in 1550. Its
founder was Hasan Naziri, the
Turkish controller of state lands
and finances in Herzegovina. It
was designed by Ramadan Aga, an
architect trained in the Persian art

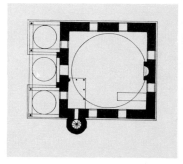

circles. The ground plan is almost
square (11.22 × 11.30 metres). It
is surmounted by an octogonal drum
with a dome measuring 11 metres
across. The harmonious transition
from the square to the octogonal
drum and on to the round dome is
achieved by means of a system of
arches, semi-domes and Persian
squinches. The height from the
floor to the crown of the dome is
19.85 metres. Three sides are
pierced by five windows each; the
lower ones are quadrangular and
the ones above have the upper part
in the form of a pointed arch, as
do the windows on the drum.
A porch resting on four marble
pillars, with pointed arches and
three blind domes, runs along the
whole front of the mosque. The
minaret is attached to the right
front part and is 36 metres high.
The portal is framed by massive

FOČA, ALADŽA MOSQUE, MINBER

stone posts which are connected
by a shallow arch. Above it is a
pointed arch which forms a niche.
It contains a stone tablet with an
inscription commemorating the
building of the mosque. In the
interior, the mihrab, minber and
mahvil are adorned with the finest
carved stone decoration in the
Balkans. It was sculptured by
Dubrovnik masters, who also took
part in the building of the mosque.
The minber (7.90 metres high and
4.20 metres wide) has three parts:
the portal with the stairs, an upper
pyramidal portion, and triangular
lateral surfaces. Everything is
decorated with rich floral and
geometric ornaments in shallow
relief. The Aladža Mosque also has
lavish painted decoration. It includes
a floral ornament in the roesette
on the north-eastern wall and wall
paintings in the porch. A stone

fountain is in front of the building.
The tomb of the founder of the
mosque and the turbeh of Ibrahim
Bey are in the courtyard. The turbeh
is square in plan (3.70 metres) and has
four slender columns at the corners,
which support the drum and a small
dome.

GAMZIGRAD [I, 4]
*Romuliana, the Late Classical
Palace*

The Roman name of Gamzigrad was
Romuliana. The palace was built on
the site of the settlement in which
Roman Emperor Galerius was born
and which was named after his
mother. The palace was an imperial

GAMZIGRAD, MOSAIC

residence and an important administrative centre which controlled the economy and mining of the Roman province Dacia Ripensis. The palace was twice demolished by the Huns, Avars and Slavs. The fortifications round the palace are in the form of an irregular quadrangle, 300 × 200 metres. The thick encircling walls were built in the first half of the 4th century and represent a typical example of the late classical art of building, which influenced the beginnings of medieval architecture. Several large buildings have been discovered within the walls. The imperial palace was built in two stages, at the end of the 3rd and at the beginning of the 4th century A. D. It had several spacious halls and two courtyards with porches, baths and auxiliary rooms. Mosaics with geometric and figural designs have been preserved in them. The mosaic representing hunters fighting with a panther and a lion (now in the May 25th Museum in Belgrade) is an example of the representative style of the imperial art of the 4th century.

GAMZIGRAD, SETTLEMENT

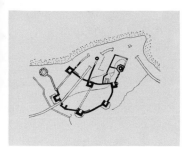

GOLUBAC [I, 3]
The Fortress

The fortress is built on a cliff above the Danube at the entry to the Iron Gates gorge. It is first cited in 1337 as a Hungarian fortress. It was held for some time by the Serbs in the 14th century, and at the beginning of the 15th century it was handed over to Despot Stefan Lazarević by the Hungarians. It had been agreed that upon the despot's death it was to be restituted to the Hungarians, but Captain Jeremija surrendered it to the Turks in 1427. During the Turkish conquests in the 15th century the fortress changed hands several times to become finally a Turkish stronghold. It was abandoned in the second half of the 19th century. Golubac was a military fortress of strategic importance, and it had no suburbs. Its ground plan is irregular and adapted to the lie of the ground. The keep is on the top of the rock and two rows of massive walls with eight square towers descend from it in a fan-like way. After the introduction of cannon warfare the outer towers were reconstructed, so that they became circular or polygonal. The Turks also built an octogonal tower with platforms for guns on the very bank of the river to protect the port.

GOLUBAC, FORTRESS

GORNJAK. MONASTERY

GRAČANICA, FRESCO, ST JOHN THE BAPTIST

GORNJAK [I, 4]
The Monastery

The monastery is situated in a pictoresque setting by the Mlava river. The monastery with the church dedicated to the Presentation to the Temple was founded by Prince Lazar about 1379. The church is trefoil in plan. It was restored several times, the last time in mid-19th century. There are no old frescoes. Above the church is a small cave-church with the remains of 14th century frescoes.

GRAČANICA [H, 6]
The Church Dedicated to the Annunciation

The church is located in the vicinity of Priština. It was constructed about 1315 on the foundations of an earlier building. Its founder was King Milutin. The church is in the form of a double inscribed cross (25 metres long) with five domes. This provides for a vertical silhouette and graded elaboration of masses. The central dome rests on four free-standing pillars. The apses are on the eastern side and are three-sided without, while the prothesis and the diaconicon are designed as separate parekkleseions. The outher narthex was added some time later and was in the form of a porch open on three sides. It was walled up in the 16th century, but its original appearance has been recently restored. The facades are built in alternate courses of brick and stone and are enlivened by lesenes, shallow niches and windows. The painting

of the frescoes was completed in 1321. They belong to the court style which was wide-spread during the first two decades of the 14th century. Liturgical scenes are shown in the apse, while the paintings in the nave illustrate the Great Feasts, the Passion, and Christ's miracles and parables. The narthex contains the founders' portraits, the genealogy of the Nemanjić family and a monumental composition of the Last Judgement with picturesque and fantastic details. The frescoes in the outer narthex date from 1570/71. Several valuable 16th century icons have been preserved in the church. The monastery was heavily damaged on two occasions: at the end of the 14th century and in mid-15th century. It was restored in the 16th century, when it began to develop as a major centre of culture. For a brief period it had a printing press, in which a well-known Octoechos was printed in 1539.

GRAČANICA, FRESCO, SIMONIDA

GRADAC [H, 5]
The Church of the Annunciation

The church was built in 1275 on the foundations of an earlier building. Queen Helen of Anjou, wife of King Uroš I, was its founder and she was buried in the church. The entire monastery was fortified and surrounded with walls, remains of which are still extant. The church is a single-nave building (25 metres long) of the Raška type, with elements of Gothic style in its structural details. The tripartite sanctuary with semicircular apses is on the eastern side, and the narthex, with ribbed vaulting and two lateral parekkleseions is on the western side. To the north and south are the choir spaces with tunnel vaulting, which form a low transept. The dome is octogonal both within and without. The apse is reinforced on the outside by four countreforts. The facades are made of roughly hewn blocks of tufa and enlivened by large and small Gothic windows. A frieze of small blind arcades runs below the roof cornice. The carved decoration is of excellent workmanship and has been preserved on the portal and the windows. The frescoes are for the most part damaged or destroyed. Their arrangement reflects the influence of Studenica. The surviving frescoes include the Communion of the Apostles, the founder's composition and parts of the Great Feasts. Another group of frescoes, dating from the end of the 13th century and illustrating the life of the Virgin, has been preserved in the narthex. The church was restored in the 16th century, but it was neglected soon afterwards. It was thoroughly restored after the Second World War.

GRADAC

HERCEGNOVI [F, 6]
The Town Fortifications

The first small fortress was built
in 1382, when the town was founded
by King Tvrtko I of Bosnia. It was
enlarged and new fortifications were
added to it in the time of Herceg
Stjepan Vukčić-Kosača in the 15th
century. The town was held by the
Spaniards for a time (1538), when
the fortress called the Španjola was
built, and then it came under Turkish
sway (1539—1687). After that it
passed under Venetian rule
(1687—1797). The Venetians built
the fortress called the Fortemare
on the sea coast.

HRASTOVLJE [A, 2]
The Church of the Holy Trinty

The date of the building of this
church has not been precisely
established. It is not earlier than
the 12th or later than the 13th century.
It belongs to the Istrian group of
churches. It is a Romanesque
pseudo-basilica with a nave, two
aisles (11.70 × 6 metres) and three

HRASTOVLJE, CHURCH OF THE HOLY TRINITY

apses on the eastern side. The middle apse is longer, semicircular within and polygonal without. A bell-tower is on the western end. In the interior two pairs of columns are linked longitudinally with round arcading. The nave and the aisles are covered with tunnel vaults, and the apses have semi-cupolas. The church is built of well-fitted stone blocks. All the interior surfaces of the walls are covered with typical Istrian frescoes of the late Gothic style. They were commissioned by Tomić Vrhović, and were painted by Janez of Kastav (Johannes de Kastua) in 1490, as testified by a Glagolitic and Latin inscription on the northern wall. The iconography is very rich: the Throne of Grace and the apostles are in the apse, the Genesis, prophets and saints are on the wall of the nave, and the months are shown on the vaults of the aisles. Along the entire northern wall runs a representation of the Adoration of the Magi with a number of genre scenes, while the Passion and Danse macabre

are illustrated on the southern wall. A fortification of the Renaissance type was built round the church in 1581.

HVAR [D, 5]
The Fortress

The building of the town fortifications began after Hvar had passed into Venetian hands in 1278. A fortress was built on the top of the hill. It was subsequently reconstructed several times, and in the 16th century it was remodelled as a quadrangular building and reinforced with three towers. It was damaged in an explosion in 1579, and it was repaired only in the 18th century. Crenellated walls run down from the fortress on the eastern and western sides. A little way off is the fortress called Napoleon, built in 1806.

CHURCH OF THE HOLY TRINITY

HVAR, BELL-TO

HVAR [D, 5]
The Bell-Tower of the Church of St Mark

The Gothic church of St Mark was built for the Dominican order at the end of the 14th century. It was demolished in 1806 and the only surviving part, apart from the front facade and the lateral walls, is the bell-tower. It is in pseudo-Romanesque style and it was built in the middle of the 16th century.

HVAR [D, 5]
The Church of Our Lady of Mercy (Crkva Gospe od milošti)

The church is located within the Franciscan monastery. It was built at the end of the 15th century and was restored for the first time at the end of the 16th century. A cloister is on its northern side. A relief of the Virgin with Christ, attributed to Niccolò of Florence, has been preserved in the lunette of the front wall. On the western side is a bell-tower, built by brothers Marko and Blaž Andrijić at the beginning of the 16th century. The church has a rich treasury.

HVAR [D, 5]
The Church of St Stephen

The cathedral church of Hvar. It was built at the end of the 16th and the beginning of the 17th century on the site of the earlier Romanesque cathedral. It is the

THE CHURCH OF ST MARK

HVAR, CHURCH OF OUR LADY OF MERCY

HVAR, HEKTOROVIĆ PALACE

HVAR, CHURCH OF ST STEPHEN

first monument of the early Baroque in Dalmatia, and it incorporates certain Renaissance elements. The building has a nave and two aisles. The upper part of the front wall ends in three arches, and the lower part features four pilasters with Corinthian capitals. In the middle is the portal surmounted by a round arch and flanked by two windows. The architects were Ivan Pomenić from Korčula and Baldisser Mechisedech from Italy. A pseudo-Romanesque campanile, made by the masters of the Karlić family, adjoins the cathedral. In front of the cathedral is the town well from the 16th century.

HVAR [D, 5]
The Hektorović Palace

This Gothic palace was built for the family of the poet Petar Hektorović at the end of the 15th century. The structure is adapted to the sloping site. it had a ground floor and two upper storeys. Only the external walls and two elaborate threelight Gothic windows on the main facade have been preserved. It is supposed that the building was never completed.

HVAR [D, 5]
The Town Loggia

The building of the loggia was completed in 1497. It was built on the site of an earlier, 13th century loggia. It has the features of Renaissance architecture. The

HVAR, TOWN LOGGIA

Leroj, the town clock-tower, adjoins the loggia. It was begun in Gothic style in 1466, and it was completed in Renaissance style in the second half of the 16th century. Behind the loggia and the Leroj tower stood the early 16th century Governor's Palace. It was damaged by fire in 1571 and it was completely pulled down in 1903, when Palace Hotel was built on its site.

HVAR [D, 5]
The Arsenal

The construction of this building began in 1579 and it was completed in 1611. It has a large vaulted space (the diameter of the arch is 10 metres) on the ground floor, which was used for the keeping of galleys. In 1612 the governor of Hvar Pietro Semitecolo built a storehouses for grain and victuals with a terrace alongside the Arsenal and also added a storey to the Arsenal, which was used as a theatre. Plays and operas were performed in it as late as 1796. The interior of the theatre was restored in 1800. The Arsenal now accommodates the town archives and a picture gallery.

ILOK [G, 3]
The Old Fortress

The fortress is in Srem, on the right bank of the Danube, and among the foothills of Fruška Gora. The

HVAR, ARSENAL

building of the medieval fortifications began in 1365, when Nikola Kont was the lord of Ilok. It is in the form of an elongated and irregular quadrangle. The strong and thick walls are built of brick and reinforced with quadrangular towers, half-towers and bastions. The walls have crenellations and a frieze of masonry brackets. The Gothic Church of St John (restored in 1907) and the foundations of some other old building have been preserved in the fortress. The fortress fell into Turkish hands in 1525. At the beginning of the 18th century, after the withdrawal of the Turks, a Franciscan monastery was built on the town walls. The western part of the fortress is demolished.

JAJCE [D, 4]
The Medieval Fortress

The fortress is located at the confluence of the Pliva and the Vrbas rivers. It is first mentioned in historical sources in 1396, although it may be inferred from the classical remains incorporated into it that a Roman settlement had existed on this site. At the beginning of the 15th century the town was in the possession of Duke Hrvoje Vukčić, and in 1463 the last king of Bosnia, Stefan Tomašević, was executed in its vicinity. King Matthias Corvinus of Hungary seized the town from the Turks and established the Jajce County in it as a centre of the struggle against the Turks. At the beginning of the 16th century (in 1527) it was recaptured by the Turks and in the middle of the 17th century it was heavily damaged by fire. It remained in the possession of the Turks until the Austrian occupation of Bosnia in 1878. The fortress is in the form of an irregular quadrangle with one small and two large towers. It also has a walled suburb, and a citadel with Romanesque features on the hilltop. The ruins of a Franciscan church dedicated to the Virgin and dating from the end of the 14th or the beginning of the 15th century have been preserved within the walls. The only surviving part of this church is the bell-tower, which has open threelight windows with double colonnettes on all three upper storeys. The late Romanesque belfry of the Church of St Luke has also been preserved.

JAJCE, MEDIEVAL FORTRESS

JAJCE, BELFRY OF ST LUKE'S

JAZAK [G, 3]
The Church of the Holy Trinity

The church is situated in Fruška Gora. The monastery was founded at the beginning of the 16th century, and it is first mentioned in historical records in 1522. The only remains of the original three-conch church are the lower portions of its walls, up to the height of 2—3 metres. The present church was constructed between 1736 and 1758, and the Baroque bell-tower was built in 1753. The church is in the form of a domed trefoil and has apses which are five-sided without. The facades are built in the traditional way, in alternate courses of brick and stone. They are divided into two zones by a cordon cornice. Two rows of blind arcades (large and small) are in the upper zone. The building shows traces of the influence of Islamic architecture (the pillars supporting the dome, the stone portal, the windows). The iconostasis was painted by Dimitrije Bačević and his assistants in 1769.

The church was restored for the first time in 1926—1930. It was damaged in the Second World War.

KABLAR [G, 4]
The Church of the Annunciation

The church was built on the foundations of an earlier building in the gorge of the Zapadna Morava river in 1602. Its founder was heugomenos Nikola. It is a typical example of church architecture from the time of Turkish rule. It is cruciform in plan, with a dome

JAZAK, CHURCH OF THE HOLY TRINITY

resting on four pillars. A semicircular apse is on the eastern side, and a wooden porch on the western side. The frescoes were painted in 1632 and their arrangement is typical of the 17th century. Especially noteworthy is the composition of the Last Judgement on the western wall. The church had a representative iconostasis (dating from 1633), which was heavily damaged in the First World War.

KALENIĆ [H, 4]
The Church Dedicated to the Entry into the Temple

The church was constructed at the end of the first decade of the 15th century. Its founders were protovestiaros Bogdan, his wife Milica and his brother Petar. The building is in the form of a compressed trefoil (18.90 metres long) and has a dome on a high square base, which emphasizes the vertical lines of the building. A narthex with a blind dome is on the western side. Kalenić is the most lavishly adorned church of the Morava School. The facades are in alternate courses of brick and stone, with thick mortar joints. Two cordon cornices divide the building into three zones: the windows are in the middle zone, and framed arches and rosettes are in the upper zone. The vertical division of the facades is accomplished by means of colonnettes and small pillars. The polychromatic effects are very rich. The arches, windows, portals and rosettes have carved decoration. The most

KALENIĆ

common ornaments are geometric. Human figures and animals are represented only in the lunettes of the twolight windows. The finest example is the window on the southern facade of the narthex. Its lunette shows the Virgin with Christ flanked by two six-winged seraphs. The frescoes date from c. 1413 and rank among the highest achievements of the Morava School. The Communion of the Apostles and the Procession of the Church Fathers have been preserved in the apse, and Imago pietatis is in the prothesis. In the nave are the standing figures of warrior saints and anchorites, and scenes from Christ's miracles. The founder's composition and scenes from the life of the Virgin are in the narthex. The church was laid waste and damaged several times, but it was rebuilt in the 18th and 19th century. It was restored in 1929.

KAMENI VRH [B, 1]
The Church of St Peter

The church is located above Ambrus in Suha Krajina. It is a typical early Gothic single-nave village church with a coffered wooden ceiling and a vaulted presbytery. The frescoes in the presbytery were painted by Janez Ljubljanski, son of painter Fridrih Beljaški, in 1459. He worked in the Dolenjsko region under the patronage of the monastery at Stična. The frescoes at Kameni Vrh are his last signed work. In the vault is a representation of Christ in the mandorla with angels and the symbols of the Evangelists. The upper zone of the walls shows St Mariette, St Catherine, the Virgin with Christ,

KALENIĆ, TWOLIGHT WINDOW

KALENIĆ. FRESCO. THE WEDDING IN CANA

St Barbara and St Dorothea. The middle zone contains representations of the Apostles. The Annunciation, St Magdalen and St John the Baptist are shown on the triumphal arch.

KAMNIK [B, 1]
The Church of St Primus (Crkva sv. Primoža)

The church is situated 12 kilometres from Kamnik. Iz was built in 1459 on the foundations of an earlier pre-Romanesque church which was enlarged in the Romanesque age. It was originally a twin-nave hall which had straight wall on the eastern side. A large, well-lit presbytery, reinforced by countreforts on the outside, was added in 1507. Along the middle of the church runs a colonnade of columns (4) with elaborately adorned capitals, which support Gothic stellar vaulting with figural and decorative sculptures. It was built by native masters from a workshop active in Kamnik and its neighbourhood from the middle of the 15th century onwards. High-quality frescoes, which mark the beginning of the Renaissance in Slovenia, are on the lateral walls. They were painted in 1504. On the northern wall are the Adoration of the Magi and the Virgin with a cloak, the protectress from the plague and other afflictions. The cycle illustrating the Virgin's life is on the southern wall. Some scenes, such as that with the Virgin as the protectress, contain allusions to contemporary events (the plague, grasshoppers, the Turks). The frescoes show traces of influences from Venice and the Netherlsands. A skilfully carved Gothic baldachin and 17th century "golden altars" have been preserved in the church.

KAMNIK [B, 1]
The Double Chapel in Mali Grad

The medieval fortress Mali Grad, located on the steep slopes in the centre of the town, was first mentioned in 1202, although it had been built much earlier. The two-storied chapel is a typical example

KAMNIK, CHURCH OF ST PRIMUS

of castle chapels such as were built in the Romanesque age. The lower chapel and the crypt were built at the end of the 11th century; it resembled a tower and had a carved portal. A rectangular nave was added in the 12th century, so that the old church became the presbytery of the new church. The upper chapel, with a semicircular apse, a Romanesque triumphal arch and a separate portal, was added in the first quarter of the 13th century, when the Kamnik feudal lord Henry IV Andeški visited Mali Grad. Both chapels had originally a flat timber ceiling. It is supposed that the earlier chapel was built by itinerant masters from Lombardy. When the chapel was enlarged for the first time, the old portal, decorated with the earliest Romanesque sculpture in Slovenia, was incorporated into the new facade. The brackets, decorated with a carved lion and a dragon, support a tympanum with the relief of a cross flanked by two angels. It represents a symbolic illustration of the Nineteenth Psalm, which glorifies the victory of Christ over the lion and the dragon.

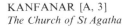

KANFANAR [A, 3]
The Church of St Agatha

The church was built at the end of the 11th and the beginning of the 12th century. It is a single-nave building with a semicircular apse, three-sided without, on the eastern side. Pre-Romanesque frescoes, dating from the 11th and 12th centuries, have been preserved in the apse and on the triumphal arch. The scenes are arranged in the usual way: the Maiestas Domini with St Agatha and St Lucia are in the semi-calotte, the Apostles are below them and Cain and Abel are shown on the arch. The frescoes exhibit traces of Byzantine influence.

KATRAN [G, 4]
The White Church (Bela crkva)

The church was built between 1332 and 1337 as the family tomb of Peter, called Brajan, a local feudal lord. It is a single-nave building with a dome

KARAN, WHITE CHURCH, FRESCO, VIRGIN WITH THREE HANDS

and an apse on the eastern side. The interior space is covered with a tunnel vault. In addition to the two basic cycles — the Great Feasts and the life of the Virgin — there are numerous portraits: Brajan with the members of his family, Dušan, Jelena and other persons who were involved in the building of the church. As regards their style, these frescoes continue the tradition of the early 14th century. The original masonry iconostasis with frescoes-icons is still extant.

KARLOVAC [C, 2]
The Fortress

The construction of the fortress began in 1579, during the rule of Charles. Habsburg, the Grand Duke of Steiermark, after whom the town was named. The first architects were M. Gambona and his assistants. About the middle of the 17th century the fortress was reconstructed and modernized by M. Stier, a military civil engineer. The fortress is in the form of a six-pointed star, with massive walls and bastions (now demolished), which girdle an urbanised settlement with a regular layout. A number of Baroque palaces and public and religious buildings has been preserved within the fortress. In the 18th century Karlovac expanded beyond the town walls and spread to the adjacent settlements, the most important of which was Dubovac, a place with a 13th century fortress, which has an irregular ground plan, and one quadrangular and three round towers.

KAŠTEL LUKŠIĆ [D, 5]
The Tomb of Blessed Arnerius

The tomb is now in the new parish church, to which it was transferred in 1835. Originally, it stood in a separate chapel of the Benedictine Church of St Euphemia (1069) in Split. Both the chapel and the tomb were made by Juraj Dalmatinac in 1446—1448 for Rastoje, a nobleman and a protovestiaros of the Kingdom of Bosnia. On the top of the tomb is the carved effigy of Bishop Arnerius on the bier, with a mourning woman and an angel who spreads a canopy over him. A deep relief on a lateral side shows the peasants of Poljica stoning the bishop who has come with his suite to collect the tithe. A stylized landscape is in the background.

KLIS [D, 5]
The Fortress

The fortress was an old Roman settlement. It is first mentioned in historical sources in 852 as an estate of the rulers of Croatia, who had their seat in the town. From the 13th century onward it was held by several feudal families in succession (Šubić, Svačić and Nelipić). King Bela IV of Hungary sought shelter in Klis during an invasion of the Tartars. The fortress offered stubborn resistance to the Turks, who captured it only in 1537, after a siege lasting several months. It remained in Turkish hands until 1648, when it was seized by the Venetian general Leonardo Foscolo. It fell under Austrian rule in the 19th century. The fortress was built in the 14th

and 15th centuries and two local masters, Marko Pavlović and Ivan Karlović, took part in its construction. The Turks continued to strengthen the walls and also built a mosque, which was later turned into a church. The fortress was remodelled according to the Vauban system during the Venetian rule, in the 17th century. It consists of three graded circles of walls.

KONČE [H, 7]
The Church of St Stephen

The church is in the neighbourhood of Radovište. It was founded by Vojvoda Nikola Stanjević in the 1360s. A charter of 1366 mentions it as a present of Emperor Uroš to the Chilandar monastery. The building is in the form of an inscribed cross, with a dome and an altar apse which is five-sided without. It is built of rubble and mortar and covered with plaster. The frescoes are considerably damaged. They have been preserved in the sanctuary (parts of the Communion of the Apostles and the Procession of the Church Fathers) and on the pillars along the iconostasis (Christ and the Virgin).

KOPER [A, 2]
The Cathedral

The church was built in several stages and it underwent several reconstructions. The front facade is in the Gothic-Renaissance style. The lower part is from the second half of the 15th century, and the upper part dates from mid-16th century. The bell-tower was built in 1480. In the 17th century the church was enlarged and remodelled in Baroque style by Giorgio Massari. The frescoes in the interior were painted by Kristofor Gusić in the 16th century. The paintings in the church include three works by Vittorio Carpaccio.

KOPER [A, 2]
The Belgramoni-Tacco Palace

The palace was built in the 16th century in high Renaissance style. Especially remarkable for their fine workmanship are the portal and the balcony with a fourlight window. The palace bouses the Municipal Museum, and there is a lapidarium in the courtyard.

KOPER [A, 2]
The Loggia

The loggia was built across the road from the old loggia. It was

constructed in 1462—1464 according to the designs of Nikolaj from Piran and Tomaso from Venice. It was then that it got its predominantly late Gothic appearance. In the 17th century (1698) it was reconstructed: another storey was added and the arcade was extended by two arches.

KOPER [A, 2]
The Baptistry

The year 1317 which is carved in the church refers to some reconstruction, although the building itself is considerably older and may date from the 12th century. It belongs to the type of the north Italian Romanesque rotundas (diameter 10.60 metres). It is built of grey-greenish stone and it is surmounted by an 18th century dome built of brick, which probably replaced an earlier one. The walls are enlivened by lesenes, which are connected with small blind arcades. It has seven windows. A portal with a semi-circular top is on the southern side.

KOPER, LOGGIA

KOPER [A, 2]
The Pretorian Palace

The palace originally consisted of two
edifices which were joined later.
The construction lasted from 1386
to 1452, when the building got
Gothic features. The Gothic windows
on the upper storey date from that
time. During the reconstruction in
1482 a new entrance stairway was
built, the windows were reconstructed
in Renaissance style, and a crenellated
parapet was added along the roof.

KOPER, PRETORIAN PALACE

KOPORIN [H, 4]
The Church of St Stephen

The church is in the neighbourhood
of Smederevska Palanka. It was
built at the beginning of the 15th
century, during the rule of Despot
Stefan Lazarević. It is a single-nave
building with a dome resting on
four pilasters. An irregular
semicircular apse is on the eastern
side, and a narthex, added in the
19th century, on the western side.
The facades are enlivened by shallow
niches. The frescoes are partly
damaged. The ones that have been
preserved include parts of the Great
Feasts, several scenes from the
Passion, standing figures and a
portrait of Despot Stefan on the
southern wall. The iconographic
content, the arrangement of subjects
and the style conform to those of
the Morava School. The church
was dilapidated, but it was restored
in 1880.

KORČULA [D, 6]
The Town Fortifications

Archaeological evidence shows
that a settlement existed in Korčula
in the Neolithic and the Bronze Age.
The Greeks established a colony there
in the 6th and 5th centuries B. C.,
and in 35 B. C. Korčula was
incorporated into the Roman Empire.
Later it was under the dominion
of Byzantium, Venice and the
Hungarian-Croatian crown. In 1214
it was granted the status of an
autonomous town. In 1420 it came
under the rule of Venice, which held
the town until 1797, although it did
not abolish its autonomy. This was
also a period of great economic
and cultural prosperity of Korčula.
The town was badly struck by plague
in 1529, when many infected houses
were set on fire, so that only their
walls and front facades (the so-called
kućišta) have survived. After the
fall of Venice the town passed under
the dominion first of Austria, then

of France, then England, and finally Austria again (1815—1918). After the Second World War Korčula became a part of Yugoslavia. The town fortifications, which originally encompassed the entire settlement, were built in the 14th, 15th and 16th centuries and were reinnforced by a series of towers, of which the bastions called Barbarigo, Balbi, Tiepolo and Cappello are still extant. The town was entered through two gates. Above the western gate rises the Revelin tower (1499) and the road passing through it gives access to the small square with the town hall. Its ground floor with arcading was constructed in 1520, and the upper storey was added in 1866. A representative entrance to the town (the Porta Terraferma), built in Baroque style in 1650 in honour of Leonardo Foscolo of Venice who had won a battle against the Turks, is also on this square. The town walls were considerably damaged in the 19th century.

KORČULA [D, 6]
The Church of St Mark

The cathedral church of Korčula was built on the foundations of an earlier Romanesque basilica, of which three semicircular apses are still extant on the eastern side. The Church of St Mark was built during the 15th century and completed in the early 16th century. Its first architect was Hranić Dragošević, and he was succeeded by Ratko Ivančić and Ratko Brajković. J. Carrer took part in its building about the middle of the 15th century, and Marko Andrijić, a master from Korčula, completed the nobly proportioned Renaissance bell-tower towards the end of the 15th century. The building consists of a nave and two aisles; the nave has a timber ceiling, and the aisles have cross

KORČULA, TOWN FORTIFICATIONS

KORČULA, GABRIELIS PALACE

vaults and galleries above them.
The front facade is simple and has
a frieze of small blind arcades
below the roof cornice, sculptured
water spouts, a large rosette and
a portal with carved decoration
in the Apulian Gothic style. The large
Chapel of St Roch was added to
the northern aisle in 1525.

KORČULA [D, 6]
The Church of All Saints

The church is a single-nave building
constructed in 1306. It has a flat
coffered ceiling painted by Tripo
Kokolja in 1713. Two important
works are preserved in the church:
a polyptich painted by Blažo Jurjev
of Trogir and a large wooden
Pietà, the work of an anonymous
master.

KORČULA [D, 6]
The Church of St Nicholas

The church forms a part of the
Dominican monastery. It was built
towards the end of the 15th century.

It was restored for the first time
in 1573, and for the second time in
1655, when another nave was added
to the originally single-nave
building, and when the bell-tower
was reconstructed.

KORČULA [D, 6]
The Gabrielis Palace

The palace is designed in Renaissance
style and was built at the beginning
of the 16th century. A cordon
cornice divides it into two zones.
Outstanding features of the facade
are the four windows and the richly
ornamented balcony resting on
brackets. A low round column
decorated with an escutcheon and
used for the setting up of flags was
placed in front of the building in
1515, Since 1957 the palace houses
the Municipal Museum.

KORČULA, CHURCH OF ST MARK

KORIŠA [H, 6]
The Hermitage of Peter of Koriša

The hermitage is in the foothills of Šar Planina, in the vicinity of Prizren. It is in a cave formerly occupied by Petar of Koriša. Two layers of frescoes, typical of the medieval cave painting, have been preserved in it. The earlier layer contains the Procession of the Church Fathers and the figures of warrior saints under painted arcades in the lower zone, and a representation of the Deesis, with unusual iconographic details, in the upper zone. The inscriptions on the frescoes are in Greek and Serbian. It is supposed that this layer was painted during the lifetime of Petar of Koriša, c. 1220, although some scholars think that it is earlier, since it exhibits some elements typical of the Comnene art (painted arcades round the saint). The later layer is from the 14th century. The compositions that have been preserved include the Divine Liturgy, the Ancient of the Days, and, on the external wall of the rock, scenes illustrating Christ's miracles and the life of the Virgin. During the reign of Emperor Dušan, Grigorije from Chilandar added a new church (now in ruins) to the hermitage.

KOSTANJEVICA [C, 2]
The Abbey of the Virgin

This Cistercian abbey was founded by Bernard Spanheim, Duke of Koruška, in 1234. Its stylistic and structural features make it one of the earliest monuments of the transitional style from the Romanesque to the Gothic. The church was modelled on the Cistercian buildings in Burgundy (Fontenay). On either side of the rectangular choir is a lateral chapel. The nave is higher and separated from the aisles by arcades with pointed arches resting on columns which have capitals richly carved with leaves and flowers. The church was covered with ribbed cross vaulting. Parts of the cloister with a Gothic portal have also been preserved. Considerable reconstruction work was carried out on the building in subsequent times. Like other Cistercian churches in Slovenia, this one was shortened at the western end. It was then that a Gothic chapel was built; an early Baroque bell-tower was constructed later (1632) and new Baroque vaulting was added in the 18th century. Especially impressive is the monastic courtyard surrounded

KOSTANJEVICA, ABBEY OF THE VIRGIN

by buildings with two-storied arcading. The entire complex was heavily damaged during the war, but it was completely restored after the war. A part of the abbey houses a gallery of paintings, and a collection of sculptures, the so-called "Forma Viva", is exhibited in front of the abbey.

KOSTANJEVICA [C, 2]
The Parish Church of St James

The church was built as a parish church in the middle of the 13th century. It is a single-nave building with a presbytery square in plan. It has two Romanesque portals. Especially noteworthy is the main portal on the western facade, with remains of early Romanesque stonework. Slender columns support a frieze of richly carved capitals.

In the 15th century the rectangular presbytery was remodelled as a long Gothic choir, to which Baroque features were added later. Important reconstruction work was carried out in the 17th and 18th centuries, when the church got Baroque vaulting. A painting of St Christopher, dating from the latter half of the 14th century, is on the southern facade, and a fresco of Christ, flanked by the Virgin and St John, which dates from about 1400, is in the lunette of the southern portal.

KOTOR [F, 6]
The Medieval Town

A town in the Gulph of Kotor (Bokokotorski zaliv). It existed already in the time of the Greek colonization, and it is mentioned by Pliny the Younger in Roman times.

KOSTANJEVICA, ABBEY OF THE VIRGIN

KOTOR, MEDIEVAL TOWN

It belonged to Byzantium, then to the rulers of Zeta, and in 1186 it became a part of the Serbian state of Stefan Nemanja. It was an important economic and cultural centre and its builders, masons, goldsmiths and painters were well known. After the fall of the Serbian state it came under Hungarian rule for some time, and then it was captured by the Venetians (1420). The Fortress of St John is located on a cliff above the town and the port. A wall, up to ten metres thick and up to 15 metres high, descends from it and encompasses the settlement in a triangle. The three large entrances were built in the middle of the 16th century, when the major part of the existing fortifications was also constructed.

KOTOR [F, 6]
The Church of St Triphon

The Church of St Triphon is the cathedral church of Kotor. The original church, referred to by Constantine Porphyrogenitus, was circular in plan and founded by Andreja Saracenis, a citizen of Kotor. A new church in the form of a Roman basilica with the nave and two aisles (28 metres long) was built on its site in 1166. It has cross vaulting. Originally it was surmounted by a dome, but it was pulled down in the 16th century and replaced by a bay with a ribbed vault. On the eastern side were three apses (two are extant) and on the western side was a vestibule and two bell-towers added in the 17th century. The church was considerably damaged in the 1667 earthquake, and its original appearance was altered in subsequent reconstructions. Especially rich is the carved decoration, which dates from various epochs. The 11th century baptismal font has carved reliefs illustrating early Christian themes: two peacocks with a cantaros on one side, and a lion and an eagle with the Tree of Life on the other side. The arcading of the original ciborium also dates from the 11th century. In addition

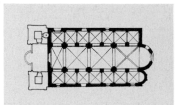

to the pre-Romanesque plaitwork, the corners are decorated with representations of lions pursuing an antelope. The threelight window in the eastern apse is Romanesque-Gothic, and the monumental ciborium, dating from the middle of the 14th century, belongs to the same style. It rests on four slender pillars, and is in the form of a three-storeyed structure octogonal in plan. The paired columns, capitals, foliage and the figures supporting the structure at the corners were the work of one master, while another artist, closer to Romanesque style, carved the

KOTOR, CHURCH OF ST TRIPHON
KOTOR, ST TRIPHON'S, CIBORIUM

ST TRIPHON'S, THREELIGHT WINDOW

scenes from the life of St Triphon, The sanctuary contains a masterpiece of old craftsmanship — a gilt silver altarpiece, the central part of which was made by Hans from Basle in 1440, while the lateral sides are the work of local masters. The frescoes in the apse date from the 14th century.

KOTOR [F, 6]
The Church of St Luke

The church was built in 1195. Its founders were Mavro Casafranco and his wife, as an inscription carved in stone testifies. It also mentions the feudal lord Nemanja and his son Vukan. It is a single-nave Romanesque building (13 metres long) with a dome which emerges directly from the roof and does not have a square base. The

KOTOR, CHURCH OF ST LUKE

facades are made of stone and are enlivened by shallow lesenes at the corners. The western portal has a rampant arch and two stone jambs with carved pre-Romanesque tendrils with foliage. It is supposed that they had been taken from some other building. The frescoes in the church date from the end of the 12th century.

KOTOR [F, 6]
The Church of the Virgin Collegiate (Crkva sv. Marija Koledjata)

The church was built in 1221. It is a Romanesque building (19 metres long) with the Byzantine spatial arrangement: it is domed and has the ground plan in the form of an inscribed cross. An apse is on the eastern side, and a bay with a cross vault is on the western side. The facades are built of alternate courses of white and purple marble. A frieze of small blind arcades runs beneath the roof cornice. The archivolt on the southern portal is moulded and dates from the 13th century. A chapel dedicated to St John, extending the entire length of the church, was added in 1434, so that an aisle was formed. The bell-tower was built in the second half of the 18th century.

KOTOR [F, 6]
The Pim Palace

The palace was built towards the end of the 16th century. It is the finest monument of civic architecture in Kotor. In front of the palace is an entrance porch with lateral loggias and a terrace. The building has two storeys with six windows each. The balcony on the second floor, running the width of the window, rests on richly moulded brackets.

KOVILJ [G, 2]
The Monastery

The monastery of Kovilj is first mentioned in the middle of the 17th century, when a Church of the Holy Archangel Michael, which was later pulled down, was attached to it. The present church was built from 1741 to 1749 and its founder was Petar Andrejević from Sremski Karlovci. It was built by German masters, who imitated the style of Serbian medieval churches, although they also used many Baroque elements. The iconostasis was painted by Aksentije Marodić and dates from 1870—1890.

KRANJ [B, 1]
The Parisch Church of St Cantianus

The construction of the church makes an unusual story. A long choir, supported on the outside by four countreforts, was added to an old Romanesque building in 1400. Somewhat later, in 1430, a new church with a bell-tower was built in front of the choir, which was retained. The interior is divided by four slender octagonal pillars into a nave and two aisles, which are covered with stellar vaults resting on elaborately carved brackets. Frescoes showing angels playing music, painted around 1460 by an artist from the school of Janez of Ljubljana, have been preserved in the central part of the vault. The front facade is enlivened

KRANJ, PARISH CHURCH OF ST CANTIANUS

KRK, CATHEDRAL

by three entrances and two windows. Especially attractive is the western portal, with a scene of the Agony in the Garden in the lunette. The painted windows are the work of Stane Kregar, a contemporary artist.

KRATOVO [J, 7]
The Medieval Towers

A settlement in Macedonia. It was a well-known mining centre already in the time of the Romans, who called it *Cratiscara*. After that it was held by the Byzantines, and from 1282 it was in the possession of Serbian feudal lords. Numerous Saxons, famed and skilful miners, lived in the town. There was also a colony of Ragusan merchants. From 1390 onwards it was under the domination of the Turks, who re-opened the old mines and encouraged the development of metal-working crafts. In the 16th century the town was one of the most important Macedonian centres for the copying of manuscripts. The settlement was formerly encircled by walls with twelve towers, dating probably from the 14th and 15th centuries. Several of the towers are extant: the Simić Tower, the Emin Bey Tower, the Hadži-Kosta Tower, the Krsta Tower and the Clock-Tower. They have two or four floors with timber floors. Several stone bridges were built across the Tabačka river in the Turkish times.

KRK [B, 3]
The Town Fortifacations

The town of Krk is situated on the island of the same name. It was an urban settlement as early as the

Roman times *(Curicum)*, and from the 4th century onwards it 'was an archiepiscopal seat. In the Middle Ages it was ruled successively by Byzantium, Venice and Hungarian-Croatian kings. At the beginning of the 12th century the feudal lords of Krk became its rulers. The best known of them was the Frankopan family, which ruled the island and the town for two centuries. From 1480 to 1797 the town was under Venetian sway. Parts of the town fortifications which originally encompassed the town are in a comparatively good state of preservation. They were built in several stages. The earliest part is the quadrangular tower on the site called Kamplin (1191). The walls and bastions along the shore were constructed in the time of Nikola Frankopan (1407), and the remaining parts of the town walls, as well as the cylindrical tower and the three town gates date from the period of the Venetian rule. Remains of Roman baths and several early Romanesque and Romanesque churches have been preserved in the town.

KRK [B, 3]
The Cathedral

The present building was constructed at the beginning of the 12th century on the foundations of a 6th century cathedral, which had a baptistry and rested on old Roman baths. It is in the form of a Romanesque basilica with the nave and two aisles, but it was partitioned several times

later. Roman and early Christian materal was used for the pillars. A Gothic chapel with stellar vaulting for the Frankopan family was added to one of the aisles at the beginning of the 15th century. The bell-tower was built in several stages between the 16th and the 18th century. The church furniture is rich and stylistically varied. Especially noteworthy is the silver altar-piece made by P. Koler in 1477. An 11th century two-storeyed Romanesque basilica dedicated to St Quirinus adjoins the cathedral. Romanesque carved ornaments have been preserved on the facade of the basilica, and there are fragments of frescoes in its interior.

KRKA [C, 5]
The Church of the Holy Archangel Michael

The church is located in the area between Knin and Šibenik. It represents a combination of various architectural styles: the domed church is Byzantine, and the bell-tower is Romanesque. It is first mentioned in the time of Emperor Dušan, in the middle of the 14th century. It underwent reconstruction in the 17th and 18th centuries. The monastic complex includes a rich treasury with a collection of old books.

KRUPA [D, 4]
The Monastery

According to some unverified sources, the monastery was founded by Orthodox monks in the middle of the 17th century. It is a single-nave building with a dome resting on free-standing pillars and a bell-tower on the western side. The frescoes in the church were painted by the well-known Chilandar artist Georgije Mitrofanović at the beginning of the 17th century. The church contains a collection of icons, including four particularly fine paintings by the Cretan icon-painter Jovan Apaka.

KRUŠEDOL [G, 3]
The Church of the Virgin

The church was built at the instance of Bishop Maksim Branković between 1509 and 1514. It is in the form of a three-conch and has a dome resting on four pillars. The nave and the narthex have tunnel vaulting. The entire church was remodelled in Baroque style in the 18th century. Monastic residences, the bell-tower (1726) and the porch (1745) were added at that time. The old frescoes dating from the middle of the 16th century (1543 and 1545) were replaced by wall paintings painted in oil. The sanctuary and the narthex were painted by Jov Vasilijević, a painter from Ukraine (1750/51) and the nave was painted by Stefan Tenecki from Arad (1756). These wall paintings are based on purely Baroque conceptions. The first zone shows individual saints, including some Serbian

saints (St Simeon, St Sava, St Stefan Protomartyr, St Stefan Dečanski). The Divine Liturgy, the Last Supper the Washing of the Disciple's Feet and scenes from the Passion are shown in the sanctuary, and scenes from Christ's life are illustrated in the upper zones of the nave. The most impressive of the compositions in the narthex is the Dormition of the Virgin. The iconostasis was made in several stages during the 17th and 18th centuries. It contains nine old icons from 1512, and the main icons are from 1745. The monastery has a rich treasury.

KRUŠEVAC [I, 5]
The Church of St Stephen

The church was built about 1380 as the court church of the medieval town of Kruševac. The founder was Prince Lazar, after whom the church was named the Lazarica. It is one of the earliest buildings of the Morava School. It is in the form of a domed compressed trefoil (18 metres long). The dome rests on a high square base, so that the building has an elongated silhouette. A narthex with a quadrangular tower is on the western side. The facades are picturesque and elaborately ornamented. They are built of alternate courses of dressed stone and brick, and are divided by two cordon cornices into three horizontal zones: the windows are in the middle zone, and rosettes and chequered panels are in the upper zone. Colonnettes and shallow niches with round arches form vertical panels. Especially rich is the carved stone decoration on the arches, rosettes, windows and portals. The ornaments may be divided into two groups: one consists of representations of fantastic birds and animals, and the

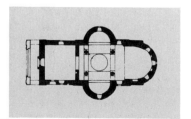

KRUŠEVAC, OLD TOWN

CHURCH OF ST STEPHEN

other is made up of vegetable and geometric ornaments. The most elegant example of this sculpture is the window on the southern facade. The church was damaged in the 15th century; it was painted anew in the 18th century, but the frescoes from the 14th and 18th centuries have perished. The church was restored in 1904.

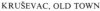

KUČEVIŠTE [I, 7]
The Church of St Saviour

The church was founded by an unknown aristocratic family (Radoslav, Asen, Vladislava) in the time of Stefan Dečanski (1330). It is a single-nave building with a dome which rests on four pillars and has a tall, decorated drum. The altar apse, five-sided without, is on the eastern side, and the narthex with towers, built somewhat later, is on the western side. The facades are built in alternate courses

of brick and various plaster ornaments. The altar apse is enlivened by blind niches in the lower zone. The frescoes have the usual early 14th century subjects. They were painted by Greek artists who followed the style of Mihail and Evtihije, emphasizing even more the narrative character of the scenes. The frescoes in the narthex date from about 1437. In 1956 the original paintings were cleaned and restored.

KUČEVIŠTE [I, 7]
The Church of the Holy Archangel

The church was built in the 1360s. Its founder is not known. It is in the form of a trefoil with a dome resting on four pillars. The apses are three-sided without. The narthex on the western side was added later. It is built of alternate courses of dressed stone and brick. Cruciform pottery elements were also

KURBINOVO, FRESCO,

KURBINOVO [Ħ, 8]
The Church of St George

The church is situated on the shore of Prespa Lake. It was built in the late 12th century as a simple single-nave building ending in a shallow apse. It may have been vaulted originally. There is no historical evidence concerning it apart from a Greek inscription on the mensa, which says that the frescoes in the church were painted in 1191. The frescoes are arranged in three zones. The Holy Healers, Constantine and Helena, Joachim and Anna are in the lower zone; bishops, deacons and the Adoration of the Lamb are in the lower zone; the middle zone contains the representations of the Great Feasts and Ezekiel's Vision on the western side, while the Enthroned Virgin with Christ and two angels are in the niche of the apse. In the upper zone only fragments of some scenes have been preserved. The frescoes are the work of several masters whose names are unknown. The finest frescoes are on the eastern side. They include the Harrowing of Hell, the Ascension, the Visitation, the Dormition of the Virgin and the Entry into Jerusalem. They are close in style to the paintings of Nerezi, although they have a more dramatic interplay of lines. The church was damaged by fire at the end of the 17th century, and extensive reconstruction was carried out in the 19th century. It was restored after the Second World War.

used for the decoration of the facades. The frescoes in the narthex were painted in 1631, and those in the nave in 1701, as testified by an inscription in the church. The door of the iconostasis, made of carved wood, probably dates from the 16th century.

KURBINOVO, FRESCO, ANGEL FROM THE ANNUNCIATION

KUTI [F, 6]
The Church of St Thomas

The church is in Boka Kotorska. It is a single-nave pre-Romanesque building constructed probably in the 11th century. As regards its spatial arrangement and the elements of the facades, it is similar to the Church of St Michael at Ston. The church is in ruins, but the 11th century altar screen has been preserved and is now on display in the Town Museum of Hercegnovi. It has a representation of the Adoration of the Cross in shallow relief, in which Byzantine iconographic elements are combined with pre-Romanesque stylistic features.

LEBANE [I, 6]
Caričin grad

An early Byzantine town built in the Justinian times (6th century). It is identified as Justiniana Prima. It was an archiepiscopal seat and a major cultural and administrative centre of Illyricum. The town itself has three separately fortified parts: the Lower Town, the Upper Town and the Acropolis. The Lower Town had two streets, a cistern, baths, a double basilica and a monumental basilica with a transept (45 metres long). In the Upper Town there were four streets, a circular square, several churches (a basilica with a crypt and a cruciform basilica) and a number of public edifices and private villas. The Acropolis was the most important part of the town. The walls of the episcopal palace, of the *consignatorium* and of a large episcopal church (a triple-nave basilica, 64 × 22 metres) are still extant. A baptistry with four conchs and a vault resting on four pillars was built next to it. The finest floor mosaics are in the basilica with the transept in the Lower Town. In addition to ornaments, birds and Christian symbols, they show hunters fighting with wild beasts, the Good Shepherd and the battle of the Amazons and Centaurs, all represented in the style of the Constantinopolitan court workshops. The town began to decay in the 7th century, and the Slavs settled on its remains, but they, too, abandoned it in the 8th century because of a conflagration and the shortage of water. The first archaeological excavations were initiated in 1912, and they were continued in 1936—1939 and after the Second World War, when conservation work was carried out on the site.

LEBANE, CARIČIN GRAD

LEPENSKI VIR [I, 4]
The Prehistoric Settlement

A large Mesolithic and Early Neolithic settlement, with elements of a new and unknown culture in European prehistory, was discovered in the Iron Gates gorge, on the banks of the Danube, in 1965. The site covers an area of about 3000 square metres. Four chronological layers have been distinguished: Proto-Lepenski Vir, Lepenski Vir I, II and III. The earliest layer has been dated into 5800 B.C., and the latest into 4400 B.C. The first three layers belong to the pre-pottery Neolithic, and the fourth, Lepenski Vir III, contains the Starčevo culture material. The earlier layers contained more than a hundred buildings, which were all built on the same architectural principles: they were dwellings trapezoid in plan, with the floor coated with red plaster and a hearth surrounded by stones. Because of the sloping ground, the wider part

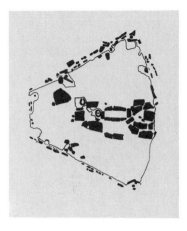

of the floor was raised on small platforms, and the narrower end

LEPENSKI VIR, SETTLEMENT

dug into the ground. In the Lepenski Vir I and Lepenski Vir II layers monumental stone sculptures, usually set into the floor round the hearth, were discovered. Some have ornamental designs and some represent the human figure, especially a fish-like human head.

The character of the sculptures and their siting suggest that they had a cult and ritual significance. Numerous bone objects (pins, awls, blades), polished and decorated with ornaments, were also found, while the upper horizons yielded decorative pottery. A number of skeletons was discovered in the cemetery or beneath the floors of the houses. In 1970 the entire settlement was removed to another place, 17 metres higher than the original site, because of the rising of the level of the Danube. This has been the most extensive conservation undertaking in Yugoslavia to date.

LEPENSKI VIR, SCULPTURE

LEPOGLAVA [C, 2]
The Church of the Virgin

The church belongs to the complex of the Pauline monastery founded by Hermann of Celje c. 1400. The monastery was heavily damaged in the fights with the Turks, and it was restored and reinforced by towers in 1489. It was the centre of the cultural and spiritual life in Slavonia from the 16th to the 18th century, but it began to decay from the end of the 18th century. In 1854 it was converted into a jail. The church is a single-nave Gothic building, which had a bell-tower and an elongated sanctuary with a three-sided termination, reinforced by countreforts, on the eastern side. The church has Gothic stellar vaulting. Fragments of Gothic frescoes are extant on the walls. The church underwent extensive reconstruction in the 17th and the beginning of the 18th century, when it got Baroque features. The nave was enlarged and added to on the western side between 1663 and 1676. The bell-tower was reconstructed twice (in 1640 and 1711). The Balagocić, Drašković, Ratkaj and Patačić families built the four lateral chapels on the northern and southern sides of the church between 1673 and 1705. At the beginning of the 18th century two porches were added, and the front facade was reconstructed in Baroque style. The facade is ornamented with lesenes, baroque plaster ornaments and eight statues in shallow niches. The interior of the church contains very attractive Baroque furniture, including several 17th and 18th century altars. Some frescoes painted by Ivan Rangor in 1742 have been preserved in the sanctuary. The old monastery was reconstructed in the middle of the 17th century, in the time of the Pauline vicar Pavo Ivanović. It was then that the building was remodelled as a closed Renaissance palace with an inner courtyard.

LESNOVO [J, 7]
The Church of the Holy Archangel Michael and Gavrilo the Hermit

The church was built in 1341 by Grand Duke Jovan Oliver, who was given the title of despot some time later. In 1349 he added a narthex, as an inscription in the church shows. The site had been an old shrine in which Gavrilo, a local hermit, to whom the church is consecrated, had lived and was buried. The church, 18.5 metres long, is in the form of an inscribed cross with a dome which rests on

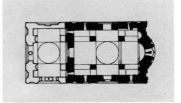

four free-standing pillars. The tall drum of the dome is octogonal without. Another dome, of almost equal size and height, surmounts the narthex. The apse on the eastern side is quite shallow within and six-sided without. The facades are built of alternate courses of dressed stone and brick, with high shallow niches. The decoration in the form of meanders, crosses, chequered patterns and rays is made of brickwork. The outer narthex was added in 1558. The frescoes in the nave date from 1347—48. The

LESNOVO, FRESCO, EMPEROR DUŠAN

subject-matter is usual: the Pantocrator and the Divine Liturgy in the dome, the Great Feasts, the Passion and Christ's miracles and parables on the walls. The lower zones were painted by the most accomplished artist. Especially striking is the cycle of the miracles of Archangel Michael. A portrait of the founder, Despot Oliver, in rich aristocratic robes and with the model of the church in his hand, is on the northern wall. The frescoes in the narthex date from 1349 and their learned iconography is quite exceptional in the Byzantine art of the 14th century. Scenes showing the Fathers of the Church as sources of wisdom which nourishes the people are below the Pantocrator in the dome. The northern end contains a cycle of St John the Baptist, and the western end shows the Forty Martyrs of Sebast. In the northern part is an illustration of the last three psalms. Especially impressive and full of life is the fresco representing Psalm

LESNOVO, FRESCO, FOUNDER DESPOT OLIVER

CIL. An exceptionally fine carved iconostasis, made by Petar Filipović of Debar and his companions between 1811 and 1814, is also in the church. The monastery had an eventful and tragic history, and it was abandoned in the 18th century. It was restored at the beginning of the 19th century, when new monastic residences were added.

LEŠAK [H, 7]
The Monastery

The monastery is in the vicinity of Tetovo. Two churches were built in the monastic complex in the 14th century: the Church of St Anastasia (1345—1355) and the Church of the Virgin. The former is cruciform in plan and has stone capitals with human and animal heads, a feature which points to the coastal carving tradition. The latter is in the form of a trefoil with apses which are three-sided without. Both churches were reconstructed and painted several times. They were restored after the Second World War.

LIPLJAN [H, 6]
The Church of the Entry into the Temple

The church was built at the beginning of the 14th century on the foundations of an earlier Byzantine basilica. It was founded by an unknown nobleman. It is first mentioned in a charter of Emperor Dušan in 1331. It is a single-nave building in which two partition walls separate the nave from the altar apse on the eastern side and from the narthex on the western end. It is covered by a tunnel vault. It was restored after a fire towards the end of the 14th century. Especially striking is the iconostasis made of masonry. Two layers of frescoes have been preserved. The earlier layer, heavily damaged by fire, dates from about 1380 (parts of the Great Feasts, the Passion and the bishops in the sanctuary) and it is ascribed to the masters of Marko's Monastery; the later layer dates from the end of the 16th and the beginning of the 17th century (1621). The church was restored between 1955 and 1958.

LJUBLJANA [B, 2]
The Old Town

The old Illyrian settlement Emona
became a colony in Roman times.
It had a castrum with two streets,
discernible even in the present
layout of old Ljubljana. Remains
of the foundations of Roman
buildings and floor mosaics
have been preserved in the centre
of the town. In the Middle Ages
the town spread on both sides
of the main road, between the
Ljubljanica river and the fortress
on the hill. The Stari trg (Old
Square), Novi trg (New Square)
and Mestni trg (Local Square)
were encompassed by massive walls,
so that the settlement looked as if
it consisted of three towns. The
old castle on Grajski Grič is
first mentioned in 1144. It was
fortified and surrounded by ditches.
The present towers are round and
date from the 16th century, and
the belvedere tower was built
in the 19th century. Restoration
work is in progress.

LJUBLJANA, OLD TOWN

LJUBLJANA

4. Church of the Holy
   Trinity
5. Fountain of the Kranjska
   Rivers
6. The Schweiger House
7. Opera

8. The Gruber Palace
9. Town Hall
10. People's Centre
11. Seminary
12. National
    and University Library

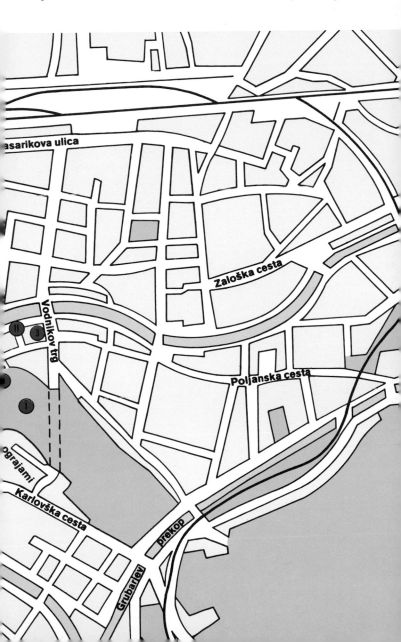

LJUBLJANA, FRANCISCAN CHURCH

LJUBLJANA [B, 2]
The Franciscan Church

The church was built in high
Baroque style between 1646 and
1660. It is a single-nave building with
lateral chapels and an elongated
rectangular presbytery. It has two
bell-towers. The roof cornice divides
the front facade into two parts: the
lower facade is enlivened by six
pilasters, a rich portal and niches, and
the upper zone contains the attic with
graceful volutes and a triangular
gable. The architect of the church is
not known, but he is supposed to
have belonged to the circle of
Lombardian masters acquainted with
the work of Carlo Maderno of Rome.
The main altar is the work of
Francesco Robba and dates from
1736.

LJUBLJANA [B, 2]
The Church of St Nicholas

The cathedral church of Ljubljana.
It was built on the foundations of an
earlier Romanesque-Gothic building.
It was designed by Andrea Pozzo

and was built between 1700 and 1707. It is modelled on Roman Baroque buildings. It is a single-nave church with a transept and a dome built in 1841 by Matej Medved. A series of chapels, with galleries above them, extends along the northern and southern sides. The presbytery has a straight termination. The interior is richly decorated. The frescoes in the vaults and in the lateral chapels were painted by Giulio Quaglio in 1703—1706 and in

LJUBLJANA, CHURCH OF ST NICHOLAS

FRANCISCAN CHURCH (INTERIOR)

CHURCH OF ST NICHOLAS (INTERIOR)

1721—1723, and those in the dome are the work of Matvež Langus (1843—1844). The angels on the altars were sculptured by Francesco Robba. Fine examples of Baroque church furniture (the organ, the pulpit, etc.) have been preserved in the church. The statues of Emona bishops under the dome are the work of Angelo Pozzo.

LJUBLJANA [B, 2]
The Church of the Holy Trinity

The church is also known as the Ursuline Church. It is a fine example of Slovenian Baroque. It was built between 1716 and 1727 in the tradition of Palladian architecture. The architect is not known, but he is supposed to have belonged to the school of the North Italian architect Frigimelizzo. It is a vaulted single-nave building with four shallow lateral chapels on the northern and southern sides. The

LJUBLJANA, CHURCH OF THE HOLY TRINITY

presbytery is straigth-ended and covered by a dome. The front facade is divided by six colossal semicolumns. The interior of the church is articulated by a series of large and small columns with elaborately decorated capitals. The main altar is the work of Francesco Robba and dates from 1744. Paintings of the Baroque artist Valentin Meteinger are in the four lateral sanctuaries, and three paintings of Palma Giovane are on the wall.

LJUBLJANA [B, 2]
The Fountain of the Kranjska Rivers

The fountain is on the square in front of the old town hall. A fountain with the figure of Neptune was installed on this site in 1660, on the eve of a visit by Emperor Leopold I, but it was dismantled twenty years later and replaced by another, popularly

LJUBLJANA, FOUNTAIN OF THE KRANJSKA RIVERS

known as the Fountain of the Kranjska Rivers, made by the well-known Baroque sculptor Francesco Robba (1698—1757). It is modelled on Bernini's Fountain of the Four Rivers in the Piazza Navona in Rome. It is Robba's masterpiece. Three seated figures of old men, with dolphins below their feet and spouting jugs in their hands, are at the edges of a three-sided obelisk rising out of a shell.

LJUBLJANA [B, 2]
The Schweiger House

The house is on Stari trg (Old Square) No.11a, and it was built about 1755. It is a three-storeyed building with an attic. The facade is enlivened by shallow lesenes and stuccowork. The windows on the middle floor have elaborate stucco ornaments and triangular, slightly

curved gables. The portal with
a balcony of wrought iron is placed
asymmetrically. The crown of
the portal arch is surmounted
by the figure of a man holding
his finger to his mouth, an allusion
to the owner's surname (*Schweiger*
means "the silent one" in German).

LJUBLJANA [B, 2]
The Opera

The opera was designed in
neo-Renaissance style by Jan
Vladimir Hrasky and Anton Hrubý
and built in 1892. The sculptures
on the facade are the work of Alojz
Gangl.

LJUBLJANA [B, 2]
The Portal of the Seminary

The building of the Seminary, which
houses the first public library
in Ljubljana, was designed by
C. Martinuzzi and constructed
at the beginning of the 18th
century. The portal was designed
in the workshop of L. Mislej in
1714, and the sculptures were
made by Angelo Pozzo. Two giants
support a moulded architrave.
Above it is a small angel who points
to a cartouche bearing the inscription
Virtuti & Musis. Above the entrance
is an arch with a mask on the
top. The interior contains a
Baroque library with frescoes
painted by Giulio Quaglia (1721).

LJUBLJANA, OPERA HOUSE

LJUBLJANA [B, 2]
The National and University Library

The building was designed by Jože Plečnik and constructed in 1939. Special attention was dedicated to the treatment of the spaces and the material, which is enlivened by rusticated accents. Especially impressive are the monumental stairway and the main reading room.

LJUBLJANA [B, 2]
The Town Hall

The front part of the building was designed by Gregor Maček and built in 1718. It is a typical Baroque edifice. Among its outstanding features are the porch with columns in front of the entrance, and the two-storeyed arcading with 17th century sgraffiti facing the courtyard.

LJUBLJANA, SEMINARY, PORTAL

LJUBLJANA. PEOPLE'S CENTRE

LJUBLJANA [B, 2]
The People's Centre (Narodni dom)

The building, designed in an
eclectic style by Františko Skabront,
a Czech architect, was constructed
in 1883—1896. It is typical of the
age of the Slovenian national
revival. In 1933 the building was
restored and converted into the
National Art Gallery.

LJUBLJANA [*B, 2*]
The Gruber Palace

The palace is in Zvezdarska street.
Its construction began in 1772, and
its owner and designer was Gabriel
Gruber, a Viennese, who came to live
and work in Ljubljana. It is built
in an ornate style. In addition to
the ground floor, which is rusticated,
it has two storeys. Especially
attractive is the portal with a scalop
on the top. The palace has a splendid
interior with a Baroque
staircase and varied stuccowork.
A chapel, with paintings by
Kremser-Schmidt, is incorporated
into the palace.

LJUBOSTINJA, CHURCH DEDICATED TO THE DORMITION OF THE VIRGIN

LJUBOSTINJA [H, 4]
The Church Dedicated to the Dormition of the Virgin

The church is in the vicinity of Trstenik. The founder of the monastery was Princess Milica and its construction began in 1388/89. The building is in the form of an inscribed cross (22.5 metres long) combined with a trefoil. It has a dome resting on four free-standing pillars. A narthex with a large blind calotte is on the western side. The facades consists of alternate courses of stone and brick, and they are divided into two horizontal zones by a cordon cornice. Shallow pilasters and colonnettes form the vertical division, common in the buildings of the Morava School. The drum has small torded columns. The name of the architect, Rad(e) Borovič, is chiseled into the threshold of the passageway between the narthex and the nave. The carved stone decoration is very rich and adorns arches, windows, portals and rosettes. Geometric ornaments predominate. The frescoes were painted at the end of the 14th century, but they are for the most part destroyed, and the surviving fragments are greatly damaged. The extant paintings include the prophets in the drum, parts of Christ's miracles in the choir, and the Ecumenical Councils and the founder's portrait in the narthex. The frescoes are the work of master Makarije (his signature has been preserved).

LJUBOSTINJA, SCULPTURED DECORATION

LJUBOTEN [H, 7]
The Church of St Nicholas

The church is in Skopska Crna Gora.
It was founded by a noblewoman
called Danica, as shown by an
inscription above the western
entrance. It was built in 1337. It
is in the form of an inscribed cross
and has a dome resting on four
columns with capitals and bases.
An apse, five-sided without, is
on the eastern side. The facades
are built of alternate courses of
stone and brick and are enlivened
by shallow niches and elaborate
brick ornaments. A round
window-rosette is above the door
on the western facade. The
frescoes have been for the most
part either destroyed or heavily
damaged. Those that are in a
somewhat better state of preservation
include the Communion of the
Apostles and the Procession of the
Church Fathers in the sanctuary, and
parts of the Great Feasts and of the
Passion in the nave. Especially
interesting is the portrait of
the imperial family — Dušan, Jelena
and Uroš — who are represented
next to an abbreviated Desis.
The church lay in ruins until 1930,
when it was restored.

LOVRAN, THE CHURCH OF ST GEORGE

LOMNICA [I, 5]
The Church of St George

The church is in the vicinity of
Vlasenica. It was built on the
foundations of an earlier church
in the 1570s. It is a single-nave
building with a low dome, a
five-sided apse on the eastern side
and a narthex on the western end.
The iconostasis was painted by
Longin, who is also the author of
the frescoes in the upper zones of
the church (the Ascension, the
Descent of the Holy Ghost,
Abraham's Hospitality, the Nativity,
the Harrowing of Hell, the Entry
into Jerusalem) (1578/79). The later
layer of frescoes, in the lower zones,
was completed in 1608 by four
artists: two Jovans, Georgije and
Nikola. They were commissioned
by monks Genadije and Akakije.

LOVRAN [B, 3]
The Church of St George

The church was built in the 14th
century. It has a choir rectangular
in plan with a stellar vault, modelled
on that of Pazin. During the
reconstruction in the Baroque age, the
lateral chapels were joined to the
nave. The frescoes were completed in
1479 and were painted by the artists
from an Istrian workshop. They show
scenes from Christ's life, the
Last Judgment, the Tree of Jesse,
and the legend of St George, the
patron of the church.

MAČE NEAR PREDVOR [B, 1]
The Church of St Nicholas

A Romanesque church reconstructed in the Gothic era as a single-nave building with a flat coffered ceiling, which was painted with Renaissance motifs in 1649. The church is best known for its frescoes dating from 1467, which are the most representative examples of the late Gothic idealistic style in Slovenia. They are the work of an unknown artist called the "Mače Master". The Adoration of the Magi and the Coming of St Ursula to Bologne are on the northern side, and St Christopher and Christ on the Cross between Mary and St John are on the external wall of the southern facade. The frescoes on the external wall betray traces of the influence of the graphic art of Master E. S.

MAGLAJ [E, 4]
The Medieval Fortress

The fortress is on the right bank of the Bosna river, at the foot of mountain Ozren. It was built as a strategic stronghold at the beginning of the 15th century. It has massive walls, four defensive towers, accommodation for the garrison and prisons. The Turks captured it in 1503. During Turkish rule it underwent several reconstructions. It was during one of them that the clock-tower was added. A garrison was maintained in the fortress until the Austrian occupation in Bosnia in 1878.

MAGLIČ [H, 5]
The Fortress

The fortress is in the Ibar valley, 16 kilometres from Kraljevo. It defended old Rascia from the north. The historical evidence concerning it is very scarce. The biography of Archbishop Danilo II, dating from the beginning of the 15th century, says that he restored the Church of St George and "exquisite palaces and other cells" in the fortress. The fortress has an elongated form, adjusted to the lie of the ground. On the eastern side is a high keep, and there are seven square towers on the thick walls. The foundations of the Church of St George and of a large edifice with a hall of unknown use have been preserved within the fortress.

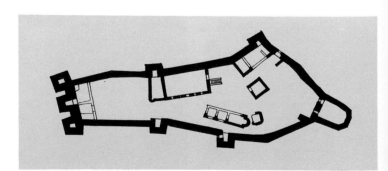

MAGLIČ, FORTRESS

MALA REMETA [G, 2]
The Church of the Virgin

The church is in Fruška Gora.
A monastery has existed on this
site since the XVI century. The
present church was built in 1739, and
its founder was Stanko Milinković
from Šuljam. It was built by masters

MALA REMETA, CHURCH OF THE VIRGIN

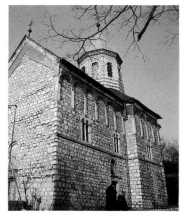

Todor and Nikola, whose building
contract, concluded with the
monastic community, has been
preserved. The church is in the
form of a domed trefoil. The altar
apse is three-sided without, and the
lateral spaces are rectangular. The
facades are built of stone of
various colours. A cordon cornice
divides them into two zones: the
upper zone contains twolight
windows and blind arcades. The
church got the iconostasis in 1757;
the main icons on it were painted
by Janko Halkozović, and the others
are by an unknown asistant of his.

MANASTIR [I, 8]
The Church of St Nicholas

The church is in the neighbourhood
of Prilep. A new and large church
was built in 1266, during the reign
of Michael VIII Palaeologus, on the
site of a smaller 11th century church.
The founder was heugomenos
Akakije. It is in the form of an
aisled basilica with three apses on the

eastern side. The Greek inscription, of major importance both from the historical and palaeoraphical view, runs the length of the nave and says that the frescoes in the church were completed in 1271 under the supervision of deacon Jovan, who had engaged "skillful and excellent masters". In the sanctuary are the Procession of the Church Fathers, the Communion of the Apostles, and the Virgin with two archangels; in the nave are scenes from Christ's life, warrior saints and martyrs; the last Judgment and the founder's composition are in the northern aisle; and the Tree of Jesse, the Ladder of John the Ladderer and a cycle devoted to St Nicholas are in the southern aisle. As regards the treatment of the figures, the frescoes follow earlier models and traditional patterns dating from the 11th and 12th centuries.

MARIBOR [C, 1]
The Church of St John the Baptist

This is the cathedral church of Maribor. It was built c. 1260, and it is a Romanesque basilica with the nave, two aisles, flat timber ceilings and three semicircular apses. The wide arcades separating the aisles from the nave rest on massive pillars. The southern arcade has round arches, while the northern one has slightly pointed arches. A long choir was added to the eastern side towards the end of the 14th century. It is supported from without by a series of countreforts and has a stone partition within. The aisles were vaulted at the same time, while the nave got vaulting in 1520. The bell-tower on the western side is in Renaissance style. Fine late Gothic stone pews and a wooden sculpture representing the Virgin with Christ (c. 1510) are in the choir, and several 16th century memorial tablets can be seen in the southern aisle.

MARIBOR [C, 1]
The Church of St Aloysius

The church, built in pure Baroque style, was completed in 1769, and its architect was P. Holy. It is in the form of a domed octagon. The vestibule is separated from the square by Baroque wrought-iron railings. A classical portal was added in 1831. It was used as a military storehouse for a time, and it was restored in 1859.

MARIBOR, CHURCH OF ST JOHN THE BAPTIST

CHURCH OF ST JOHN THE BAPTIST, THE VIRGIN WITH CHIRST AND PEWS

MARIBOR [C, 1]
The Fortress

In the 12th century the earlier small farming settlement grew into the seat of the regional feudal lords. It was in the possession of the Spanheim family and later it passed under Austrian rule and developed as an important strategic stronghold in the Habsburg expansion towards the Adriatic. The town walls and the towers were completed in the 16th century. The building of the town-castle began in 1478, but it was later (1560) remodelled in Renaissance style by Domenico dell'Allio, who added new fortifications, bastions and a loggia. The great hall was given a Baroque appearance in the 17th century (the stucco ceiling and historical compositions), and the Rococo stairway was added in 1749. The building now houses a museum.

MARIBOR [C, 1]
The Town Hall

It is located on the main square. It has been rebuilt and reconstructed several times. The Renaissance front facade with a portal and a balcony dates from the 16th century, and the courtyard side is Baroque. The main hall is also decorated in Baroque style.

MARKO'S MONASTERY

MARKOV MANASTIR [I, 7]
Marko's Monastery, Sušica

A monastic church near Skopje, dedicated to St Demetrius. The construction of the church began in 1345, in the time of Emperor Dušan; it was resumed during the reign of King Vukašin, between 1366 and 1371, and it was completed in the eighth decade of the 14th century, in the time of King Marko, after whom it was named. Its ground plan is in the form of an inscribed cross (16th metres long) and it has a dome resting on four free-standing pillars. An apse, five-sided without, is on the eastern side, and a narthex with a blind cupola is on the western side. The narthex is separated from the church by a tripartite opening with two columns, a structural element known also from monastery Matejče. The facades are built of brick and stone and have rich brickwork decoration in the form of chessboard patterns, zig-zag lines, rays and crosses. The decorative elements include shallow niches, walled up twolight windows and rosettes. A moulded cornice runs round the entire church at the level of the socle. An open porch was added in front of the church. The frescoes were painted in the eighth decade of the 14th century, and their iconography is based on religious poetry. The entire lower zone is occupied by saints and rulers approaching Christ-Emperor and the Virgin-Empress, which is in fact an illustration of the songs sung during the liturgy. Several cycles are illustrated in the middle and upper zones of the walls of the church: the Great Feasts, the Passion, Christ's miracles, and a cycle illustrating the Acathist Hymn (a song in praise of the Virgin).

These cycles include some new and unusual subjects, such as the Massacre of the Innocents with a very expressive fresco of the Weeping of Rachel. Four cycles are shown in the narthex: the cycle of the Virgin, the cycle of St Nicholas, the cycle of St Demetrius and the Songs of the Canon with Christ the Logos. The common features of the paintings of Marko's Monastery are a tendency to lively movement, vigorous expression and deformed physiognomies. Parts of a 14th century stone iconostasis and of a bronze candelabre have been preserved in the church.

MARKO'S MONASTERY, FRESCO, ST BAZIL

MARTIJANCI [D, 1]
The Church of St Martin

The church is a single-nave Gothic
building with a bell-tower on
the western side and a narrow
presbytery on the eastern side.
The presbytery is supported by
countreforts on the outside.
The church was built and painted
with frescoes by Janez from
Radgona in 1392, as an inscription
on the southern wall of the
presbytery testifies. They include
scenes from the legend of St Martin,
the patron saint of the church, an
interesting founder's composition,
which shows the parish priest
Erasmus kneeling in front of the
apostles, and a self-portrait
of the painter.

MATEJČE [I, 7]
*The Church of the Nativity of the
Virgin*

The church is near Kumanovo in
Skopska Crna Gora. The building of
the church began during the lifetime
of Emperor Dušan, but it was
completed by Empress Jelena and her
son Uroš between 1355 and 1360.
The monastery was a centre of
literary and copying activity in
the 15th century. Vladislav
Grammaticus worked in it for
some time. The church is in the
form of an inscribed elongated cross
with five domes. The central dome
rests on four pillars and is
twelve-sided without, which is
very rare in the architecture of this
type. Three semicircular apses are

MATEJČE, CHURCH OF THE NATIVITY OF THE VIRGIN

on the eastern side, and a narthex, separated from the nave by a tripartite opening with two lower pillars, is on the western side. The interior is spacious and extremely well lit. The facades are built of roughly hewn stone and enlivened by pilasters and shallow niches. The domes are built of brick. The frescoes were painted immediately after the completion of the building. In addition to the portraits of the founders, Jelena, Uroš and Dušan, and the standing figures of saints in the first zone, almost fifteen cycles are illustrated. They include the Great Feasts, Christ's miracles and parables, the Passion, the life of the Virgin, the Acathist Hymn, the Acts of the Apostles, the miracles of the Archangels, the Legend of Abgar, and the Seven Ecumenical Councils. The frescoes of Matejče are of an encyclopaedic and narrative character. The monastery was damaged and abandoned in the 17th century. It was restored in 1926 and 1934.

MATKA [H, 7]
The Church of the Virgin

The church is situated on the left bank of the Treska river. It was built in mid-14th century for Bojko, the son of Danica, the noblewoman who founded the church at Ljuboten. It is in the form of a compressed inscribed cross with a dome and an apse, which is three-sided without. It is built of broken stone and brick, and the facades are enlivened by lesenes. The original frescoes have not been preserved and the later ones

MILEŠEVA, CHURCH OF THE ASCENSION

were painted in 1497. An inscription refers to Milica and Tošnik, who, together with their son Nikola and Metropolitan Atanasije, restored and repaired the church and built the narthex. The paintings are of indifferent quality. They include standing figures, medallions and, in the upper zones, the great Feasts and the Passion. The founders, Milica and Nikola, are represented in citizens' clothes on the western wall.

MILEŠEVA [G, 5]
The Church of the Ascension

The church is in the vicinity of Prijepolje. It was built in 1218—19, during the reign of Prince Vladislav, who became King of Serbia in 1234. The monastery played an important

MILEŠEVA, FRESCO, ANGEL AT CHRIST'S TOMB (DETAIL)

historical role in the Middle Ages. The body of St Sava was transferred from Trnovo and buried in it. In 1377 the Ban of Bosnia Tvrtko had himself crowned in Mileševa as King of Serbia and Bosnia. In the 16th century the monastery had a printing press which published church books (psalters and prayer-books). The church belongs to the architectural style fostered by the Raška School.

It is a single-nave building (30 metres long) with a drum resting on a cubic base. A tripartite apse is on the eastern side, and a narthex on the western end. The wall between the narthex and the nave was pulled down later. Choirs, of smaller height, are on the northern and southern sides. A domed outer narthex with two small lateral parekkleseions was added soon after the completion

MILEŠEVA, FRESCO, ANGEL AT CHRIST'S TOMB

of the church. The facades are covered with plaster and enlivened by a frieze of small blind arcades running below the roof cornice. The church had originally a stone portal with sculptured decoration, of which only a lion has been preserved. The church underwent several reconstructions, so that it has lost much of its original appearance. The surviving frescoes date from various periods. The earliest and finest were painted when the church was built, before 1228. The background of the frescoes in the nave is covered with pieces of gold foil with drawn squares imitating mosaic. The Angel at Christ's Tomb, a masterpiece of Serbian medieval painting, belongs to this type of frescoes.

Below this mural, which is on the southern wall, is the founder's composition, which shows Vladislav

MILEŠEVA, FRESCO, ST SAVA

with a model of the church being led to Christ by the Virgin. The frescoes in the narthex and the sanctuary have a blue background. Archbishops, warrior saints, martyrs and monks are represented in the lower zone. The usual arrangement of the compositions in the middle and upper zones is slightly modified. The most imposing are the monumental compositions of the Great Feasts. The monumental appearance of the figures is best illustrated by the Virgin in the Annunciation. On the northern wall of the narthex is the remarkable gallery of portraits of the Nemanjić family — Stefan Nemanja (as monk Simeon), St Sava as Archbishop, Stefan the First-Crowned and his two sons, Radoslav and Vladislav. It is supposed that the main painters of these frescoes were Greek. The frescoes in the outer narthex were painted c. 1236. They are not so good as those in the nave for they were the work of local masters seeking to imitate the style of the artists who painted the earlier layer. Some of these frescoes, e. g. the Last Judgment, have a red background. In the 16th century the frescoes in

the church were painted anew, and several compositions from that phase have been preserved (the Last Supper, the Forty Martyrs of Sebast).

MLJET [E, 6]
The Church of the Virgin

The Benedictine abbey on the island of Mljet was founded by Desa, the lord of Raška, in 1151. The church was built a little later, at the end of the 12th century. We know this because King Stefan the First-Crowned of Serbia is mentioned as its donor already at the beginning of the 13th century. It is a single-nave building with three semicircular apses on the eastern side. A blind dome, submerged in the cubic mass of the wall and covered with a pyramidal roof rises above the central part. The facades are built of dressed stone and have a frieze of small blind arcades below the roof cornice. The architectural style of the church is similar to that of Apulian Romanesque, but it is also associated

MLJET, CHURCH OF THE VIRGIN

MORAČA, ICON, SS SAVA AND SIMEON OF SERBIA

with the monuments of the Serbian Raška School, especially with Studenica, which was built at the same time. The church underwent reconstruction in the 15th and 16th centuries, when the two lateral choir spaces were probably added.

MORAČA [G, 6]
The Church of the Dormition of the Virgin

MORAČA, CHURCH OF THE DORMITION OF THE VIRGIN

The church is in the vicinity of Kolašin. It was built in 1251/52.

Its founder was Prince Stefan, the
son of Duke Vukan. In the period
of the Turkish conquests the
monastery was abandoned, but it
was restored in the 16th century
and a lively artistic activity
developed in it. The church is
a single-nave building (24.40
metres long) with a dome, a low
choir transept and a semicircular
apse on the eastern side. A
diaconicon and a prothesis, built
as separate rooms, adjoin the
building laterally. The narthex
is on the western side. The
parekkleseion of St Stephen
adjoins it on the northern side.
The church is built of stone and
covered with plaster. Below the
roof cornice runs a frieze of
small blind arcades. Carved
ornaments with the
representations of gryphons have
been preserved on the western

MORAČA, FRESCO, ST ELIJAH PERFORMING ANOINTMENT

portal and on the bishop's throne. The earliest surviving frescoes (c. 1260) are in the diaconicon: the Virgin, the Annunciation, Deesis and scenes from the life of St Elijah. The other frescoes date from the 16th (the central part of the sanctuary, the nave and the narthex) or the 17th century (the prothesis, the outer facade, the parekkleseion of St Stephen and the small church of St Nicholas in the monastic courtyard. The carved iconostasis dates from the very beginning of the 17th century. The monastery has a large collection of icons. Especially worthy of scrutiny, because of its high artistic quality and the beauty of its carved wooden frame, is the icon of SS Sava and Simeon with the scenes from St Sava's life.

MOSTAR [E, 5]
The Old Stone Bridge

The construction of this bridge spanning the Neretva river was completed in 1566 on the orders of Suleyman the Magnificent. Its architect was mimar Heyrudin Junior, a disciple of mimar Sinan. The bridge has a single arch with a span of 28.70 metres, so that it raises steeply towards the centre. It is four metres wide and its height is 21 metres when the water level is normal. The materials used for its construction were a kind of stone called *tenelija* and, to a lesser extent, limestone. At each end of the bridge is a tower, built some time previously: Herceguša, which was used as a powder magazine, and Ćelovina, which was a watch-tower and a prison. The bridge is one of the finest examples of the bold designs of Turkish architects and of the skill of Herzegovian and Dubrovnik builders.

MOSTAR [E, 5]
The Karadjoz Bey Mosque

The mosque was built by Mehmed Karadjos Bey, the brother of two Turkish high officials, in 1557. The structure is a complete replica of that of the Aladža Mosque in Foča, and the transition from the square plan (10.65 × 10.65 metres) to the circular base of the dome is effected in the same way. The mihrab, minber and mahvil are of the same dimensions, but they lack the floral decoration of the mosque in Foča. Dubrovnik masters took part in the building and decoration of the mosque.

MOSTAR, STONE BRIDGE, NORTHERN TOWER

MOTOVUN [A, 3]
The Old Town

The old town is on the top of
a hillock above the Mirna river.
A settlement existed on this site
as early as the prehistoric times.
It was in the possession of the
bishops of Poreč and the Patriarch
of Aquileia in the early Middle
Ages, and it fell under Venetian
rule in 1278. The town fortifications
with bulwarks, towers and gates
were built from the 13th to the
17th century and consist of three
circles. The earliest is the
innermost zone encompassing
the core of the settlement, with
a massive 13th century
Romanesque bell-tower on the
main square. Near it is a
Renaissance church designed by
A. Palladio and built in 1600,
and the town loggia, dating from
the early 17th century.

MOTOVUN, OLD TOWN

MULJAVA [B, 2]
*The Church of the Dormition of the
Virgin*

The church is in the neighbourhood
of Stična. It was built in the first

MOSTAR, STONE BRIDGE

NEREZI, CHURCH OF ST PANTELEIMON

half of the 15th century as a
single-nave building with a
presbytery with ribbed vaulting.
It is famous for its large ensemble
of frescoes painted by Janez
of Ljubljana in 1456, as an
inscription in the church shows.
The arrangement and iconography
of these frescoes are typical of
the middle of the 15th century:
Christ in the mandorla is painted
on the vault of the presbytery, and
symbols of the Evangelists and
angels are round him. The Passion
is illustrated in the upper zone
of the walls in the presbytery
and the Apostles are
represented in the middle zone.
The Tree of Jesse is on the
triumphal arch, Cain and Abel and
the Adoration of the Magi are on
the northern wall, scenes from
the life of St Paul are on the
southern wall, and the Last
Judgment is depicted on the
western wall. A cycle illustrating
the life of the Virgin is shown
in the presbytery. A Gothic
wooden sculpture, the Virgin
with Christ (c. 1450), and the
Baroque main altar, made by

Jernej Plumenberger from
Ljubljana and gilt by Jakob
Menhar in 1674, have been
preserved in the church.

NAUPARA [I, 5]
*The Church of the Nativity of the
Virgin*

The church is in the vicinity of
Kruševac. It was built in the 1370s.
There is no historical evidence
of its founder. The building is in
the form of a domed compressed
trefoil. The narthex on the
western side has two storeys. The
facades are built of rough stone,
and the most noteworthy
ornaments are the two
monumental rosettes, featuring
the signs of the Zodiac, on the
western side. The church was
restored and remodelled at the
beginning of the 19th century,
so that it has lost its original
appearance. Its frescoes have
not been preserved.

NEREZI. FRESCO, ST PANTELEIMON

NEREZI [I, 7]
The Church of St Panteleimon

The church is in the vicinity of Skopje. It was built by Alexius Angelos, the Prince of Byzantium and son of Constantine Angelos and Theodora, the daughter of Emperor Alexis I Comnenus. An inscription in the church refers to this. The building is 15 metres long, and its ground plan is in the form of an inscribed cross. It has five domes, the central one being higher and wider than the others. The corner spaces are separated from the central cruciform design. The narthex on the western side has transverse vaulting. Three apses are on the eastern side: the two lateral ones are shallow, while the central apse is deeper and five-sided without. It is built in the Byzantine fashion, in alternate courses of stone and brick.

Threelight windows are in the lower zone of the lateral facades and in the central apse, and twolight windows are on the southern and northern sides. The drums of the lateral cupolas are quadrangular on the outside, and the drum of the central dome is octagonal. The original marble iconostasis, decorated with stylized acanthus leaves, intertwined bands, palmettes, tendrils and symbols of the Eucharist, has been preserved in the church. The frescoes of Nerezi represent one of the most important monuments of 12th century Byzantine painting. Christ in four different iconographic aspects is shown in the lateral calottes, and the Communion of the Apostles and the Adoration of the Hetimasia are illustrated in the sanctuary. The lower zone of the nave

contains standing figures, and the upper zones show scenes from the lives of Christ and the Virgin. They include such anthology pieces of Comnene painting as the Deposition, the Lamentation, the Transfiguration, the Raising of Lazarus, the Entry into Jerusalem, the Nativity of the Virgin and the Presentation in the Temple. Their linearism shows the characteristic features of the 12th century style and betray the Constantinopolitan origin of the unknown Nerezi master. In mid-16th century the monastery was damaged by an earthquake and the main dome collapsed. The church was restored a little later. The earliest frescoes were painted over in the 19th century, and the entire church was restored after the Second World War.

NEREZI, FRESCO, THE LAMENTATION

NIN, CHURCH OF THE HOLY CROSS

NIN, CHURCH OF ST NICHOLAS

NIN [B, 4]
The Classical Temple

The temple was built on the forum, in the vicinity of the amphitheatre, in the 1st century A. D. The remains that have come down to us show that it was a monumental building with high quality carved decoration. It is supposed that the temple served as an Augusteum and contained the emperor's statues in the imperial times.

NIN [B, 4]
The Church of the Holy Cross

Nin played an important role in the Middle Ages as the centre of a bishopric and a seat of Croatian rulers. The church was built in the 11th century and an inscription carved on the architrave says that it was the foundation of Godežav, a Croatian feudal lord. It is a pre-Romanesque building (9.20 metres long) with a cruciform ground plan. It has a central dome supported on squinches, which is a characteristic structural element of pre-Romanesque architecture. Quadrangular spaces are on three sides round the dome, and three apses, extending the entire width of the building, are on the eastern side. The church is built of broken stone and its facades are enlivened by shallow, low niches with semicircular tops. Above the entrance is a bell-tower.

NIN [B, 4]
The Church of St Nicholas

The church is located on a small hill 3 kilometres from Nin. It dates from the 11th century. It is trefoil in plan and it has a rectangular narthex on the western side. Above the nave is a blind dome surmounted by a massive octagonal tower with an indented cornice. The church is built od dressed stone.

NIŠ, MEDIANA

NIŠ [I, 5]
Mediana

A settlement with villas five kilometres from the Roman town of Naissus. It was an imperial residence and its construction lasted, with interruptions, from the end of the 3rd to the end of the 6th century, when the entire region was deserted. The settlement contains villas, palaces, baths, and a building with a monumental floor mosaic decorated with late classical geometric designs.

NIŠ [I, 5]
The Tomb with Frescoes

A tomb dating from the end of the 4th century was discovered in the courtyard of the hostel for secondary school pupils in Jagodin-mala in 1953. An entrance on the eastern end gives access to a rectangular chamber (2.63 × 2.23 metres) covered with a tunnel vault and divided by low partition walls into three graves in the form of lidless coffins. The walls are covered with frescoes. On the eastern and western walls is Christ's monogram surrounded by a garland. Next to it are the standing figures of SS Peter and Paul (on the eastern wall) and a representation of paradise (on the northern and southern walls). The stylistic features of the frescoes are based on the late classical tradition, and the iconography is influenced by the early Christian painting of the catacombs. The tomb was restored and made open to the public in 1955. Seven other tombs have been discovered in the vicinity, but their decoration has been destroyed.

NIŠ, MEDIANA, MOSAIC

NIŠ [I, 5]
The Fortress

The fortress was built during
Turkish rule in the 17th century,
on the site of an earlier Roman
castrum and a medieval castle. It is
seven-sided in plan and has five
bastions. The gates are on the
northern and southern sides. Several
other structures from Turkish times
have been preserved within the walls:
a mosque, parts of Turkish baths
and an armory which has been
converted into an exhibition gallery.

NOVA PAVLICA [H, 5]
*The Church Dedicated to the
Entry into the Temple*

The church was built before the
battle of Kosovo in 1389. The
founders were brothers Stefan and
Lazar Musić, sons of Musa, a
military commander, and Prince
Lazar's sister Dragana. The
ground plan is in the form of an
inscribed cross combined with a
trefoil. The dome rests on four
free-standing pillars. A new
narthex was built in the 15th century
to replace the old one, and a
bell-tower was constructed in
front of it in the 19th century.

NOVI PAZAR, CHURCH OF ST PETER IN RAS

The church was built of stone and whitewashed. The facades are enlivened by shallow niches. The church underwent several reconstructions, so that it has lost its original appearance. The arrangement of the frescoes is the same as in the majority of the churches of the Morava School. The standing figures (warrior saints and hermits) are in the lower zone; above them is a frieze with the busts of saints, and the Great Feasts and the Passion are in the upper zones. The Communion of the Apostles and the Church Fathers are represented in the sanctuary. Several masters worked in the church, and the most gifted of them painted the expressive portraits of the founders, the Musić brothers. Frescoes from 1464 have been partly preserved in the narthex. They were commissioned by Joanikije, Metropolitan of Raška, who is represented holding a model of the narthex.

NOVI PAZAR [H, 5]
St Peter in Ras

The church is located near old Ras. It has had a long, complex and eventful history. A Greek-Illyrian hoard (now in the National Museum in Belgrade), containing objects and vessels ornamented in the archaic style and made of glass, bronze, silver and gold, was found during the restoration of the church. The date of the church has not been established, but it is supposed that its basic architectural core dates from the 9th or 10th century. It was enlarged and rebuilt several times in subsequent periods. It was the centre of the bishopric of Ras and it was later elevated to the rank of archbishopric. The historical sources show that two important councils were held in the church in the 12th century: at one of them it was decided that the bogumils should be expelled, and at the other Stefan Nemanja renounced the throne in favour of his son Stefan. The church is in the form of a rotunda with a wide dome resting on four squinches. Round this core runs a storeyed gallery which girdles a part of the building. The internal decoration has been only partly preserved. The ornaments made by scratching in fresh mortar and by painting date from the earliest layer, as do parts of the frescoes in the drum with the scenes illustrating the Great Feasts. The second layer was painted in the 12th century and it is in the sanctuary. In the half-calotte is the Virgin, in the middle area the standing figures of the Apostles, and in the lower zone is the Procession of the Church Fathers. There are also some fragments of 13th century frescoes in the church. The church was reconstructed for the last time in 1718, but it was abandoned at the beginning of the 19th century and turned into a Turkish military storehouse. It was restored after the Second World War.

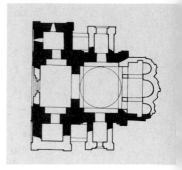

NOVI PAZAR [H, 5]
Djurdjevi Stupovi

The church is consecrated to St George and it is situated on a hilltop near old Ras, i. e. Novi Pazar. Originally, it had two rows of defensive walls. It was built in 1170/71 by Stefan Nemanja, after he had become the Grand Župan. Further work on the church and the monastic buildings was done in 1282/83, during the reign of King Dragutin, who was buried here. The building is 16.5 metres long and has three separate parts. In the centre is a rectangular nave with a dome

and vestibules on the northern and southern sides; on the eastern side is a tripartite sanctuary, and a narthex with two towers is on the western side. The church is built of stone and covered with plaster. A frieze of small blind arcades ran below the roof cornice on the facade, and fragments of stone sculptures have been found round the church. This shows that the church was decorated with carved ornaments. The drum of the dome is enlivened within by arcades and marble colonnettes which have Romanesque capitals. The frescoes are heavily damaged. The earliest layer dates from c. 1175 and its frescoes were skillfully arranged in real or painted architectural settings. The prophets are in the drum, the Evangelists on the squinches, and scenes from the Great Feasts are on the walls of the nave. In the lower zone standing figures are shown under painted arcades, which is quite unusual in Serbian medieval art. The surviving frescoes exhibit the stylistic features of the Comnene art. The second layer of frescoes was painted in 1282/83. A part of it is in the narthex, which contains the cycle of St George, including a splendid representation of St George on a white steed. The other part of the second layer is in the chapel, in one of the towers in the monastery. It represents the

NOVI PAZAR, DJURDJEVI STUPOVI

procession of the Nemanjič family and four Serbian state councils — an arrangement meant to show in a visual way the continuity of the Nemanjić rule. The church was heavily damaged first in 1689 and on several subsequent occasions, particularly in the First and Second World Wars. It was completely deserted in the 19th century. It was restored between 1972 and 1977.

NOVI PAZAR [H, 5]
The Ras Fortress

The fortress is seven kilometres distant from Novi Pazar. It is supposed that an old Byzantine settlement existed on this site. It was held by Serbian feudal lords from the 9th century. The Byzantines captured it twice in the 12th century, but the Serbian rulers re-established their sway from 1172 and held it until the Turks captured it in 1455. It was an important political and cultural centre of the Serbian state in the Middle Ages. Old Ras had a large suburb, a town (Pazarište) and a fortress on the hill of Gradina. It is in the form of an irregular triangle, the longest side being 170 metres. The massive walls were reinforced by several semicircular towers. Remains of the foundations of three towers are still extant. The fortress is heavily damaged.

NOVI SAD [G, 3]
The Church of St Nicholas (Nikolajevska crkva)

The church was built in the first half of the 19th century. The oil wall paintings are the work of Nikola Dimšić. The original iconostasis has not been preserved and the present one was painted by Pavle Simić in 1862.

NOVI SAD [G, 3]
The Almaška Church

The church was built in Baroque style at the end of the 18th century.

NOVI SAD, CHURCH OF ST NICHOLAS

NOVI SAD, ALMAŠKA CHURCH

It is a single-nave building with a semicircular apse on the eastern side and a bell-tower on the western side. The ornate carved iconostasis is the work of Aksentije Marković, and the icons on it were painted by Arsa Teodorović in 1810—1811.

NOVI SAD [G, 3]
The Church of the Dormition of the Virgin (Uspenska crkva)

The building of the church began in 1755, but it was completed only at the end of the eighth decade of the 18th century. The wooden iconostasis was carved by the members of the Novi Sad family Marković (Aksentije and Arsenije). The majority of the paintings, except those on the doors of the iconostasis, were painted by Janko Halkozović. It is supposed that they were his last works.

NOVO BRDO [I, 6]
The Medieval Town

The town is 20 kilometres distant from Priština. It is known in old sources as Novus Mons, Novomonte, Monte Novo and Nyeberghe. It was a large and well-known mining centre in the Middle Ages and it had about 40 000 inhabitants at one time. There were colonies of Saxon miners and of Dubrovnik merchants in it. The town had a statute and a mining law, it issued some charters and it even minted its own money for some time. It is first mentioned in 1326, but its economic and cultural prosperity dates from the time of the despotic state, from the end of the

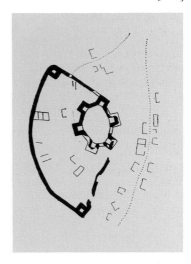

14th and the beginning of the 15th century. The Turks captured it for the first time in 1441, but they agreed to cede it to Despot Djuradj

NOVO BRDO, MEDIEVAL TOWN

Branković three years later. It was definitely subjugated by Mohammed II in 1455, after a siege lasting forty days. The Turks continued to work the mine until the middle of the 17th century, when the town lost its importance and was gradually deserted. Novo Brdo consists of three parts: the citadel, the main suburb, which is surrounded by a fan-like wall with two corner towers on the western side, and a smaller suburb on the eastern side. The citadel is on the top of a hill, at the altitude of 1124 metres above sea level. It is oval in plan and has six towers arranged radially. The cathedral church of St Nicholas, later turned into a mosque, and a Saxon church with an old cemetery, were discovered during the archaeological excavations in the eastern suburb.

NOVO HOPOVO [G, 2]
The Church of St Nicholas

The church was built in 1576, when the monastery Hopovo was restored. The founders were Lacko and Marko Jovišić from Kovin. At the beginning of the 18th century a painting school was founded in the monastery. It was directed by painters Arsenije and Nil. In 1758 the great Serbian writer Dositej Obradović took monastic orders in this monastery and lived for some time in it. The church is trefoil in plan and has three apses on the eastern side. The lateral conchs and the central apse are five-sided without. The narthex is covered with a tunnel vault, and the nave has

NOVO HOPOVO, CHURCH OF ST NICHOLAS

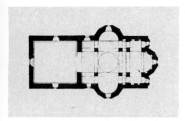

ridge-rib vaulting, in conformity with the pointed arches in the structure under the dome. This shows the influence of Islamic architecture. The dome is interesting from an architectural point of view. A cordon cornice divides the facade into two parts. The upper zone carries blind arcades and blind windows, and the doors and windows are in the lower zone. A high Baroque bell-tower was built in front of the entrance on the western side in 1753/54. The monastic guest-houses were built in the first half of the 18th century. The church was painted in the 17th century. The frescoes in the nave date from 1608 and those in the narthex were painted in 1654. The earlier paintings are the work of Greek painters who followed Cretan models, while the frescoes in the narthex were painted by masters who had come to Novo Hopovo from northern Greece. The church had a gilt iconostasis, carved by Paul and Anton Rezner, while the icons were painted by Teodor Kračun in 1776. The entire monastic complex was heavily damaged during the Second World War, but it was restored later.

OHRID [H, 8]
The Classical and Medieval Town

The town is on the north-eastern side of Lake Ohrid. The old classical settlement Lichnydos, on the Via Egnatia which led from Drač to Salonica, became the seat of an archbishopric in the 4th century. In the 9th century it became a major centre of Slavonic culture, because of the activity of two teachers and preachers, Clement and Naum. It was the capital of Samuilo's state, and an archiepiscopal centre. Later it came under the rule of Byzantium, the Normans, Bulgarians and Serbs. The Turks captured it in 1395. The medieval town from Samuilo's time was built on the site of classical Lichnydos. Walls up to 16 metres high encompassed the entire suburb and extended as far as the shore of the lake. There were two gates, the Upper Gate and the Lower Gate (Gornja i Donja porta). The citadel, called Gornji Saraj, is on the most elevated ground and its representative gateway is flanked by two semicircular towers. The town has a total of 13 towers. A number of medieval churches, built between the 11th and 15th century, is in the suburb.

OHRID [H, 8]
The Church of St Sophia

The church was built in the time of Emperor Samuilo, and it was originally domed, but it was completely remodelled in the time of Archbishop Lav (1037—1056). It was the cathedral church of Ohrid for a long time. It is in the form of a basilica with a nave and two aisles (32 metres long), ending in three semicircular apses. The middle apse is larger and wider, three-sided without. It is enlivened by eight shallow niches in the upper zone. A narthex is on the western side. It has the ground floor, with cross vaulting, and an upper storey reached by a staircase on the northern side.

Above the stairway is the
parekkleseion of St John the
Forerunner, dating from the 14th
century. Two other parekkleseions
were built above the diaconicon and
the prothesis at the end of the 12th
and the beginning of the 13th century.
In 1317 Archbishop Grigorije built
the outer narthex. It has a pillared
porch on the ground floor and an
open gallery with arcading on the
upper storey. Two towers are at the
lateral sides; each has a dome and
two twolight windows. The facades
conform to the Byzantine tradition
and are built in alternate courses of

OHRID, CHURCH OF ST SOPHIA

OHRID, CHURCH OF ST SOPHIA, FRESCO, THE ASCENSION

stone and brick. The inscription of Archbishop Grigorije, commemorating the building of the outer narthex, is also made of bricks. A frieze of shallow niches forms a decorative element in the middle zone of the front facade. Fragments of an 11th century altar screen made of stone and an early 14th century ambo with representations of animals and vegetable ornaments in shallow relief have been preserved in the church. The most valuable part of this church are its frescoes. Two groups of wall paintings are particularly interesting: the earliest

OHRID, CHURCH OF ST SOPHIA, FRESCO, THE SACRIFICE OF ABRAHAM

frescoes, painted in the 11th century, and a group of wall paintings dating from mid-14th century. The earlier frescoes are in the sanctuary, on the western wall of the nave and in the narthex. The frescoes in the main apse show standing figures of Church Fathers in the lower zone; the Eucharist and the Office of St Basil are in the middle zone; and the enthroned Virgin with Christ is in the upper zone. Scenes from the Old Testament and liturgical scenes are illustrated in the sanctuary, and the Ascension is depicted on the vault above the sanctuary. The legend of the Forty Martyrs of Sebast is illustrated in the prothesis, and the cycle of St John the Forerunner is shown in the diaconicon. The frescoes in the

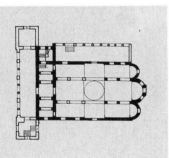

narthex show female saints, the Ascension of Elijah and the Seven Sleeping Youths of Ephesus. The iconographic content and the expressive and dramatic psysiognomies of the saints indicate that the artists were from Constantinople. The later layer of frescoes was painted in two phases during the 14th century; those in the parekkleseion of St John the Forerunner were painted by Konstantin and Jovan, and the much more competent frescoes on the upper storey of the narthex and in the outer narthex were the work of Jovan Therianos. When the

Turks came, the Church of St Sophia was converted into a mosque. Some parts of it were torn down, others were reconstructed, and the frescoes were painted over with whitewash. Extensive restoration work was carried out after the Second World War.

OHRID [H, 8]
The Church of the Virgin the Peribleptos

The church was built at the end of the 13th century and adorned with frescoes in 1294/95. A Greek inscription shows that its founder was Progon Zgur, a relative of Emperor Andronicus II Palaeologus. It is a domed building with the

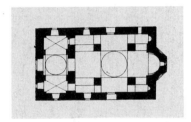

ground plan in the form of an inscribed cross. At the western end is a vaulted narthex, and on the eastern side are two lateral, shallow apses and a central, wider and deeper apse, three-sided without. The facades are picturesque, with bricks laid in the form of shallow niches and various geometric ornaments. The church underwent several reconstructions and an outer narthex, with the so-called Grigorije's Chapel, was added in the latter half of the 14th century. The outer narthex was reconstructed in the 17th and 19th centuries. The frescoes are of high artistic quality

OHRID, CHURCH OF THE VIRGIN THE PERILEBTOS

and are the work of two masters, Mihailo Astrapus and Evtihije, who left their signatures at several places in the church. The famous Procession of the Church Fathers and the Communion of the Apostles are in the altar apse; Christ as a priest in the Temple of Jerusalem and Abraham's Hospitality are in the prothesis; and the Three Children in the Furnace and scenes from the life of St John the Forerunner are in the diaconicon. Distinguished monks, hermits and warrior saints are represented in the lower zone of the nave, and Great Feasts and scenes illustrating the Passion and Christ's miracles and parables are in the upper zones. St Clement, the patron saint of Ohrid, and Archbishop Constantine Cavassilas of Ohrid, were accorded a prominent place in the church, on the northern wall, near the iconostasis. Scenes from the life of the Virgin are illustrated in the frieze on the northern and southern walls, and a monumental Dormition of the Virgin is on the western wall. The Christmas Hymn and scenes from the Old Testament are illustrated in the narthex, and Christ Angel of the Great Council is painted in the shallow calotte. As regards their iconography, painted architecture and modelling, these frescoes obviously belong to the »Palaeologue Revival«, a style which was to spread to other parts of the Balkans later. The frescoes in the outer narthex were painted in the 1360s, as were those in the parekkleseion of St Gregory, added to the northern side of the church. After the conversion of the Church of St Sophia in Ohrid into a mosque, the centre of the archbishopric was transferred to the monastery of the Virgin the Perilebtos. The archiepiscopal treasury was also transferred to the church of the Virgin at this time. In 1916 most of its valuables were plundered. After the Second World War the monastery was restored, and the outer narthex now contains the finest collection of medieval icons in Yugoslavia.

OHRID [H, 8]
The Church of the Virgin the Perilebtos. The Double Icon of the Virgin Hodeghetria

A double processional icon dating from the second half of the 13th century. Tempera on wood, 97 × 67 cm. One side shows the Virgin in the iconographic type of Hodeghetria with small Christ who confers blessings and holds a scroll in his left hand. The background is covered with silver decorated with vegetable ornaments, the busts of St Demetrius and St George, and scenes from Christ's life. On the reverse side is the Crucifixion.

DOUBLE ICON, THE VIRGIN HODEGHETRIA

Crucified Christ is shown against a
golden background, with the Virgin
and St John to the right and left of
him; above him are two angels, and
remains of Adam's grave are at the
foot of the cross. The inscriptions
are in Greek. The icon was restored
after the Second World War.

OHRID, CHURCH OF THE VIRGIN THE PERILEBTOS, ICON, THE CRUCIFIXION

OHRID [H, 8]
The Church of the Virgin the Perilebtos. The Icon of St Matthew

This is one of the main icons on the iconostasis. It dates from the end of the 13th or the beginning of the 14th century. Tempera on wood, 106 × 56 cm. St Matthew is shown with the Gospels in his hand. The background is pale ochre, and the halo is golden. The inscriptions are in Greek.

OHRID [H, 8]
The Church of the Virgin the Perilebtos. The Icon of the Doubting of Thomas

Tempera on wood, 46 × 38.5 cm. Christ has risen his right arm and is showing his wound to Apostle Thomas, who is extending his hand towards Christ's breast. Behind them is an architectural element with a shallow niche flanked by arcades. The background and Christ's halo are golden.

OHRID, CHURCH OF THE VIRGIN THE PERILEBTOS, ICON, THE DOUBTING OF THOMAS

OHRID [H, 8]
The Church of the Virgin the Perilebtos. The Icon of the Harrowing of Hell

The icon dates from the beginning of the 14th century. Tempera on wood, 46.5 × 38.5 cm. Christ, dressed in a gilt mandorla, descends into hell. He extends his arm towards Adam, behind whom is Eve. Beneath Christ's feet are the gates of hell, and, on the right side, David and Solomon, crowned, and St John the Forerunner. Above the mandorla are angels, and behind them is a rocky landscape. The background and the halos are golden.

OHRID, CHURCH OF THE VIRGIN THE PERILEBTOS, ICON, THE HARROWING OF HELL

OHRID [H, 8]
The Church of the Virgin the Perilebtos. The Icon of the Virgin Saviour of Souls

A double processional icon dating from the beginning of the 14th century. Tempera on wood, 94.5 × 80.3 cm. The icon is supposed to have been sent from Constantinople as a present to Archbishop Grigorije, who built the outer narthex of the Church of St Sophia. One side shows the Virgin in the iconographic aspect of Psychosostria (the Saviour of Souls) with infant Christ on her left arm. He confers blessings and holds a

OHRID, CHURCH OF THE VIRGIN THE PERILEBTOS, ICON, THE VIRGIN

scroll. In the corners above them are Archangels Gabriel and Michael. The background is mounted with silver, which shows traces of enamel. The silver frame is decorated with a relief showing Christ in the middle, Jacob and prophets Aaron and Gideon to the left of him, and St John Chrysostom and prophets Ezekiel, Daniel and Habakkuk on the right side. The inscriptions are in Greek.

On the reverse side is the Annunciation. The enthroned Virgin is on the right, and Archangel Gabriel is on the left. The background is golden. The inscriptions are in Greek.

OHRID, CHURCH OF THE VIRGIN THE PERILEBTOS, ICON, THE ANNUNCIATION

OHRID [H, 8]
The Church of the Virgin the Perilebtos. The Icon of Christ the Saviour of Souls

A double processional icon dating from the beginning of the 14th century. Tempera on wood, 94.5 × 70.5 cm. One side shows Christ in the iconogoraphic type of Psychosostis (Saviour of Souls), blessing with his right hand and holding the Gospels in his left hand. The background is mounted with silver decorated with vegetable and geometric ornaments. The relief on the frame shows busts of Apostles, six of which have been preserved: Peter, Andrea, Paul, John, Matthew and Mark. The inscriptions are in Greek. On the reverse side is the Crucifixion. To the left and right of Christ are the Virgin and St John, and two weeping angels are above him. Part of a wall with ornaments is seen behind him. The background is golden. The inscriptions are in Greek. It is supposed that the icon was a present sent to Archbishop Grigorije from Constantinople.

OHRID [H, 8]
The Church of the Virgin the Perilebtos. The Icon of St Clement

A carved wooden icon, 140 × 36 cm. It was made at the beginning of the 14th century in very high relief (depth 13.5 cm), which is rare in Byzantine art. It was originally painted. It shows St Clement, the patron saint of Ohrid, blessing with his right hand and holding a closed book in his left hand. The icon is damaged (the right hand, the tip of the nose and the background). It is supposed that it stood originally in the Church of St Panteleimon in Ohrid, above the saint's tomb, and that it was later transferred to the Church of the Virgin the Perilebtos.

OHRID [H, 8]
The Church of the Virgin the Perilebtos. The Icon of Christ's Baptism

The icon dates from the beginning of the 14th century. Tempera on wood, 47 × 38.2 cm. Christ is in the Jordan. St John stands on a rock to the left of him, and angels are on his right side. Beneath Christ's feet is a personification of the Jordan and a fantastic animal, and above him is the ray of the Holy Ghost. The background and the halos are golden. The inscriptions are in Greek.

OHRID [H, 8]
The Church of St John the Divine Kaneo

The church is perched on a rock above Lake Ohrid. The name Kaneo comes from a fishing village of the same name. The church was built in the 13th century and its history is little known. Its ground plan is in the form of an inscribed cross (11.5 metres long) and it has a dome resting on a tall octagonal drum. On the eastern side are the shallow niches of the prothesis and the diaconicon, and the central apse, which is three-sided without. The church is built in alternate courses of stone and brick, and there is rich sculptured pottery decoration in the upper zones.

OHRID, CHURCH OF ST JOHN THE DIVINE KANEO

Porches were added on the western and southern sides in the time of Turkish rule. Frescoes have been preserved only in the sanctuary and the dome. They were painted c. 1290 and are stylistically close to the frescoes in Manastir near Prilep. The church was restored after the Second World War.

OHRID [H, 8]
The Church of St Nicholas Bolnički

It is supposed that this church was founded by Jakov, the heugomenos of the Monastery of St Clement. It was built in the 1360s. Originally a simple single-nave building, its nave is cut across by a high transverse nave added later, as in the Church of SS Constantine and Helena. The frescoes that have been preserved include medallions with the busts of martyrs, scenes from the Procession of the Church Fathers, the Annunciation and the Ascension. The artist who painted these frescoes was also the author of the later

wall paintings in Marko's Monastery. The carved wooden iconostasis, made in 1833, is another noteworthy monument in the church.

OHRID [H, 8]
The Church of SS Constantine and Helena

The church was built in the 1360s as the family mausoleum of monk Partenije. It is a simple

OHRID, CHURCH OF THE VIRGIN BOLNIČKA

building with a vaulted nave (interior 5 × 3 metres). The niches of the diaconicon and the prothesis are shallow, and the middle apse is three-sided without. The nave is cut across in its upper part by a high transverse nave. A small parakkleseion was added to the southern side and a spacious narthex of irregular shape was built subsequently in front of both buildings. The facades are built of alternate courses of stone and brick and have a richly moulded roof cornice. The original wooden doors of the parakkleseion and the southern entrance, adorned with geometric ornaments, have been preserved. The wooden iconostasis, which has painted, not carved decoration, also dates from the time of the building of the church. The walls of all three chambers are covered with frescoes. Two cycles dominate the main church: the Passion and the Great Feasts. The parekkleseion contains, in addition to the standing figures and the usual scenes in the sanctuary, illustrations of the Great Feasts. In the porch are two layers of frescoes, including a cycle of St Paraskevi, which is very interesting from the iconographic point of view. The later layer of frescoes dates from the middle of the 15th century.

OHRID [H, 8]
The Church of the Virgin Bolnička

The church was built in the 1330s at the instance of Archbishop Nikola of Ohrid. It is a single-nave building with tunnel vaulting and an apse on the eastern end. It was painted in 1335/36. The arrangement of its frescoes became a model for other small churches of this type: the Virgin, flanked by two angels,

and the Procession of the Church Fathers are represented in the apse; medallions with various iconographic representations of Christ are on the vault; the Great Feasts are on the walls, and below them are medallions and the standing figures of saints. As regards the artistic quality of these paintings, they are not above the level of competent craftsmanship. A procession of the Nemanjić family headed by SS Sava and Simeon Nemanja was painted on the southern facade in 1345. The wooden door, a masterpiece of 14th century carving, also dates from the time of the construction of the church. It is divided into sixteen panels and two horizontal bands, with reliefs showing warrior saints, gryphons, snakes, lions, centaurs and illustrations of Aesop's fables. During the First World War the Bulgarians took the door away, and no trace of it has been found since then.

OHRID [H, 8]
Monastery Zaum

The monastery is the foundation of Grgur, a brother of Despot Vuk Branković and a nobleman, who brought the cult of the Virgin of Zahumlje from Herzegovina to Ohrid, It is built on the very shore of the lake. Its ground plan is in the form of an inscribed cross and it has a dome resting on four free-standing pillars. The facades have rich picturesque brick ornaments in the form of meanders, crosses and zig-zag lines. The frescoes date from 1361, and were commissioned, as an inscription says, by Bishop Grigorije. Those that have been preserved include the prophets in the dome, the Virgin in the apse, parts of the Great Feasts (including the Dormition of the

OHRID, MONASTERY OF ST NAUM, THE CHURCH OF ARCHANGEL MICHAEL

Virgin), the Passion on the vaults and in the upper zones, and a cycle of the life of the Virgin. A representation of the Deesis can be discerned in the narthex. The author of these frescoes is supposed to have been trained in a Byzantine centre, presumably Salonica. The church was restored in 1930.

OHRID [H, 8]
The Monastery of St Naum

The monastery is located on the southern shore of Lake Ohrid. It was founded by Clement's disciple Naum, who died in 910 and was buried in the monastic church dedicated to Archangel Michael. It played an important role as a religious and cultural centre. It was laid waste several times and was damaged by fire in 1802. The present monastic church dedicated to Archangel Michael was built in the 14th century on the foundations of an earlier building dating from Naum's time. It is a combination of a basilica with a nave and two aisles and an inscribed cross. The central part is surmounted by a dome, which has a tall octagonal drum with windows. The narthex and a small chapel containing Naum's grave are at the western end. Chapels were added above them subsequently. The facades are built of brick, laid in the Byzantine way. The church was partitioned and remodelled at the end of the 15th and the beginning of the 16th century. The frescoes are of a more recent date. They were painted by Trpe, a master from Korča, in 1806. They are of no particular artistic value. The same can be said of the icons on the iconostasis made by zograph Konstantin in 1711, when the wooden iconostasis was carved.

OLOVO [F, 4]
The Cemetery Jelen Šuma

The cemetery is in eastern Bosnia. In a small area there are eleven sites with 262 *stećci* (medieval gravestones), which have uniform stylistic features, so that they were probably the products of the same school of carving. The forms are usual (sarcophagus, tablet, casket), but the sarcophagi are lower than on other sites, elongated and narrowing towards the bottom, so that they resemble a log-cabin. Unlike the *stećci* of the school of Herzegovina (Radimlja), they are devoid of figural decoration. The most common motifs are spirals, rosettes, garlands, crescents, circles and a hand holding a sword or a spear. They were carved from the end of the 14th to the end of the 15th century.

OMIŠ [D, 5]
The Church of St Peter at Priko

OMIŠ, CHURCH OF ST PETER AT PRIKO

The church was built in the 10th century and it is mentioned in documents of Croatian national rulers. It is a single-nave pre-Romanesque building with a blind dome which is supported, via squinches, on four strong pillars. The dome is enveloped without in a cubic mass. The altar apse is semicircular within and four-sided without. The eastern and western bays have cross vaulting. The church is built of broken stone and whitewashed. The facades are enlivened by windows and lesenes which are connected by double blind arcades. The church was restored in 1961.

OSIJEK [F, 2]
The Fortress

This is the old core of Osijek. In the 16th century, during Turkish rule, this site was occupied by a town with a castle. At the beginning of the 17th century a new and modern fortress with eight bastions was built on the old foundations. This fortress was pulled down in 1923 and the only surviving parts of it are the Water-Gate and Water-Tower. In the first half of the 18th century a distinct group of Baroque buildings, including the town hall (1702), the Main Guard (1709), the military headquarters (1726) and the Jesuite Church of St Michael (1725—1748), grew up round the main square in the fortress. A number of private buildings designed in Baroque style was constructed round this core.

OSIJEK [F, 2]
The Church of SS Peter and Paul

The church was designed by F. Landenberg from Bonn and built between 1894 and 1898 under the auspices of Archbishop Josip J. Strossmeyer. It is built of brick and its forms are purely neo-Gothic. Especially noteworthy are the frescoes in the interior, which were painted by Mirko Rački.

OSIJEK [F, 2]
The Theatre

The building which houses the theatre was designed in pseudo--Moorish style, especially evident in the decoration of the facades. It was constructed in 1866 and its architect is not known. It has the ground floor and an upper storey, and the entrance is particularly imposing. The building was converted into a theatre in 1907.

OSTROŽAC ON THE UNA RIVER [C, 3]
The Old Fortress

The fortress is first cited in historical sources in 1286. It was held by the Hungarians for a long time, and the Turks captured it in 1577. It underwent considerable alterations in the 17th and 18th centuries. Its ground plan is in the form of an ellipse. At the beginning of the 20th century it was remodelled in the spirit of historism and reconstructed as a palace.

PAG [B, 4]
The Town Fortifications

The town fortifications are on the island beearing the same name. A Roman settlement with a castrum

PAG, TOWN FORTIFICATIONS

PAG, CHURCH OF THE VIRGIN

and fortifications existed here as early as the 1st century A. D. From the 11th century onwards one part of the island belonged to the church of Rab and the other to the church of Zadar, a situation which led to friction and conflicts (1311). In 1244 the town of Pag was granted the status of a free royal town by King Bela IV, and in 1376 it was given full autonomy by Lodovik I. From 1409 to 1797 it was under Venetian rule. Since the old town and settlement were not sufficiently fortified, it was decided that a new fortress should be built a kilometer away, on a site called Katena. The construction of these fortifications began in 1443 and it was completed in 1470. The new settlement was encompassed by strong walls with nine towers and bastions, and it had four gates. One of the chief masters who took part in the building of the fortifications was Juraj Dalmatinac. The town is divided into four parts by two main streets, and the seats of the political and religious authority, with the rector's palace, the residence of Bishop Palčić and the new parish church, are located at their

intersection. A large part of the fortifications was torn down in the 19th and 20th centuries.

PAG [B, 4]
The Church of the Virgin

The Church of the Virgin is also called the New Parish Church. Its construction began in 1443, at the same time when the new settlement of Pag was founded, and the main work was completed by 1488, although construction continued as late as the 16th century. The architects were brothers Juraj and Pavle from Zadar, who reproduced, at the request of the founder, the dimensions and form of the Church of the Dormition of the Virgin from the old town. Its ground plan retained the old Romanesque form of a basilica with a nave, two aisles and three semicircular apses on the eastern side. The facades and the capitals of the columns (14) which separate the nave from the aisles are in the transitional Gothic-Renaissance style. The front facade is divided by a cordon cornice into four zones. In addition to a rosette and the portal, it has five sculptures: an angel with folded wings on the top, the Virgin and Archangel Gabriel (Annunciation) below it, and in the second zone, St George and Archangel Michael. A relief of the lion, symbol of St Mark, the patron saint of Venice, is also on this wall. The lunette contains a representation of the Virgin protecting the men and women of Pag under a broad cloak. The front facade was designed by Juraj Dalmatinac. A Renaissance bell-tower with four storeys was added in 1552. The church underwent alterations in the 17th and 19th centuries.

PANČEVO [H, 3]
The Church of the Dormition of the Virgin (Uspenska crkva)

The building of the church began in 1807 and was completed in 1811. Especially noteworthy is the iconostasis, carved by Mihailo Janić and painted by Konstantin Danil from 1828 to 1832.

PANČEVO [H, 3]
The Church of the Transfiguration (Preobraženska crkva)

The church was designed by Svetozar Ivačković (1844—1924) and it was built between 1874 and 1878. It is an attractive example of Romantic architecture with some medieval elements in its structure. The iconostasis was painted by Uroš Predić and the frescoes are the work of Stevan Aleksić and date from the beginning of the present century.

PANČEVO, CHURCH OF THE DORMITION OF THE VIRGIN

CHURCH OF THE TRANSFIGURATION

PAZIN [A, 3]
The Church of St Nicholas

A single-nave bulding to which a late Gothic polygonal presbytery with stellar vaulting was added in 1441. The high quality frescoes were painted in the 1460s by an anonymous Tirolian master, who is supposed to have belonged to the circle of Leonard from Brixen. The frescoes from this church exercised a strong influence on the development of late Gothic painting in Istria.

PEĆ, THE PATRIARCHATE

PEĆ [H, 6]
The Patriarchate. The Church of the Apostles

The complex of the Patriarchate of Peć consists of several buildings which were built one next to the other in the 13th and 14th centuries. The Church of the Apostles is in the middle, the Church of St Demetrius is on the northern side, and the Church of the Virgin Hodeghetria with the small Church of St Nicholas, is on the southern side. An open narthex with a tower was constructed in the 14th century in front of the three churches, linking them into a unified range.

From the middle of the 13th century Peć was the seat of the Archbishopric, and from 1346 the seat of the Patriarchate. The Church of the Apostles, known also as the Church

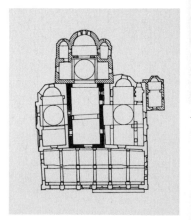

PEĆ, THE PATRIARCHATE, CHURCH OF THE APOSTLES, FRESCO, THE DEESIS

of the Saviour, is the oldest. Its founder was Archbishop Arsenije and it dates from the 1230s. Its design follows that of Žiča: it is a domed single-nave building with a transept. On the eastern side is a spacious altar apse, the prothesis and the diaconicon, which also have a semicircular termination. The western part is covered with a tunnel vault. The facade was covered with plaster and painted red. The earliest layer of frescoes was painted in the middle of the 13th century. The Deesis and the Procession of the Church Fathers are in the sanctuary, the Communion of the Apostles is above the altar, scenes from Christ's life are in the space below the dome, and the Ascension, with the expressive figures of the Virgin and angels, is painted in the dome. The paintings in the prothesis show Old Testament scenes. The frescoes have a monumental quality in spite of the fact that the forms are modelled in a technique which is closer to icons than to wall-paintings. The scenes from the Passion in the western part of the church were painted at the very end of the 13th century, and the standing figures and the Great Feasts in the choir date from the second half of the 14th century. A few wall paintings from 1634 have been preserved in the western part of the church. The building was restored in 1932, and the frescoes were cleaned and restored after the Second World War.

PEĆ, THE PATRIARCHATE, CHURCH OF THE APOSTLES, FRESCO, CHRIST

PEĆ [H, 6]
The Patriarchate. The Church of St Demetrius

The church was founded by Archbishop Nikodim and built against the northern side of the Church of the Apostles between 1321 and 1324. It is a single-nave building with a dome and a semicircular apse. The western bay has cross vaulting. The facades are made of alternate courses of brick and tuffa, and the exterior of the dome is decorated with colonnettes and cornices. The altar window has a pointed Gothic arch. The frescoes were painted in the time of Archbishop Joanikije, about 1345. In addition to the Great Feasts and the usual scenes, they include scenes from the life of St Demetrius with numerous lively details, the Ecumenical Councils and the

PEĆ, THE PATRIARCHATE, CHURCH OF ST DEMETRIUS, FRESCO, THE VIRGIN

councils of Serbian saints. The Greek signature of a painter in an unusual but characteristic phrase "The gift of God from Jovan's hand" has been preserved in the apse. In 1620 Georgije Mitrofanović restored the frescoes which had become dilapidated. The carved decoration has been preserved on the parapet panels of the old iconostasis, on the western portal and on the sarcophagi. Especially remarkable is a sarcophagus from the second half of the 14th century with triple figures-of-eight and plastic pellets. The church also contains objects from the monastic treasury. They include many precious things, but especially noteworthy is an icon of SS Cosmas and Damian with their lives, painted by master Radul in 1674.

CHURCH OF ST DEMETRIUS, FRESCO, THE NATIVITY OF THE VIRGIN (DETAIL)

PEĆ [H, 6]
The Patriarchate. The Church of the Virgin Hodeghetria

The church was founded by Archbishop Danilo II and it was built against the southern wall of the Church of the Apostles between 1330 and 1337. The building is in the form of a shortened inscribed cross with a dome resting on four free-standing pillars. The facades are built of alternate courses of brick and tuffa. The frescoes were painted about 1337. The great Feasts are depicted in the nave, and the lives of St Arsenije of Serbia and St John the Forerunner are illustrated in the northern and southern lateral parekkleseions respectively. The founder's composition, showing Archbishop Danilo II with a model of the church and Prophet Daniel who leads him

PEĆ, THE PATRIARCHATE, CHURCH OF ST DEMETRIUS, ICON, ST COSMAS

to the Virgin is on the western wall. The stone sarcophagus of Danilo II, decorated with a floral cross and the symbols of resurrection and the Last Judgment in shallow relief, has been preserved in the church.

PEĆ [H, 6]
The Patriarchate. The Narthex

Archbishop Danilo II caused, about 1337, a narthex to be built in front of all three churches in the complex of the Patriarchate. It was designed in the form of a porch with double arcading. A bell-tower, which has not been preserved, was at its

CHURCH OF THE VIRGIN HODEGHETRIA, SARCOPHAGUS OF DANILO II

western end. Remains of the original frescoes have survived on the eastern wall. Especially remarkable is the one showing the Nemanjić dynasty.

The other frescoes were painted in 1565, when Patriarch Makarije restored this part of the Patriarchate.

CHURCH OF THE VIRGIN HODEGHETRIA, FRESCO, THE NATIVITY

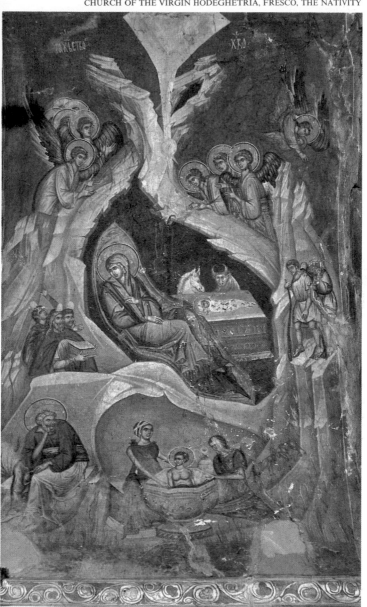

PETROVARADIN, FORTRESS

PERAST [F, 6]
*The Church of Our Lady of the Rocks
(Gospa od Škrpjela)*

The church is situated on an artificial
island off Perast. The construction of
this Baroque building began in
1630. A dome designed by Ilija
Katičić was added between 1720 and
1725. The walls and ceilings of the
church are decorated with
sixty-eight paintings by the Baroque
painter Tripo Kokolja. They were
painted in the last decade of the
17th century.

PEŠTANI [H, 8]
The Church of the Virgin

The church is on the very shore of
Lake Ohrid in the vicinity of Ohrid.
It is a small cave church and its
eastern part is considerably damaged.
The frescoes were painted about
1370 and are adapted to the small
dimensions of the church. Those that
have survived show parts of the
Great Feasts, some Ohrid Saints,
warrior saints and monks.

PETROVARADIN [G, 3]
The Fortress

The fortress is located on a small
hill on the right bank of the Danube
opposite modern Novi Sad. A
Roman settlement called Cusum
was located in its vicinity. In the
12th century, when the fortress
was built, this region was the scene
of battles between the Hungarians
and the Byzantines. King Bela IV
of Hungary donated the fortress
and his royal palace to a Cistercite
monastery. It was here that the
treaty between King Matthias
Corvinus and Venice against Turkey
was concluded in 1463. The Turks
captured the fortress in 1526 and
held it until 1687, when it passed
into the hands of the Austrians. This
marked the beginning of several
successive reconstructions and
enlargements. The last ones were
made in the time of Maria Theresa
between 1754 and 1766, when the
fortress got its final appearance.
Its massive walls built of brick to
resist heavy artilery encompass the
lower garrison town and extend to
the bank of the Danube. Subterranean
galleries run beneath the walls,
and there is a number of buildings

within the fortress, which were formerly used as barracks and now house a museum, the archives and art studios.

PIRAN [A, 2]
The Venetian House

The building was constructed as a private residence in the middle of the 15th century and it is designed in Gothic style. It is called »Mlečanka« (the Venetian house). It has a richly decorated threelight window and a balcony at the corner of the first floor. On the second storey are windows on brackets with lion-heads and a tablet with the initials of the first owners of the house, the Del Bello family.

PIRAN [A, 2]
First of May Square (Prvomajski trg)

A square typical of maritime towns, with buildings dating from various epochs. The balcony of the »Venetian House« dates from the 15th century, and the Baroque building is from the end of the 18th century, when the public fountain was also constructed. The monument to the violin player G. Tartini was made by A. dal Zotto in 1896.

PIVA [F, 7]
The Church of the Dormition of the Virgin

The church is situated on the bank of the Piva river. It was built between 1573 and 1586 and its founder was Savatije, the Metropolitan of Herzegovina and later Patriarch. It is in the form of a basilica with the nave, two aisles and tunnel vaulting. A semicircular apse is on its eastern side, and a narthex on the western end. The frescoes in the nave were painted between 1604 and 1606, and those in the narthex date from 1604 and 1626. A monumental gilt iconostasis (1638/39) with icons painted by master Jovan has been preserved in the church. The monastery has a rich treasury. The monastery has been transferred to another place because of the construction of a hydro-electric power plant.

PIRAN, VENETIAN HOUSE

PLJEVLJA [G, 5]
The Church of the Holy Trinity

The church in the monastic range
was built on the foundations of an
earlier building in the 1530s. Its
founder was monk Visarion. The
building is almost square in plan
and has a wide semicircular apse
on the eastern side. The nave is
divided into three parts by four
columns. The central part has
tunnel vaulting. A narthex with a
dome was added on the western
side at the end of the 16th century,
and in 1876 an outer narthex was
built and the entire building was
reconstructed: the dome was
heightened, and all three parts of
the church were covered with the
same roof. The frescoes were
painted in 1592 (the narthex) and
1595 (the nave and the sanctuary).
The frescoes in the sanctuary
represent the Virgin with Christ,
the Adoration of the Lamb and
individual figures of archbishops;
in the nave are the Great Feasts, the
Passion and the cycle of the Virgin
(in the western part), while the
paintings in the first zone show
warrior saints, the founder's
composition and the procession of
the Nemanjić family. Hermits and
founders are represented in the lower
zone of the narthex, while the upper
zone contains two cycles: an
illustration of Christ's miracles and
the cycle of the Gospels of the
Resurrection. The monastery has
a rich treasury, a large library
with old manuscripts and a valuable
collection of icons.

POČITELJ, MOSQUE

PLJEVLJA [G, 5]
The Husein Pusha Mosque

The mosque was built in 1569 in
classical style. It was founded by
Husein Pasha Boljanić, the sanjakbey
of Bosnia. The ground plan is
square, and the dome rests on

mahvil are richly ornamented with geometric designs in shallow relief. Dubrovnik masters took part in the construction of the mosque, but its chief architect is not known. It is inferred, from its stylistic and structural features, the he was Heyrudin, the same master who built the bridge in Mostar and the fortress at Makarska. — The mosque was restored in 1880.

POČITELJ [E, 5]
The Old Town

Počitelj is first cited in 1444, and after the fall of the kingdom of Bosnia in the second half of the 15th century King Mattias Corvinus, the Ragusans and Vladislav Hercegović reinforced its defences, preparing themselves for the struggle against the Turks. One of the masters who worked on the fortifications of Počitelj was Paskoje Miličević from Dubrovnik. The Turks captured Počitelj in 1471 and enlarged the settlement several times from the 16th century. The settlement was walled in again towards the end of the 17th century. It was deserted in the 20th century. After the Second World Was its more important buildings were restored.

web-like squinches. The octagonal drum is reinforced by countreforts. The corners above the squinches are surmounted by two smaller blind cupolas. A porch supported on four columns runs the entire length of the north-western side. It is covered with three smaller domes, the middle one being a little higher than the other two. The portal is decorated with rosettes and stalactite decoration. The mihrab, minber and

POGANOVO [J, 5]
The Church of St John the Theologos

The church is situated south-west of Dimitrovgrad. It was built at the end of the 15th century and its founders were Konstantin and Jelena, of whom there is no historic evidence. The building is a domed trefoil and has a narthex on its western side

POGANOVO, CHURCH OF ST JOHN THE THEOLOGOS

with a gallery giving access to a bell-tower. The church is built of stone and brick. The frescoes were painted in 1490, as shown by an inscription above the entrance. Two cycles are illustrated: the Great Feasts and the Passion. The church was heavily damaged in the First and Second World Wars. It has been recently restored.

POLOŠKO [I, 7]
The Church of St George

The church was built at the beginning of the 14th century and it was donated to monastery Chilandar by a charter of King Dušan from 1340. In 1378 brothers Dejanov presented the Pološko monastery and church to the monastery of St Panteleimon on Mount Athos. It is a domed single-nave building with a three-sided apse on the eastern side. The facades are built of stone and brick and are enlivened by shallow niches. The frescoes date from about 1370 and seem to have been painted under the supervision of Chilandar monks. The frescoes in the altar apse show the Virgin and the Communion of the Apostles, and those in the nave represent the Great Feasts and the Passion. On the western wall is the Dormition of the Virgin with Christ in an unusual position, bending over the Virgin for the last kiss. The scenes contain new and uncommon iconographic details. In the 17th century the original frescoes were partly painted over, and some new ones were painted in the narthex.

POREČ [A, 3]
The Cathedral of the Euphrasiana

The main edifice, a basilica with the nave and two aisles, was built by Bishop Euphrasius between 535 and 550, as shown by an inscription on the mosaic in the main apse. The Euphrasiana represents a developed type of basilica, its nave being broader and higher than the aisles and separated from the aisles by two rows of arcades. The nave and the aisles end in semicircular apses, and the ciborium is located in the middle apse, which is wider and deeper than the lateral ones. A narthex, atrium and baptistry are on the western side. Carved decoration has been preserved on parts of the church furniture and on the capitals, which are either in the form of a stylized Corinthian capital or in the form of a reversed truncated pyramid with vegetable and zoomorphic decoration. The mosaics in the main apse are representative examples of Byzantine monumental style, which spread along the Adriatic coast from Constantinople and Justinian's workshops in the 6th century. The triumphal arch shows Christ with apostles and has a frieze of 13 medallions. The central medallion contains a symbolical representation of Christ as Lamb and the medallions to the left and right of it represent martyrs. The half-dome contains a representation of the enthroned Virgin surrounded by angels; to the right of her are three unknown martyrs, and to the left is martyr Maurus leading the founder, Bishop Euphrasius, with the model of the

POREČ, CATHEDRAL (INTERIOR)

POREČ, CANONS' HOUSE

church in his hand, to the Virgin. He is accompanied by Archdeacon Claudius and a boy who bears the Bishop's name. The founder's inscription is below this composition. In the lower zone are the Annunciation, the Visitation and the figures of St Zachary and John the Baptist. The Euphrasiana was built on the foundations of an earlier basilica with the nave and two aisles from the 5th century (the Basilica pre-Euphrasiana), which rests on the foundations of a sacred building from the early 4th century. North of the main basilica another church was built in Euphrasius's time, but it was adapted as the bishop's residence in the Middle Ages. The other buildings in this complex were built from the 13th century onwards: the sacristy, the bell-tower, and the first church; parallel with this, considerable adaptation and reconstruction took place which altered the original appearance of the earlier buildings. The entire complex was heavily damaged in the 18th century, so that many parts of it were ruined or fallen into disuse. After the Second World War the buildings were completely restored.

POREČ [A, 3]
The Canons' House (Kanonička kuća)

A dwelling house in late Romanesque style built in 1251. Especially noteworthy are the portal, the niches with inscriptions and the double Romanesque windows.

POREČ [A, 3]
The Gothic Palace

The palace was built in the late Venetian Gothic style towards the end of the 15th century. It has a ground floor and two upper storeys. The remarkable features of the facade include two elaborately ornamented windows.

PRILEP. CHURCH OF ST NICHOLAS

POREČ [A, 3]
The Sinčić Palace

This representative Baroque palace was built in the second half of the 17th century. Its architect is not known. The building now houses the Town Museum.

PRČANJ [F, 6]
The Parish Church

The church was designed by the Venetian architect Bernardino Maccaruzzi and its construction began in 1790. The first stage of building was completed in 1807. The second stage began in 1867 and lasted until 1909. The church is a triple-nave building with a massive dome. The front facade is designed in Baroque style. It is divided into two zones: the portal flanked by Corinthian columns is in the lower zone, and in the upper zones the columns become pilasters which support a triangular gable. The frescoes and paintings in the church were painted by Milo Milunović in the 1920s, and the marble Lamentation was sculptured by Sreten Stojanović in 1926.

PRILEP [I, 8]
The Church of St Nicholas

The church was built in the 12th century and it is a simple single-nave building with an apse. All the facades are decorated with brick ornaments in the form of blind arcades or zig-zag designs. The frescoes were

PRILEP, CHURCH OF ST DEMETRIUS

painted in two stages. The earlier group dates from about 1200 and includes the Virgin in the apse and the Procession of the Church Fathers. Their style belongs to the Comnene art of the 12th century. The later frescoes date from 1298, when the entire church was painted anew. A Greek inscription above the southern window says that the frescoes were painted in the time of Emperor Andronicus and Empress Irina and that the founder were Vega Kapsa and his wife Marija, of whom there is no historical evidence. The frescoes are divided into two zones: individual figures are in the lower zone, and the Great Feasts and the cycle of the Passion are in the upper zone. The painted architecture, the increased number of figures in the compositions and the modelling show that these frescoes represent a transitional stage from the 13th to the 14th century art.

PRILEP [I, 8]
The Church of St Demetrius

The church was built in the latter half of the 13th century and it was first adorned with frescoes about 1290. It underwent several reconstructions, and the southern aisle and the narthex were added in the 14th century. It has a nave, two aisles and a large dome which is twelve-sided without and enlivened by blind arcades. The old frescoes were re-painted about 1380 by Metropolitan Jovan from Zrze and his assistants. He retained the old arrangement, but his figures display a new and powerful expressiveness. The frescoes were covered with whitewash in the Turkish period. They were cleaned and restored in 1970.

PRILEP, CHURCH OF THE HOLY ARCHANGEL, FRESCO, KING MARKO

PRILEP [I, 8]
The Church of the Holy Archangel

PRILEP [I, 8]
Marko's Town

The church and the monastery were built on a cliff below Markov grad, in the time of King Vukašin and his son Marko. It is a domed single-nave building. A semicircular apse is on its eastern side, and the narthex and the vestibule are on the western side. It is built of stone framed with brick. Frescoes showing King Vukašin and King Marko are painted on the facade on either side of the entrance. They were painted about 1372, after Vukašin's death in the Battle of Marica and at the time when King Marko succeeded to the throne.

This was a Byzantine town in the 10th century, and the Bulgarians held it for a time. It was taken from the Byzantines by King Milutin, and later Emperor Dušan and King Vukašin held their court here. From 1371 to 1395 it was in the hands of King Marko, after whom it was named. After his death the town was captured by the Turks. It is built of very big stone blocks and it consisted of three parts: the citadel, which was on the highest hill, and two suburbs below it. They were encompassed with thick walls with towers, eight of which are extant. An old Slavonic settlement has been discovered in the

PRILEP, THE CHURCH OF THE HOLY ARCHANGEL

suburb, which is now called Varoš, and several churches dating from the 12th to the 14th century are extant in the town.

PRIŠTINA, FATIH MOSQUE

PRIŠTINA [H, 6]
The Fatih Mosque

The mosque was founded by Sultan Mohammed II Fatih (the Conqueror) in 1416. It is built in early Constantinopolitan style. Above the entrance is an inscription commemorating its construction. The ground plan is square, measuring 14 × 14 metres. The dome is of equal span and rests on four pendentives. This was the largest dome built in the Yugoslav territory up to that time. A porch supported on four pillars and covered with three cupolas runs along the front part of the building. The mosque is built of stone without and of brick within. The painted floral ornaments are blue and black. A remarkable feature is the rosette on the top of the dome. The mosque is popularly known as »the Sultan's Mosque«.

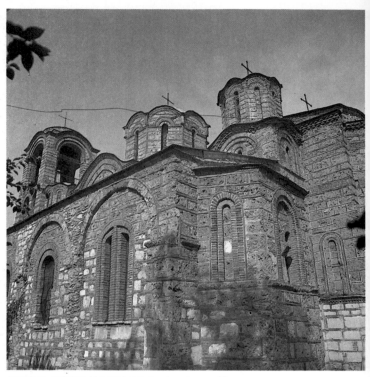

PRIZREN, CHURCH OF THE MOTHER OF GOD LJEVIŠKA

PRIVINA GLAVA [G, 3]
The Church of SS Michael and Gabriel

The church is situated in Fruška Gora. The earliest reference to the monastery dates from 1566. The old church is not extant. The present church was built from 1741 to 1760 from donations of rich merchants and officers of the frontier troops. It is trefoil in plan, with apses which are five-sided without, and it has a bell-tower on the western side. The dome is of the same type as that at Novo Hopovo: eight colonnettes encircle the drum. A two-winged building with monastic residences adjoins the church. The iconostasis, dating from 1786, is a splendid example of wood carving and gold-working. The artist is not known. The icons and the frescoes in the choirs were painted by Kozma Kolarič.

PRIZREN [H, 7]
The Medieval Fortress

The fortress is first cited in the 11th century, at the time of the insurrection of Macedonian Slavs. It was incorporated into the Serbian state from the 13th to the middle of the 15th century. It was the seat of a

CHURCH OF THE MOTHER GOD LJEVIŠKA, FRESCO, STEFAN NEMANJA

bishop and an important cultural, economic and trading centre. The Dubrovnik merchants had their colony in it. The Turks captured it in 1455. The fortress was built on a hill above the settlement in order to protect the open suburb and the market. Its ground plan is irregular, adjusted to the lie of the ground, and the walls were reinforced by towers, which were subsequently rebuilt. Remains of buildings for the accommodation of the garrison have been preserved inside the walls.

PRIZREN [H, 7]
The Church of the Mother of God Ljeviška (Bogorodica Ljeviška)

The church was built on the foundations of an earlier building in the 13th century. It was thoroughly renovated by King Milutin in 1306/1307, as testified by an inscription made of brick in the apse. The church represents a combination of a triple-nave basilica (29 metres long) and an inscribed cross with five domes. On the eastern side is the altar apse (five-sided without) and the smaller apses of the diaconicon and the prothesis. On the western side is the outer narthex with the

CHURCH OF THE MOTHER OF
GOD LJEVIŠKA, FRESCO, CHRIST
HEALING THE BLIND

open ground floor in the form of a
porch, and an upper storey. Above
the entrance rises a two-storeyed
bell-tower, lightened by large
openings. The south-eastern aisle and
the outer narthex have cross vaulting.
The facades are built of alternate
courses of brick and tuffa and are
enlivened by shallow arcades, blind
niches, windows and ceramic
ornaments in the form of crosses,
spirals and rays. The surviving
parts include the stonework on the
west portal and some carved
fragments which had belonged to
the earlier basilica and which were
incorporated into this church. The
earliest frescoes were painted in the
third decade of the 13th century and
those that have been preserved show
the Wedding at Cana, the Healing
of the Blind and the Virgin of
Tenderness. The basic group of
frescoes dates from the period

between 1310 and 1313. The frescoes
in the nave and the aisles illustrate
the Great Feasts, Christ's miracles
and parables, the Passion, the life of
St Nicholas, the Acathist Hymn and
the Ecumenical Councils. Portraits
of the members of the Nemanjić
family, including a very expressive
King Milutin, are in the narthex, and
the Last Judgment, Baptism,
prophets, classical philosophers and
a sibyl are represented in the outer
narthex. The long painted inscription
in the narthex says that masters
Nikola and Astrapa were the chief
builders of the church. It is supposed
that the authors of the frescoes were
Mihailo (Astrapin) and Evtihije.
During Turkish rule the church
was converted into a mosque, and
after the First World War it become
a church again. After the Second
World War the frescoes were cleaned
and the church was restored.

PRIZREN [H, 7]
The Church of the Holy Archangels

The church is situated in a gorge, on the bank of the Ribnica river, near Prizren. It was built as the sepulchral church of Emperor Dušan and its construction lasted from 1343 to 1352. Dušan issued a charter endowing the future monastery with lands. The church has the ground plan in the form of an inscribed cross with a dome resting on four pillars. On the eastern side are three altar apses; the middle one is wider, deeper and five-sided without, and the two lateral ones are three-sided. An open outer narthex is on the western side. The facades are built of white and red marble. The church had a rich floor made of white and blue stone in the narthex and of mosaic in the nave. It was adorned with frescoes, now destroyed, and richly decorated with ornamental and figural carvings (capitals, portals, windows, church furniture). Fragments of this decoration are now on view in the Archaeological Museum in Skopje. A tomb stood in the northern aisle, in which the body of Emperor Dušan was buried after his death in 1355. Round the church are monastic buildings (the refectory, monastic residences) and a small church dedicated to St Nicholas. The entire complex was fortified and connected with the citadel of Višegrad. With the arrival of the Turks the monastery was abandoned; by the beginning of the 17th century it had already fallen into ruin and its dressed stone was being used for the building of the Sinan Pasha Mosque in Prizren. By the beginning of the 20th century the ruins were almost completely covered with earth. They were excavated in 1927, and extensive restoration work was done in the late 1960s.

PRIZREN [H, 7]
The Church of St Saviour

The church was built for Mladen Vladojević, a nobleman, in the time of Emperor Dušan. It is first

PRIZREN, CHURCH OF ST SAVIOUR

mentioned in historical sources in 1348. It is a domed single-nave building. The facades are built of alternate courses of stone and brick. The frescoes in the church have been damaged by fire. They date from about the middle of the 14th century.

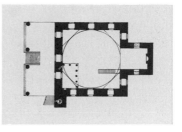

PRIZREN [H, 7]
The Sinan Pasha Mosque

The building of the mosque was completed in 1615. Its walls incorporate dressed stone blocks and carved decoration from the ruined Church of the Holy Archangels. It has all the features of classical style. The ground plan is a square (17.80 × 17.80 metres). In the upper portion the quadrangular base is formed into an octogonal drum on squinches surmounted by a dome. The mihrab space is quadrangular and covered with a

semi-calotte. A minaret 42 metres high is embedded into the mass of the wall. In front of the mosque was a porch resting on four pillars and covered with three cupolas. The porch was pulled down during the First World War. The mosque was restored in 1952.

PSAČA [J, 6]
The Church of St Nicholas

The church is situated in the vicinity of Kriva Palanka. It was built about 1354 and its founder was Vlatko, a nobleman. Its ground plan is in the form of an elongated inscribed cross. On the eastern side is the altar apse, three-sided without, and on the western side is a domed narthex. Judging by the founder's composition, there was originally a dome above the nave as well. The facades are built of alternate courses of brick and stone and are enlivened by lesenes and ceramic decoration. The frescoes were painted between 1365 and 1371 and are considerably damaged. The surviving paintings include parts of the Great Feasts, the Passion and Christ's miracles, as well as parts of the cycle of St Nicholas. The frescoes in the narthex are in a better state of preservation. Particularly expressive is the founder's composition, which looks like a group portrait and belongs to a type very rare in Byzantine painting.

PRIZREN, SINAN PASHA MOSQUE

PTUJ [C, 1]
The Church of St George

A single-nave early Romanesque building was converted in the middle of the 13th century into a triple-nave basilica with a flat ceiling and three semicircular apses on the eastern side. An entrance porch, originally surmounted by a monumental loft and dating from the second third of the 13th century, runs the width of the nave on the western side. The empora housed a chapel used by the governor of Salzburg when he came to visit this region and took up residence in Ptuj. Remains of wall paintings dating from about 1240 have been preserved in the chapel. In the Gothic period the church was reconstructed, and cross vaulting and two aisles were added. The two lateral chapels adjoining the presbytery were built in the Baroque era. A monumental bell-tower, in fact a tower incorporated into the town fortifications, was built independently of the church. The church contains Gothic wooden pews, carved in 1446.

PTUJSKA GORA [C, 1]
The Church of the Virgin

The church was built c. 1400 in fulfilment of a vow, and its founders were Bernard III of Ptuj and Ulrich Walse. It is the finest and most important monument of Gothic architecture in Slovenia. It is a basilica with a nave, two aisles and three polygonal apses on the eastern side. An octagonal bell-tower rises above the entrance. The facades are enlivened by tall windows and countreforts which reinforce the building. The nave is wider and only slightly higher than the aisles, and it is separated from the aisles by two colonnades with pointed arches.

PTUJSKA GORA, CHURCH OF THE VIRGIN, ALTAR

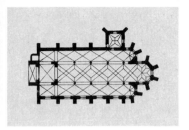

Ribbed cross vaulting rests on sheaves of columns. The masons and carvers were from a workshop influenced by the work of Peter Parler from Prague. The church furniture and carved decoration are very rich. Decorated stone stalls are in all three apses. The bracket masks in the sacristy and on the northern wall are the work of the master of the presbytery of Hajdina. The »Celje Altar« is in the southern apse (c. 1400). The slender octagonal columns which support the canopy have capitals with masks, human and half-animal figures. The angels on escutcheons, the Adoration of the Kings and the Dormition of the Virgin, above and near the main portal, belong to the same »soft style«. Especially important are the two Gothic stone altars dedicated to the Virgin and St Sigmund, which herald the later altarpieces. Several other early 15th century Gothic sculptures have been preserved in the church. Particularly worthy of scrutiny is the Virgin with the cloak on the main altar, a masterpiece of Gothic sculpture. The representation is carved in deep relief and shows eighty figures of believers under the Virgin's cloak. Some of the heads look very much like portraits. Frescoes depicting the Passion, the legend of St Nicholas, the Pentecost and the Church Fathers have been preserved in the Holy Cross Chapel. They were painted about 1420 by a master from the circle of Hans von Bruneck in the spirit of the international "soft style". The church is encircled by walls and it is approached by a Baroque stairway.

PTUJSKA GORA, CHURCH OF THE VIRGIN, FRESCOES, PASSION

PULA, AMPHITHEATRE

PULA [A, 3]
The Amphitheatre

From the middle of the 1st century B. C., when it was founded as a Roman colony, Pula had a flourishing development and grew into a large town which has left us numerous monuments of architecture (triumphal arches, temples, theatres), sculpture (a torso of Emperor Augustus and a torso of Emperor Hadrian) and painting (frescoes and mosaics). Outside the town walls is a monumental amphitheatre, ellipsoid in form and measuring 132 × 105 metres. Its construction began in Augustan times, and it was completed towards the middle of the 1st century A. D. Its western, seaward side has three storeys, rising to a total height of 32 metres. The first two zones consist of arches supported on massive pilasters, and the third zone has quadrangular windows. On the eastern side use was made of the natural lie of the ground, so that a part of the arena and some seats were dug into the hill, and the wall on this side had two storeys. Four towers are incorporated into the wall on four sides and they serve as reinforcement and decoration. Below the arena is a large room form which a vaulted corridor leads to the sea. Although still in a comparatively good state of preservation, the amphitheatre, like a number of other monuments in Pula, was damaged in the 17th and 18th centuries. As a result of minor conservation works carried out after the Second World War, it is now possible to use it as an open theatre.

PULA [A, 3]
The Temple of Augustus

The temple was built in the Augustan times, between 2 B.C. and 14 A.D. on the northern side of the former forum. It is a single-nave building with a closed quadrangular cella. It has four columns on the front side and one on each of the lateral sides. The columns have Corinthian capitals. The frieze above the tripartite architrave is decorated with ornaments in the form of flowers and akanthus leaves. A medallion with the representation of a deity was in the middle of the tympanum, and on the frieze below ran the inscription in bronze letters ROMAE ET AUGUSTO CAESARI DIVI F(ILIO) PATRI PATRIAE.

PULA [A, 3]
The Twin Gate

Three monumental gates have been preserved from classical Pula: the Hercules Gate, the Triumphal Arch of the Sergii and the Twin Gate. The Twin Gate was built in the times of the Antonini, about the middle of the 2nd century A.D. It has two vaulted passageways between thick pilasters. The facade is enlivened by half-columns with composite capitals, smooth arches and a smooth architrave. The cornice is elaborately decorated.

PULA [A, 3]
The Funeral Chapel

The chapel was built in the middle of the 6th century, at the time when Pula had a bishop and was under the jurisdiction of the Ravenna exarchate. It is a typical example of Byzantine architecture with the facades enlivened by shallow niches. Parts of its mosaics and frescoes have been preserved. The chapel belonged to the monumental basilica of St Mary Formosa.

RAB [B, 3]
The Church of St Mary Major

The cathedral church of Rab. It was consecrated in 1177, but it is supposed that it is a little earlier. It is a basilica with a nave and two aisles,

PULA, FUNERAL CHAPEL

semicircular apses and a flat ceiling. The aisles are separated from the nave by six pairs of columns. The lower part of the western facade is built of white and pale red stone and enlivened by two rows of semicircular niches. A carved Pietà, the work of Petar Trogiranin, is in the lunette. High Gothic choir stalls, carved in 1445, and the baptismal font carved in stone by Petar Trogiranin, have been preserved in the church. Especially remarkable is the Romanesque bell-tower, which is progressively lightened by increasingly large windows (onelight, twolight, threelight and fourlight). A gilt silver reliquary of St Christopher, dating from the 12th century, and parts of the cross which King Koloman presented to the church, are on the altar, below a 9th century ornamented ciborium.

RAB [B, 3]
The Church of St Andrew

The church is in the form of a triple-nave basilica and it was built as the church of a Benedictine nunnery at the end of the 12th century. Later it was heavily damaged and it was rebuilt about the middle of the 16th century, when a new frontage and the Renaissance portal were added. The Romanesque bell--tower built against the wall on the southern side dates from 1181. A richly decorated Baroque altar, made in 1765, has been preserved in the church.

RAB, CHURCH OF ST MARY MAJOR

RAB, SUPETARSKA DRAGA [B, 3]
The Church of St Peter

The church, one of the earliest Romanesque buildings in Dalmatia, was built in 1066 on the foundations of an older edifice. It is a triple-nave basilica with semicircular niches, a flat ceiling and clerestories. The columns and capitals which separated the aisles from the nave were taken from some early Christian church. The front facade is decorated

main Renaissance portal. The windows display a mixture of Gothic and Renaissance elements typical of the architecture in Dalmatia in this period. Next to the large palace is the small Nimira palace, with a fine Gothic portal featuring the family coat-of-arms in the lunette.

RAB [B, 3]
The Church of St Francis

The Franciscan monastery was founded as early as the 13th century, and its church was built in 1491. Its front facade combines Gothic and Renaissance elements. Especially decorative is the upper portion with three fan arches and a bell-tower. The monastery was abandoned in 1823, and the church is now used as a funeral chapel.

RAB [B, 3]
The Loggia

A loggia existed in Rab as early as the 14th century, but it has not been preserved. The present loggia was built in Renaissance style in 1509. It is an open hall with a porch resting on six columns with carved capitals and moulded bases. It adjoins the town tower.

by a prothyron above the portal. Next to the church is a bell-tower, the lower portion of which is original. It houses a 13th century bell.

RAB [B, 3]
The Nimira Palace

The palace was built for the rich family Dominis Nimira at the end of the 15th century. It has the ground floor, two upper storeys and a large garden. Especially remarkable is the

RADIMLJA [E, 5]
The Medieval Cemetery

Radimlja is in the vicinity of Stolac in Herzegovina. It is one of the largest and most attractive cemeteries of *stećci* and contains 133 of these medieval gravestones. They were carved in the 15th and 16th centuries, and it is supposed, on the basis of their inscriptions, that the cemetery belonged to the feudal family Hrabren-Miloradović. Two forms are predominant: high casket and sarcophagus. Sixty-three monuments have carved decoration, which can be divided into two types: ornamental and figural. The first type includes zig-zag lines, torded ropes, tendrils, rosettes, shallow arcades, shields, swords, bows and arrows. The second type of ornaments consists of representations of waggons, animals and human figures. Especially typical of this workshop are the *stećci* showing figures of *vojvodas* (military leaders). These are male figures with a raised outsized hand, dressed in medieval costume. Above the figure is the sun on one side and a bow and arrows on the other side. The carving is crude, and the designs are neither very descriptive nor detailed. Some names of the masters who carved the monuments have been preserved — Miogost, Bolašin Bogačić and Ratko Brativonić.

RADOŽDA [H, 8]
The Church of Archangel Michael

The church is in the vicinity of Struga. It is a cave church, and its structure is adjusted to the position of the rocks. It has a narthex and a nave, Some other rooms existed originally in front of the church, but now only their foundations survive. The earliest frescoes date from the 1270s. One of them is the Miracle at Hona. The later frescoes were painted in the second half of the 14th century.

RAM [I, 3]
The Medieval Fortress

The fortress is situated on a steep slope on the right bank of the Danube. It is referred to in Trajanic times as a settlement in which cavalry units were stationed. In 1128 it is mentioned as being in the vicinity of a place at which the Byzantines defeated the Hungarians. The present fortifications were built by Sultan Bayazid II (1480—1512). Its ground plan is a regular pentagon and it is constructed as a fortress for cannon warfare. The side towards the land has a low wall with a wide moat in front of it. Apart from the keep, through which the fortress is entered, there are four corner towers. Masonry fireplaces, rare in medieval buildings in this region, have been preserved in them. The interior of the fortress was demolished during Koča's rebellion in 1788. A caravanserai, built in the same way as the fortress, is in the vicinity.

RAVANICA [I, 4]
The Church of the Ascension

The church is in the vicinity of Ćuprija. It was built at the end of the eighth decade of the 14th century, and its founder was Prince Lazar. It is surrounded by a defensive wall with seven towers. The church is in the form of a five-domed inscribed cross combined with a trefoil (16.5 metres long). The central dome rests on four free-standing pillars. On the east is a tripartite sanctuary The old narthex on the western side was pulled down at the end of the 17th century, and the present one was built in 1721. The facades are built of alternate courses of stone and brick and are enlivened by windows, rosettes and ceramic decoration. The facades are divided by two cordon cornices into three horizontal zones and by colonnettes and shallow semicircular niches into vertical panels. Sculptured ornaments have been best preserved on the windows and rosettes. The main motifs are fantastic animals and a twopartite band forming various geometric and vegetable designs. The sculptured ornaments are sometimes very plastic, as in a medallion with two gryphons. The frescoes were completed by about 1385, and they mark the beginning of the so-called Morava style in Serbian medieval painting. The Virgin between angels, the Communion of the Apostles and the Procession of the Church Fathers are represented in the apse. The Great Feasts and the cycle of Christ's miracles and parables are in the nave. The middle zone and the lower zone are separated by a band with medallions containing busts of saints. The frescoes were painted by several masters, one of whom, Konstantin by name, has left his signature. The best artists painted the frescoes in the sanctuary and on the vaults and walls of the nave. The monastery was laid waste and plundered several times, and it was abandoned at the end of the 17th

RAVANICA, CHURCH OF THE ASCENSION

RAVANICA, FRESCO, WARRIOR SAINTS

century. It was restored at the beginning of the 18th century.

RAVANJSKA VRATA [E, 4]
The Upper Cemetery

The cemetery is at Ravanjska vrata near Kupres in central Bosnia. There are five sites with 163 *stećci* in this area. The Upper Cemetery has the most decorative examples. In addition to geometric ornaments and floral designs, which are most common, some *stećci* show scenes of hunting and jousting. A characteristic feature are arcades containing tournament scenes: two knights on horseback engaged in a combat. The most common forms are the sarcophagus, the casket and the tablet. No inscriptions have been preserved. The monuments were carved between the 14th and the middle of the 15th century.

RESAVA [H, 4]
The Fortress and the Monastery

The fortifications were constructed
between 1407 and 1418, during the
reign of Despot Stefan Lazarević for
the better protection of the monastery
Resava-Manasija. In the first half of
the 15th century it was the most
important Serbian literary centre in
which books were copied and
translated and the style of the
Serbian language was polished. The
Despot died in 1427 and the Turks
took the fortress for a brief period
in 1439, and definitely in 1458. The
fortress has an irregular polygonal
ground plan and eleven towers. The
largest is the keep, called the Despot's
Tower. Both the walls and the
towers have a number of defensive
machicolations connected by internal
corridors. The towers had
battlements with embrasures for
bowmen. A large monastic refectory
and the living quarters for monks
were built near the church within the
walls. The Church of the Holy
Trinity was built and adorned with
frescoes between 1407 and 1418. It

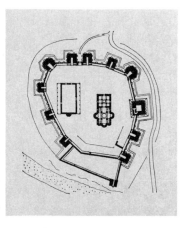

RESAVA, FRESCO, A WARRIOR SAINT

is in the form of an inscribed cross combined with a trefoil (34 metres long), and it has five domes on slender drums. The central dome rests on four free-standing pillars. On the eastern side is a tripartite altar space, and a spacious domed narthex is on the western side. Unlike the other buildings of the Morava School, the facades are built of ashlars and enlivened by colonnettes (on the lateral conchs and on the apse) and a frieze of small blind arcades on brackets running below the roof cornice, as in the churches of the Raška School. The original floor made of stone of various colours has been preserved in the interior. The frescoes are of a high artistic quality, but they are only partly preserved. The Communion of the Apostles and the Procession of

RESAVA, FRESCO, PROPHET HABAKKUK
RESAVA, CHURCH OF THE HOLY TRINITY

the Church Fathers are in the apse, prophets are shown in the dome, while the surviving frescoes in the nave include parts of the Great Feasts, Christ's miracles and, in the lower zone, warrior saints, who are very typical of the style of Manasija. On the western wall is the Dormition of the Virgin and below it is the portrait of the founder, Despot Stefan, holding a model of the church in his hand.

RIJEKA [B, 2]
The Castle of Trsat

The castle is situated on a hill called Trsat above Rijeka. It was

FRESCO, FOUNDER DESPOT STEFAN
RESAVA, FORTRESS

constructed in the latter half of the 13th century for the princes of the Frankopan family on the site of an old Roman settlement called Tarsatica. It was reconstructed and enlarged for the first time in the 17th century. In 1826 it was bought by the Austrian vice marshal Laval Nugent. He added new buildings (outer ranges, the mausoleum) and reconstructed thoroughly the entire castle, so that much of its original appearance has been lost. Beneath the castle are two churches: St George (13th century) and the Church of Our Lady Lauretana (15th century). Both have lost their original features in subsequent reconstructions. The castle has been adapted for tourist purposes, and a part of it accommodates the Museum of the People's Revolution.

ROVINJ, CHAPEL OF THE HOLY TRINITY

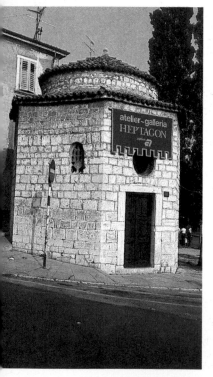

RIJEKA [B, 2]
The Town Tower

The old 15th century clock-tower, which formed part of the medieval fortifications, was reconstructed towards the end of the 18th century, when it got typical Baroque features. The upper portion incorporates reliefs with the figures of Emperor Leopold and Charles VI.

ROVINJ [A, 3]
The Chapel of the Holy Trinity

The chapel is situated on the Liberty Square (Trg slobode) in the southern part of the town. It was designed in Romanesque style, although it also shows some traces of Byzantine influence in its structure. It was constructed in the 13th century. The chapel is polygonal in plan, and its roof structure is in the form of a dome.

ROVINJ [A, 3]
The Church of St Euphemia

The church was built in 1736 on the foundations of an earlier church. It is a triple-nave Baroque building situated on a hilltop, so that it dominates the town. The southern wall incorporates a 14th century Gothic relief. The bell-tower is earlier and it belonged to the older church. Its building was completed in 1677 and it was designed by A. Manopola, who used the campanile of the Church of St Mark

ROVINJ

in Venice as his model. It is surmounted by a statue of St Euphemia. A 6th century sarcophagus of the Ravenna type and two paintings of the Venetian school dating from the 16th and 17th centuries have been preserved in the church.

SAMOBOR [C, 2]
The Church of St Anastasia

The church was built between 1671 and 1675 at the initiative of Countess Jelisava Auersperg and the citizens of Samobor on a site occupied earlier by the parish church. The architect was Hans Allio from Celje. The ground plan is modelled on that of the Jesuit church of St Catherine in Zagreb: the nave has tunnel vaulting and three lateral chapels on either side. The sanctuary has a three-sided ending and it is reinforced without by strong countreforts similar to those used in the Gothic period. The bell-tower, with Renaissance openings and a Baroque upper portion, adjoins the church on the northern side. The front facade is simple, with high windows and a Renaissance portal.

SAMOBOR [C, 2]
The Church of the Virgin

The church belongs to the Franciscan order. It was built in 1722 as a single-nave Baroque building with lateral chapels. On the eastern side is a polygonal presbytery, and a high bell-tower adjoins the front facade on the western side. A monumental illusionistic composition of the Dormition of the Virgin (1752) by Franc Jelovšek, altar paintings by Valentin Metcinger (1734/35) and two rich Baroque altars dating from 1735 and 1752 have been preserved in the church. The Baroque monastery with an inner courtyard had been built, between 1712 and 1721, before the church was constructed.

SAMOBOR [C, 2]
The Old Fortress

The fortress was built in several phases between the 13th and the 18th century. It was in the possession of many distinguished families: the counts of Celje, the Frankopans, the Erdőds, the Kulmers. As a result of successive enlargements and reconstructions, the fortress exhibits various stylistic features. Its ground plan is irregular, adjusted to the lie of the hilly ground. The massive walls are reinforced by semicircular towers, and there is a pentagonal bastion with openings for guns at the most exposed point. The typically Renaissance hearths date from the first half of the 16th century. A Gothic chapel dedicated to St Anne is within the fortress.

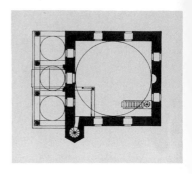

SARAJEVO [F, 4]
The Ali Pasha Mosque

One of the finest mosques in Bosnia. It was built in 1561 for the governor of Bosnia Hadim Ali Pasha, who lived in Sarajevo, where he died, a short time before the mosque was

SARAJEVO, ALI PASHA MOSQUE

completed, as shown by an inscription above the entrance. It is designed in classical style. It is square in plan and it has a large dome on squinches which dominates the entire area. The minaret is embedded into the mass of the wall. The front part has a porch supported on four marble columns with capitals and moulded bases. The porch is covered with three smaller domes, the middle one being a little higher than the other two. The columns are connected with pointed arches. In front of the porch is a fountain, and the cemetery is in the yard. The interior of the mosque is richly decorated with stalactites, moulded cornices and ornaments engraved in stone. It was restored in 1894.

SARAJEVO [F, 4]
The Brusa Covered Market (Brusa Bezistan)

The market was founded by the Grand Vezier Rustem Pasha and it was constructed in 1551. It has massive walls of stone and brick and high windows. The ground plan consists of six equal squares covered with domes. It is modelled on the "ulu-mosque", in which the domes surmounting the square areas are of the same height and size.

SARAJEVO [F, 4]
The Gazi Husrev Bey Mosque

This is the largest mosque in Bosnia and Herzegovina and a very important monument of Ottoman architecture of the early 16th century. It was built in 1530. Its founder was Gazi Husrev Bey, a nephew of Sultan Bayazit II, during whose reign several important public buildings (the Turkish baths, the mecteb, the school, the library, the covered market and the caravanserai) were constructed in the old urban core of Sarajevo. It belongs to the early classical style and its architect was Ajem Esir Ali, but Dubrovnik masters also participated in its construction. The main inner space is domed and square in plan (13 × 13 metres); it is extended by the mihrab, half-square in plan and covered with a semi-cupola. The radius of the dome is 13 metres, and the height from the floor to its top is 26 metres, or two widths of the plan. Two smaller domed chambers are placed laterally. A porch with arcades supported on four high marble columns with capitals is in front of the mosque. The porch is divided into five bays, and each bay is covered with a shallow dome. The main entrance is very decorative and has features which appear in the

SARAJEVO, BRUSA COVERED MARKET

SARAJEVO, HUSREV BEY MOSQUE, PORTAL

interior of the building as well.
A fountain and two mausolea, the
Gazi Husrev Bey turbeh and the
Gazi Murad Bey turbeh, are in the

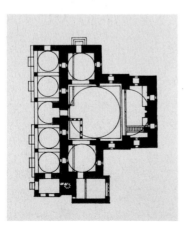

yard in front of the mosque. Both
turbehs date from the 16th century
and are examples of the closed type
of mausoleum, octagonal in plan
and domed.

SARAJEVO [F, 4]
*The Husrev Bey Covered Market
(Husrev-begov bezistan)*

The market was built in 1540. Its
plan is basilican and its length is 109
metres.The nave is higher and covers
the main passageway. The lateral
parts consist of small compartments
— shops — with tunnel vaulting.
Dubrovnik masters took part in the
construction of the building.

SARAJEVO [F, 4]
*The Husrev Bey School (Husrevbegova
medresa)*

Gazi Husrev Bey also founded a
high school (medresa), which is
situated opposite his mosque. It was
designed and built by Ajem Esir Ali
in 1537. It is rectangular in plan and
it has an atrium with an arcaded
porch covered with ten small domes.
Fourteen more domes are built
above the chambers for work and
study. A fountain is in the middle of
the yard. Tall pointed chimnes
impart a special dynamic quality to
the roof structure. The building is
popularly known as the Kuršumlija
because it was covered with lead
(*kursum* means "lead" in Turkish).

SAVINA [F, 6]
The Church of the Virgin

The church is near Hercegnovi. In addition to this cathedral church, the complex of the Orthodox monastery comprises two smaller churches, one of them with 17 century frescoes. The Church of the Virgin was founded by the monks themselves, with the permission of the Doge of Venice. The construction lasted from 1777 to 1799, and the main architect was Nikola Foretić from Korčula, who was assisted by Juraj Korčulanin. It is a single-nave building which has a semicircular apse on the eastern side and a narthex with a three-storeyed bell-tower on the western side. The central space is covered with a dome, which has a decorative octagonal drum resting on a cubic base. A frieze of small blind arcades runs beneath the roof cornice. It is a typical example of the eclectic style, combining Romanesque (the roof cornice), Byzantine (the dome) and Baroque

SAVINA, CHURCH OF THE DORMITION OF THE VIRGIN

(the decorative elements, the rosettes, the oval windows) elements. The iconostasis was painted by Simeon Lazović from Bijelo Polje in 1797. A rich library of old manuscripts and charters, a collection of icons and a treasury with parts of church

SAVINA, CHURCH OF THE DORMITION OF THE VIRGIN, FRESCO, THE DEPOSITION

furniture have been preserved in the monastery.

SELO IN PREKOMURJE [D, 1]
The Church of St Nicholas

The church was built in the first half of the 13th century and it is first mentioned in historical sources in 1366. It is a domed rotunda (inner diameter 6.60 metres). The church had an apse on the eastern side, but it was pulled down in 1845 and replaced by a bell-tower. It is built of brick and the facades are enlivened by lesenes connected by an indented frieze. The interior walls are divided into ten semicircular niches. The frescoes were painted in two phases: the earlier ones date from mid-14th century (the Adoration of the Kings) and the later ones were painted c. 1400. The Throne of Grace, the sun, the moon and the symbols of the Evangelists are represented in the dome. Below them are scenes from the Passion, including a remarkable Bearing of the Cross. On the walls are the Adoration of the Kings and individual figures of saints. The church was restored in 1956.

SENJ [B, 3]
The Nehaj Fortress

Senj is first mentioned as early as the 4th century B.C., and it was a flourishing trading port in Roman times. In the early Middle Ages the town belonged first to the Byzantines and then to the Franks. Later it became an episcopal seat and grew into an important centre of Glagolitic learning. In 1271 it passed under the rule of the feudal Frankopan family, and in 1469 it was seized by King Matthias Corvinus of Hungary. At the beginning of the 16th century, when Senj was already under the rule of the Habsburgs, and especially after the fall of Klis, numerous refugees took shelter in Senj, organized themselves as Uskoks and began to attack the Turks by land and the Venetians on sea. After 1617 (the Madrid Peace) the Uskoks were resettled in Lika, their ships were destroyed and an Austrian garrison was stationed in Senj. The walls that encircled the core of the town were built in the 15th and 16th centuries, but they were pulled down for the most part in the 18th an 19th centuries. The extant parts of the city fortifications include the walls on the northern and eastern sides, the towers Lipica, Šabac and Leon. In 1558 general Nikola Lenković had a fortress built on a hillock above the town to serve as the military headquarters. It is called Nehaj and it has an inner yard with a cistern. Its walls are strengthened on the outside with corner watch-towers. Several Glagolitic inscriptions, taken from the ruined churches in the town, are incorporated into its walls. The fortress houses the Municipal Museum today.

SENJ, NEHAJ FORTRESS

SISAK [D, 2]
The Castle

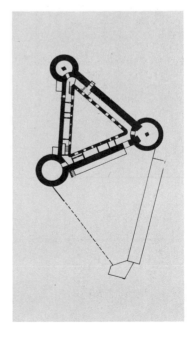

The Fortress was built by master Peter from Milan between 1544 and 1550 on the orders of the Zagreb chapter. Local masters (Blaž Belković, Mihailo from Ivanić and others) also took part in its construction. The fortress was built with the aim of protecting Zagreb from Turkish incursions. The ground plan is triangular with three Renaissance bastion towers for heavy cannon. A well and two-storeyed arcades are in the yard. The fortress also had a barbican. It was damaged during the Second World War, but it was restored later.

SKOPJE [I, 7]
Kale

The settlement called Scupi was founded as early as the Roman times, but it was damaged in an earthquake in 518. Justinian restored it and made it the seat of an archbishopric. The town was incorporated into Samuilo's state, and later it was under the rule of the Byzantines, the Bulgarians and the Normans. From 1282 it was one of the chief towns in the Serbian state. Dušan was crowned emperor and proclaimed his famous code of laws in it. The Turks seized it in 1391. The fortress — Kale — Was built in several phases and its walls incorporate numerous remains of antiquity. The surviving parts of the walls with towers date from the Middle Ages.

SKOLJE [I, 7]
The Church of St Nicholas

The church is situated 17 kilometres from Skopje. It was founded by King Milutin and erected on the foundations of an earlier building in 1307/1308. Its ground plan (11.5 metres long) is in the form of an inscribed cross and it has a dome resting on four free-standing pillars. The facades are built of alternate courses of stone and brick and are enlivened by vertical shallow niches. The altar apse is ornamented with chess-board designs, meanders and

CHURCH OF ST NICHOLAS

other motifs. The frescoes in the church were painted before 1316 and are the work of Miahilo and Evtihije, whose signature is found on the shield of St Theodore Tiro on the southern wall. The iconography is typical of the early 14th century — the Great Feasts, Christ's miracles and the Passion — the only difference being that the arrangement of the compositions is slightly altered. The frescoes of the greatest artistic worth occupy the most conspicuous places. Parts of the frescoes on the vault were damaged in the Middle Ages, so that a new layer was painted in 1483/84. The southern entrance was repaired in 1574, and the entire church was restored in 1692. A small church consecrated to St John the Forerunner stood at its southern side, but it was torn down during an inexpert restoration of the main church in 1928.

SKOPJE [I, 7]
The Andreaš Monaster

The monastery is situated above the Treska river. The church is dedicated to St Andrew. It was founded by Andreaš, the second son of King Vukašin and brother of King Marko, in 1389. It is trefoil in plan, but the lateral semicircular apses are enveloped without in the cubic mass of the wall. The central space is surmounted by a dome on a high octagonal drum. A narthex was added during Turkish rule. The facades are built of broken stone with horizontal courses of brick and they are enlivened by two rows of shallow niches. The ornaments in the niches are either made of brick or painted in the fresco technique.

SKOPJE, CHURCH OF THE HOLY SAVIOUR, ICONOSTASIS

SKOPJE, PASHA BATHS, ICON, CHRIST

The frescoes in the sanctuary and nave of the church were painted by Metropolitan Jovan and his assistant monk Grigorije. Jovan had come from Monastery Zrze, where he worked with another monk, Makarije. These two artists evolved a particular style which influenced the development of painting at the end of the 14th century. The arrangement of their monumental scenes and figures follows 13th century models. In the lower zone are the standing figures — warrior saints, Apostles and Evangelists; above them are the busts of hermits, archbishops and warriors. The middle zone contains an illustration of the Passion, which is remarkable for its excellent treatment of space, lively details and bold anatomic foreshortenings. The basic features of this style are

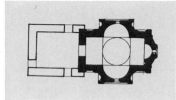

expressiveness and a monumental quality, which is most clearly seen in the fresco depicting St Peter. Remains of paintings from 1559/60 have been preserved in the narthex.

SKOPJE [I, 7]
The Church of the Holy Saviour

SKOPJE, ANDREAŠ MONASTERY

The church was built during Turkish rule, at the end of the 17th and the beginning of the 18th century. It is a low building, sunk into the ground. It has a nave and two aisles. The nave is vaulted, and the aisles have flat ceilings. It was reconstructed in the

SKOPJE, ANDREAŠ MONASTERY, FRESCO, AGONY IN THE GARDEN

19th century. The grave of the insurrection leader Goce Delčev is in the courtyard. The iconostasis, the finest example of wood-carving in Macedonia, was completed in 1824. It was made by masters Petar Filipović-Garkata, his brother Marko and Makarije Negrijev--Frčkovski from Galičnik.

SKOPJE [I, 7]
The Sultan Murat Mosque

The mosque was built in 1436 at the orders of Sultan Murat II, father of Mohammed the Conqueror. It is popularly called the Hjumkar (Sultan) mosque. It is the oldest mosque in the territory of Yugoslavia. It is built of stone and brick in Brusa style. The interior space is in the form of a basilica with a nave, two aisles and flat ceilings. It is covered with a pavilion roof. A porch with five arcades which have pointed arches is on the northern side. A Husein from Debar is cited as the chief builder. The mosque was damaged by fire twice, in 1537 and 1689, and it was reconstructed in the time of Solyman the Magnificent and Sultan Ahmed. The roof structure and the minaret were altered in these reconstructions.

SKOPJE [I, 7]
The Daut Pasha Baths (Daut-pašin hamam)

The baths were built from 1487 to 1497 as a double *hamam,* for men and women. It is one of the finest buildings of the early Constantinopolitan style. The

SKOPJE, MUSTAFA PASHA MOSQUE

SKOPJE, KURŠUMLI HAN

decorative Byzantine technique of building in alternate courses of stone and brick was used for its construction. It is rectangular in plan and has a monumental interior space surmounted by two large and eleven small domes. The domes rest on squinches with stalactites and have small perforations for lighting. The walls were decorated with picturesque ornaments. The building was heavily damaged in 1689, but it was restored in 1949, when the Art Gallery was housed in it. The Gallery possesses an icon of Christ, painted by Jovan Zograf c. 1400, and an icon of the Virgin, painted by Makarije at about the same time. The building was damaged in the 1963 earthquake, but it was subsequently repaired and restored.

SKOPJE [I, 7]
The Isa Bey Mosque

It was built in 1457 in the early Constantinopolitan style on the model of the Mahmut Pasha Mosque in Constantinople. Its ground plan is longitudinal (19 metres) and it has two domes. Two small lateral chambers were added later. The minaret is 34 metres high. The porch is covered with five cupolas, and the arcading consists of pointed arches. The mosque is built of dressed stone and brick. It was damaged in the 1963 earthquake and the top of the minaret collapsed.

SKOPJE, DAUT PASHA BATHS

SKOPJE [I, 7]
The Mustapha Pasha Mosque

The mosque was built in 1492 and its founder was Mustapha Pasha, later the Grand Vezier and favourite of Sultan Bayazed II. It belongs to the early Constantinopolitan style. Its ground plan is square (16 × 16 metres). An imposing dome rests on an octagonal drum supported by squinches. The minaret, 47 metres high, is embedded in the wall. Its balcony (sherefa) rests on stalactite projections. In front of the entrance is a porch of white marble supported on four pillars. The arcades have pointed arches. The porch is covered with three domes, the middle one being a little higher than the other two.

SKOPJE [I, 7]
The Kuršumli Han

The *han* represents the highest achievement of Ottoman secular architecture in the territory of Yugoslavia. It was built in the fifth decade of the 16th century to serve as a shelter and resting place for travellers, merchants and caravans. It is built in the Byzantine fashion, in alternate courses of stone and brick, with highly placed windows. A wide gate, for waggons and horses, is on the southern side. The *han* consists of two parts and two inner courtyards. The first part has a spacious yard with a fountain, surrounded by a porch with arcading. Storehouses are on the ground floor, and 29 rooms for travellers are on the first floor. The rooms are vaulted and have fireplaces. The other part consists of the ground floor only and it used to serve as a stable for horses. After the First World War the building was restored and it now houses the Archaeological Museum.

SLADKA GORA, CHURCH OF THE VIRGIN

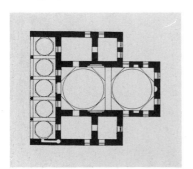

SLADKA GORA [C, 1]
The Church of the Virgin

The church is situated in the vicinity of Celje. It was built on the site of an earlier church c. 1750. It is square in plan and has a flattened dome and rounded lateral chapels. A cupola with a lantern is above the presbytery, and two bell-towers are on the western side. The facades have concave sections and are enlivened by lesenes and stuccowork. The architect is not known. Judging by certain structural elements, he may have been associated with the circle of the well-known Steiermark architect Johan Fucks. Its interior displays a unique synthesis of architecture, painting and sculpture. The illusionistic frescoes were painted by the well-known Baroque painter Franc Jelovšek in 1753. Five splendid Baroque altars, a pulpit, an organ and other pieces of church furniture have been preserved in the church.

SLEPČE [I, 8]
The Church of St John the Forerunner

The monastery with the church is located in the vicinity of Bitolj. It is first mentioned in historical sources in 1543, but it is supposed that it was founded as early as the 14th

SLADKA GORA, CHURCH OF THE VIRGIN (INTERIOR)

century. Workshops for the copying of Slavonic books and for the painting of icons existed in the monastery. The present church was constructed in 1862 on the site of a large 14th century church, which had been demolished. It does not have any architectural value, but two important wood-carvings from the 16th century have been preserved in it: a single and a double door made of chestnut. The double door (179 × 100) is covered with shallow geometric ornaments with 34 panels containing representations of saints, centaurs, winged dragons, lions, tigers, elephants and other animals. The relief was originally painted. The iconographic content of this decoration is interpreted as an illustration of Psalms CXLVIII, CXLIX and CL, which glorify God. It is very similar in style and subject--matter to the door in monastery Treskavac. The doors are exhibited in the Art Gallery in Skopje.

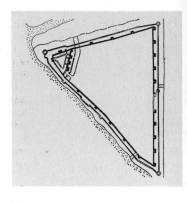

SMEDEREVO [H, 3]
The Medieval Fortress

The fortress was built by Despot Djurdje Branković, after he had transferred the capital of Serbia to Smederevo in 1430. The Turks captured it in 1439 and held it until

SMEDEREVO, THE MEDIEVAL FORTRESS

1444, when, following the Treaty of Szegedin, they ceded it to the Serbs. Mohammed II attacked it without success twice, in 1453 and 1456, and finally captured it in 1459. That marked the end of the Serbian medieval state. Later the Hungarians attempted to seize the town, but they failed and it was only the Austrians who managed to take it from the Turks. They kept their garrisons in it in 1688, 1690, 1717—1738 and, for the last time, in 1789. During the First Serbian Insurrection Karadjordje liberated Smederevo, but the Turks re-captured it a short time afterwards and remained in the town until 1867, when an agreement on the surrender of Serbian towns was concluded between Prince Mihailo and the Turks. It was very well preserved until 1941, when it was damaged by an explosion in a German ammunition depot. Smederevo belongs to the type of the "riverside fortress", and it is built at the very junction of the Jezava river and the Danube. It has an irregular triangular shape 550 × 502 × 400 metres and represents one of the finest fortresses in Europe. It was built in three phases. The "small fortress", with Despot Djurdje's residence, dates from the first phase, between 1428 and 1430. The residence contained an impressive presence hall, of which three Gothic windows have been preserved. The "small fortress" had, in addition to the keep, five other towers which reinforced the walls. A monumental inscription in brickwork commemorating the building of the fortress has been preserved on one of them. The second phase lasted from 1430 to 1439 and from 1444 to 1456. It was then that the "large fortress", strengthened with 19 towers, was built. They were open from the inner side and divided into storeys by timber structures. The towers were over 11 metres wide

and over 20 metres high. The defence walls and walls of the towers were 4.5 metres thick. They were built of stone, and brick was used for decorative elements on the facades. The fortress was designed for warfare with cold weapons. In the third phase, in 1480, the Turks built three cannon towers at the corners on the outer side. They were polygonal in plan and were connected by a low wall.

SOLIN [D, 5]
The Classical Town of Salona

A suburb of Split. It was a port and a stronghold of the Illyrian Dalmatae. It is first mentioned in historical sources in the 2nd century B.C., when the Romanization of its population began. It was granted status of a Roman colony and

SOLIN, BASILICA

became the seat of the governer of Illyricum, later Dalmatia. It was especially prosperous in the time of Trajan, Hadrianus, Antoninus and Diocletian. With the spreading of Christianity its appearance changed and it became an important religious as well as trading centre. At the beginning of the 7th century it became extinct as a town as a result of the attacks of the barbarians. Its buildings date from several phases. The urban nucleus with the port, walls, forum, theatre, temple, baths and private villas was formed in the 2nd century. The large amphitheatre from the 2nd century was incorporated into the town fortification system. The natural slope of the ground was partly used for its construction, which points to the Greek tradition. The mosaic of Orpheus from the Villa Urbana, dating from the end of the 2nd or the beginning of the 3rd century, is the finest mosaic found on this site (now in the Archaeological Museum of Split). From the 4th century to the fall of Salona ten churches of various forms and ground plans, inspired by the cult of martyrs, were built in the town. Outstanding among them is the basilica at Manastirine, which harboured the relics of Domnius, the first bishop of Salona, who was executed in the amphitheatre. A number of graves and sarcophagi has been found in the basilica. Many sculptures, portraits, reliefs and decorated sarcophagi of high artistic quality have been found elsewhere in Salona and are now on display in the Archaeological Museum of Split.

SOMBOR [F, 2]
The Bačko-Bodroška District Hall

The construction of the building began in 1802, but it got its present

SOLIN, AMPHITHEATRE

appearance only in 1882. It was designed as the centre of the district administration. A monumental composition, *The Battle of Senta,* painted by Ferencz Eisenhut in 1896, is in the assembly hall.

Especially remarkable is the main entrance above which rises a tower with a clock and a terrace with iron railings, which served as an observation point for firemen. In front of the town hall is a square with private houses in Baroque style.

SOMBOR [F, 2]
The Town Hall

SOPOĆANI [H, 5]
The Church of the Holy Trinity

The town hall was built in 1842 in classical style on the foundations of the former palace of Count Jovan Branković. It has the ground floor with shops and two upper storeys.

It is in the vicinity of Novi Pazar. It was constructed before 1263 as the mausoleum of King Uroš I and his family. The church is a single-nave building (36 metres long) with a

SOPOĆANI, CHURCH OF THE HOLY TRINITY

dome and a semicircular apse on the eastern side. The choirs on the northern and southern sides, the prothesis and the diaconicon, as well as the two lateral parekkleseions adjoining the narthex, are under the same roof, so that the church, viewed from the outside, looks like a triple-nave basilica, with the middle nave higher, broader and pierced by clerestories. The facades are enlivened by lesenes and a frieze of small blind arcades below the roof cornice. The carved decoration is very modest: the frames of the windows and doors are decorated with arches, and the twolight windows have Romanesque capitals of white marble. The outer narthex, open on three sides like a porch, was added c. 1340. A high tower rises above the entrance. The frescoes were painted between 1263 and 1268 and are the work of several masters of uneven competence. The best painter painted the frescoes in the central part of the church. The background of his pictures is covered with gold foil, with drawn lines imitating mosaic. In the apse are the representations of the Virgin with Christ and two angels, the

SOPOĆANI, FRESCO, DORMITION OF THE VIRGIN

Communion of the Apostles and the Procession of the Church Fathers, including the Serbian archbishops Sava I, Arsenije I and Sava II. The Great Feasts are arranged on the walls of the nave, in accordance with a well-planned iconographic programme. The Dormition of the Virgin, the most monumental composition in Serbian medieval painting, is on the western wall. The details of this fresco illustrate excellently the epic and heroic character of the Sopoćani frescoes. The wall paintings in the choirs represent the Forty Martyrs of Sebast, the Hospitality of Abraham and the Apostles. Especially noteworthy for their classical postures are Apostles John, Peter and Paul. The narthex, which was painted by an inferior artist, contains the paintings of the Ecumenical Councils, the story of Joseph, the Tree of Jesse, the Last Judgment, the founders' portraits and the Death of Anna Dandolo, the founder's mother, based on the composition pattern of the Dormition of the Virgin. The southern parekkleseion contains frescoes with a blue background illustrating the life of

St Simeon Nemanja. The life of
Stefan Protomartyr is represented in
the northern parekkleseion. The
poorest artist painted the prothesis
and the diaconicon. The frescoes in
the outer narthex (Christ's miracles
and parables) and in the chapels of
St George and St Nicholas were
painted between 1342 and 1345.
Sopoćani was damaged already
in 1389, and its roof structure was
pulled down in 1689, when the
monastery was abandoned. It was
restored in 1926 and after the
Second World War, when special
attention was paid to the conservation
of the frescoes.

SPLIT [D, 5]
Diocletian's Palace

Emperor Diocletian had his palace
built in the vicinity of Salona, the
capital of the Roman province of
Dalmatia, c. 300 A. D. It is the most
important classical building in
Yugoslavia. It is a combination of
a castrum, town, residence and
villa, and it is in the form of an
irregular rectangle 174.94 × 215.94
× 180,90 × 215,54 metres, covering
an area of 29409 square metres. It is
encompassed on all sides with
walls 2.10 metres thick, which are
24 metres high on the southern side
and 17 metres on the northern side.

SPLIT, PORTA AUREA

Quadrangular defensive towers stood at all four corners. In addition to them, the walls were reinforced on three sides (except the southern, seaward side) with three quadrangular and two octagonal towers which flanked the gates on each side. The interior of the palace was divided by two streets, the *cardo* and *decumanus,* which intersected at a right angle and led to the four gates *(Porta aurea, Porta argentea, Porta ferrea* and *Porta aenea).* The northern gate, the *Porta aurea,* is richly decorated, for the road through it led to Salona, while the eastern gate, the *Porta argentea* had the same structure, but was devoid of representative decoration. Servants' quarters, guard-rooms, bakeries, horse-stables and storehouses were in the northern part of the palace. The southern half included the emperor's residence. A series of open arcades with loggias ran along the entire first storey on the seaward side. Two separate structures stood in front of the emperor's apartments — one designed for the cult of god and the other for the cult of the ruler. Between them was an enlarged vestibule, the present peristyle, with two rows of columns with Corinthian capitals, made of white marble and pale red granite. To the west of the peristyle is a small square with a temple dedicated to Jove or Esculapus. In front of the simple rectangular cella of the temple, covered with a stone barrel vault, is a vestibule with six columns and a richly decorated portal. On the opposite, eastern side of the peristyle is the mausoleum. It is octagonal in plan, with semicircular and square niches and a double tier of granite and porphyry columns which end in Corinthian or composite capitals. On the wall between the columns of the upper tier is a frieze showing Eroses carrying the busts of Diocletian and

SPLIT. PROTHYRON

SPLIT, PORTA ARGENTEA

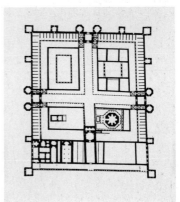

his wife Priscia. The building is surmounted by a brick-built dome. The mausoleum is encircled by a porcth with 24 columns. The southern side of ￟ne peristyle is closed by the prothyron, a structure with four columns supporting a triangular gable. The prothyron gave access to the vestibule, a circular room with a brick-built dome and walls originally faced with marble and mosaics. This was the antechamber of the imperial aparments. The architectural forms, the manner of building and many other details of Diocletian's palace are characteristic of the late classical style which heralds the Byzantine and medieval art. Life in the palace continued after Diocletian's death, until the fall of Salona in the 7th century. After that medieval Split grew up on the site of the palace.

Some structures have been preserved, but their function has been altered: the mausoleum has been turned into the cathedral and the temple into a baptistry. Scholars began to show an interest in the palace as early as the 17th century, but restoration work was initiated only in the present century.

SPLIT [D, 5]
The Church of Our Lady of the Belfry (Crkva Gospe od zvonika)

The church was probably built in the 11th century in the corridor on

SPLIT, PERISTYLE

the upper storey of the Iron Gate of Diocletian's Palace. Above the church is a bell-tower ending in a Romanesque twolight window. It was built in 1100 and it is the oldest Romanesque bell-tower in Dalmatia.

SPLIT [D, 5]
The Church of St Nicholas

The church is located in the suburb of Veli Varoš, at the foot of Marjan Hill. It is popularly known as the Church of St Mikula. According to the inscriptions above the door and on the altar, it was built towards the end of the 11th century or at the beginning of the 12th century for Ivan, a distinguished Split citizen and his wife Tiha. Its design combines elements of early Romanesque and Byzantine traditions. It is a single-nave building divided by four pillars in such a way that its ground plan is in fact a compressed cross. A presbytery rectangular in form is on the eastern side. The old altar screen was replaced by a new altar in the Baroque era.

SPLIT [D, 5]
The Church of St Martin

The church was built in the 11th century in the corridor on the

SPLIT, PROTHYRON

upper story of the Golden Gate of Diocletian's Palace. A rare work has been preserved in the church: the original altar screen *(septum)* with the characteristic plaitwork design and a chiselled inscription.

SPLIT [D, 5]
The Church of St Domnius (Crkva sv. Duje)

The cathedral church of Split. The original structure of Diocletian's mausoleum had been preserved in its entirety and it was converted into the cathedral at the end of the 8th century. The decoration of the interior continued in almost all the subsequent epochs. Adjoining the cathedral is a Romanesque bell-tower, one of the finest in Dalmatia. It was built in the 13th and 14th centuries and it was completed in the 16th century. It has five storeys which gradually taper and its volume is lightened by arcading on slender colonnettes with capitals. It was rebuilt at the end of the 19th century. A monumental door, carved in chestnut by master Andrija Buvina in 1214, is at the entrance. The 28 framed panels show scenes from Christ's life and the Passion. The basic features of Buvina's work are a tendency towards linear expression and generalization. The door was originally painted (red, blue, and gold). Two important works of Romanesque church furniture have been preserved in the church: the pulpit and a wooden stall carved in the first half of the 13th century. The rich decoration incorporates figures of saints, exotic animals and

SPLIT, DOOR OF THE SPLIT CATHEDRAL

scenes from hunting and everyday life. Two reliefs on the bell-tower, illustrating the Annunciation and the Nativity, also belong to Romanesque style. They were probably carved by masters from the workshop of master Radovan. Two important Gothic monuments have been preserved in the cathedral: The Chapel of St

of an earlier classical building. Round the central circular space are six semicircular apses. It is built of roughly hewn and broken stone, and its facades are enlivened by shallow and high niches. It is supposed that the middle part was originally surmounted by a semicalotte.

SPLIT, BELL-TOWER OF THE CHURCH OF ST DOMNIUS

SPLIT, BAPTISTRY

Domnius (1427, Bonino from Milan) and the Chapel of St Anastaius, made by Juraj Dalmatinac in 1468. It also contains a ciborium and a sarcophagus with an exceptionally expressive central scene depicting the Whipping of Christ. The cathedral has a rich treasury.

SPLIT [D, 5]
The Church of the Holy Trinity

The church is situated at Poljud, on the outskirts of Split. It was built in the 9th century on the foundations

SPLIT [D, 5]
The Church of St Roch

This church was built in 1516 in pure Renaissance style. The front facade, which has a semicircular termination, features a decorated portal, a rosette and a decorative bell-tower flanked by two volutes.

SPLIT [D, 5]
The Town Hall

A Gothic building constructed in 1443. An open loggia with arcading is on the ground floor, and two storeys rise above it. The upper portion of the building was destroyed at the beginning of the 19th century and it was restored in neo-Gothic style. The building houses the Ethnographic Museum.

SPLIT [D, 5]
The Papalić Palace

The palace was built by Juraj Dalmatinac in pure Gothic style in the midle of the 15th century for the Split humanist Papalić. It has the ground floor and two upper storeys and it is built of dressed stone. Especially noteworthy is the richly decorated main portal and the fourlight window on the southern facade. The original Gothi vaulting has been preserved in the main hall. The courtyard with an open staircase is also attractively designed. The palace now houses the City Museum.

SPLIT [D, 5]
The Baptistry

The old Roman temple of Diocletian's Palace was turned into a baptistry at the end of the 8th century. It has a coffered barrel vault. The stone font, decorated with plaitwork, dates from the 11th century and incorporates a very important work of pre-Romanesque art: a panel with the figure of a ruler. In the upper part is a triple-band plaited ornament, and below it is the enthroned ruler, with the crown and royal insignia.

SPLIT, CHURCH OF THE HOLY TRINITY

SPLIT, TOWN HALL

To the right of him is a figure in a tunic with a belt, and below is a small figure in the posture of adoration. It has been suggested that the enthroned figure represents Christ. It is a typical and rare example of pre-Romanesque sculpture with a human figure. The origin of the panel is not known. Some scholars think that it was transferred here from the Church of St Peter in Solin. Other noteworthy objects in the baptistry include the saracophagus of Archbishop Ivan Ravenjanin from the second half of the 8th century, an 11th century sarcophagus, and a panel with the figure of St Domnius, carved by Bonino from Milan.

SPLIT [D, 5]
The Milesi Palace

An early Baroque palace built in the 17th century. In front of the palace is a monument to Marko Marulić, the work of Ivan Meštrović. The building houses the Maritime Museum.

SREMSKA MITROVICA [G, 3]
Sirmium

A classical town on the bank of the Sava which the Romans captured in the 1st century A.D. It was first a

SREMSKA MITROVICA, SIRMIUM

customs station, then a colony (in the Flavian times), then the centre of the province of Lower Pannonia and finally one of the capitals of the Empire. Emperors Dacius, Probus and Maximianus were born in Sirmium, and Theodosius was crowned emperor in it. The town was especially prosperous in the 3rd and 4th centuries. In the early Christian times it was one of the centres from which the new religion spread. Constantine took up his residence here between 316 and 321 and founded a mint. The Avars seized it in 582 and resettled its inhabitants, and a year later a great conflagration destroyed the entire settlement. The town was walled in and there was a port on the Sava. Remains of the imperial palace, baths, water conduit, granary, racing courses, a street with shops and parts of many public and private houses have been found. Two pagan cemeteries, east and west of the town, have also been discovered. Systematic archaeological excavations have been in progress since 1957.

SREMSKI KARLOVCI [G, 3]
The Church of St Nicholas

The cathedral church of Sremski Karlovci. It was built by Kosta Cincarin and the German master Johannes in Baroque style. The construction lasted from 1758 to 1762, during the incumbency of Metropolitan Pavle Nenadović. It is a single-nave building with a semicircular apse, which originally had a small dome in the centre. The monumental Baroque front facade is flanked by two bell-towers. The decorative parts of the towers and of the small dome were designed by Zaharije Orfelin. It was first restored after a fire in 1799. In 1909 it underwent a radical reconstruction according to the designs of Vladimir Nikolić, who introduced neo-classical elements. The iconostasis, carved by Arsenije Marković, with icons painted by Teodor Kračun and Jakov Orfelin in 1781, has been preserved in the church. The small iconostasis dating from 1780, which stood in the choir, is now in the Gallery of Matica Srpska in Novi Sad.

SREMSKI KARLOVCI [G, 3]
The Patriarch's Residence

The residence was built in 1892, under the auspices of Patriarch Georgije Branković and was financed from a fund established as early as the end of the 17th century by Metropolitan Vladimir Nikolić. It is a typical

SREMSKI KARLOVCI, ST NICHOLAS

residence in eclectic style. The assembly hall was especially richly furnished and contained the busts of Georgije Branković and Stefan Stratimirović made by Petar Ubavkić. During the Second World War the residence was pillaged and damaged.

STARI GRAD [D, 5]
The Hektorović Mansion (Tvrdalj)

The building is situated on the island of Hvar. It was built c. 1520 as the summer residence of the poet Petar Hektorović. It is a fortified Renaissance palace with a large porch with round arches on the inner side. The closed courtyard consists of a large park and a fish-pond. The portal and the windows on the upper storey were made in the 18th century.

STARO NAGORIČINO [I, 6]
The Church of St George

The church is in the vicinity of Kumanovo. The earlier building, constructed in the 11th century by Byzantine Emperor Roman IV Diogenes, was restored by King Milutin in 1313, after a victory over the Turks. This is recorded in an inscription above the western entrance to the church. The old walls, built of dressed stone, have been preserved up to a half of the building. The ground plan, in the form of an inscribed cross, is adjusted to the earlier triple-nave basilica (20 metres long). The church has four small domes at the corners and a large central dome which rests on four free-standing pillars. The domes have octagonal drums. The altar apse is semicircular in the lower zone and

STARO NAGORIČINO, CHURCH OF ST GEORGE

five-sided in the upper portion, and it is enlivened by shallow niches. The facades are polychromatic, especially the two lateral threelight windows, decorated with brick ornaments in the form of meanders, crosses and swallow-tails. The twolight window above the western entrance has a stone colonnette tied into a knot in the middle. The old stone iconostasis has been preserved in the church. The frescoes were painted between 1316 and 1318, during the incumbency of heugomenos Venijamin. They were painted by Mihailo and Evtihije, who have left their signature on the shields of the warrior saints. Christ the Pantocrator, the Divine Liturgy and the prophets are represented in the main dome, the Virgin, enthroned and surrounded by angels, is in the apse, and below her are the Communion of the Apostles and the Adoration of the Lamb. The Great Feasts, Christ's miracles and parables and the Passion are in the nave. There are three more cycles: the cycle of St George, to whom the church is dedicated, the cycle of the Virgin and the cycle of St Nicholas. The lower zone contains individual figures of saints and the founder's portrait of King Milutin, who is shown as being presented, as the victor over the Turks, with an upheld

STARO NAGORIČINO, FRESCO, LAST SUPPER

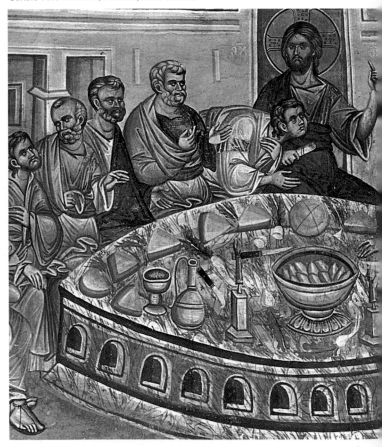

sword by St George. Beside the king is his wife Simonida. The lower zone also contains remains of the representations of Ohrid saviours Clement and Konstantin Kavasila, of Archbishop Sava of Serbia and of the local hermits Prohor Pčinjski and Joakim Osogovski. The dramatic character of the compositions, the rich painted architecture, the large number of figures and their lively movements, the colouring and modelling of forms show that the style of the "Palaeologue Revival", which dominated the painting of the early 14th century, found an unsurpassed expression in this monument.

STIČNA [B, 2]
The Cistercian Monastery

The church was built in Romanesque style for the Cistercian monastery (founded in 1136). It was consecrated in 1156 and it is in the form of a basilica with a nave and two aisles. The nave is wider and higher than the aisles and it is separated from them by seven arches supported on rectangular pillars on each side. The nave and the aisles had originally flat timber ceilings. On the eastern side is the transept with three projecting spaces, parallel with the aisles, ending in semicircular apses. Two more apses were at the ends of the transept. The facades are built of dressed stone blocks laid horizontally. The church was built by master Michael, probably a Frenchman in the service of the Cistercian order, who is referred to in documents as a "homo Latinus". South of the church is the monastic range, in the centre of which is the courtyard with a cloister, which was covered with Gothic ribbed vaulting at the end of the 13th century.

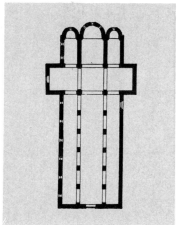

Mid-14th century frescoes of an encyclopaedic character have been preserved in it. The bay with the symbols of the four Evangelists was painted anew in the 15th century by Janez Ljubljanski. The monastery underwent extensive reconstruction in the Gothic era: the presbytery was altered, the octagonal bell-tower was added, and the entire monastery was fortified with defence walls and towers. The monastery was remodelled in the 17th and 18th centuries, when the present Baroque features were introduced and the monastery lost its original appearance. Fifteen paintings, illustrating the Procession to Calvary, the work of the Baroque painter Fortunato Berganta from 1766, have been preserved in the church.

STIČNA, CISTERCIAN MONASTERY

STOBI [I, 7]
The Classical Town

It is situated at the confluence of the Crna Reka and the Vardar and at the junction of the roads running from Salonica to Sirmium and from Heraclea to Serdica. It was an important settlement of Illyrian Peonia and the largest town in northern Macedonia in the Roman period. It became a municipium in Augustan times. At the end of the 4th and in the 6th century it was damaged by earthquake and in the second half of the 5th century it was captured and sacked by the Goths. In the 7th century it was settled by the Slavs. In the time of Emperor Basil II of Byzantium it was laid waste and deserted. A number of sculptures and fragments of frescoes have been preserved from the Hellenistic and Roman times and they are today exhibited in the National Museum in Belgrade and in the Archaeological Museum in Skopje. Stobi represents an impressive architectural and urban complex, with a water conduit, sewage, baths, a street with a porch, a semicircular square, and a number of secular and sacred buildings. The most remarkable edifice is the Parthenius Palace, built in the 5th century, which has a large peristyle and a pool. The sinagogue was built at the beginning of the 4th century on the foundations of an earlier building. It had a mosaic floor and walls decorated with stuccowork and frescoes. It was pulled down at the end of the 4th century, and a triple-nave Christian basilica with a narthex and an atrium was built on its site at the beginning of the 5th century. The monumental theatre, constructed in three stages, in the 2nd, 3rd and 4th centuries, displays the typical features of Greek theatres: the schena, the choir and amphitheatral seats cut into a hillock. Seventeen rows of marble seats have been preserved in the lower portion, and there were 19 more in the upper, now destroyed part, so that the total seating

STOBI

STOBI, AMPHITHEATRE

STOBI, MOSAIC

capacity was about 7 600. The triple-nave episcopal basilica was built in two phases: at the end of the 4th and in the middle of the 5th century. It has a narthex, atrium and a crypt in the apse, and it was adorned with frescoes, mosaics and sculptured decoration (capitals, parapet panels, ambo). Next to the basilica is the baptistry, dating from the end of the 4th century. It is quatrefoil in plan. The piscina is framed with parapets and surmounted by a canopy with six columns. High quality mosaics have been preserved on the floor of the basilica and in the palaces. Their decoration follows Oriental models, with geometric and floral ornaments framing figures of animals, birds and fishes. Archaeological investigations of Stobi were initaited in the 19th century, and were particularly intensive after the Second World War.

STOLAC [E, 6]
The Medieval Fortress

The fortress is first mentioned in historical sources in 1444, but it is considerably older. It was held by Hercog Stjepan, and after the Turkish conquests a Turkish garrison was stationed in it. Extensive reconstructions were made in the Turkish times. The position of the fortress, which has seven towers, is adjusted to the lie of the ground. Within the walls were a mosque, cisterns and dwellings. It is also known as Viodoški grad in historical documents.

STON [E, 6]
The Town Fortifications

The town is on a small isthmus connecting the peninsula of Peljašac with the mainland and it consists of two fortified settlements — Ston and

STON, CHURCH OF ST MICHAEL

Mali Ston — one looking to the sea, and the other to the land. Although a Roman military stronghold, and later a medieval settlement, was located on Sveti Mihailo hill, the present Ston and Mali Ston were founded in 1333, when the Dubrovnik citizens were given this territory by Emperor Dušan and the Ban of Bosnia. The fortifications were raised in the 14th and 15th centuries. The length of the walls is 5.5 kilometres, and they are reinforced by ten round and thirty-one quadrangular towers and six round bastions. The fortifications of Ston are pentagonal in plan, and those of Mali Ston have the ground plan in the form of a regular quadrangle. They are connected by a strong wall, extending over the hill. Three strong fortresses are incorporated into this complex: Veliki Kaštio above Ston, Pozvizd on the hill and Koruna above Mali Ston. Among the builders of the fortifications whose names have been preserved in documents are Župan Bunić, Juraj Dalmatinac and Paskoje Miličević, natives, and Michelozzo Michelozzi and Bernardi from Parma, foreigners.

STON, CHURCH OF ST MICHAEL, FRESCO, A WARRIOR SAINT

STON [E, 6]
The Church of St Michael

The church is on Sveti Mihailo hill, the top of which was encircled with strong walls in the Middle Ages. It was built c. 1080 and its founder was King Mihailo of Zeta, who was proclaimed king by the pope and who died in 1081. It is an early Romanesque single-nave and vaulted building (5.80 metres long),

with an altar apse which is three-sided
without. Three conchs submerged in
the mass of the wall are in the
interior. It is built of roughly hewn
stone, and the facades are enlivened
by lesenes, which have a semicircular
top. Above the door and round the
windows are ornaments sculptured
in shallow relief. The basic design
is the tendril with geometrized leaves.
Only fragments of the frescoes have
survived. There are individual figures
of male and female saints, the
Evangelists, prophets, St George,
St John the Baptist, the Last
Judgment, and, in the sanctuary,
the Fall of Man. The best preserved
fresco is the founder's composition,
which shows the founder with a
crown on his head and a model of
the church in his hand. If the model
corresponds to the original building,
the church had a dome and a narthex
with a tower on the western side. —
After the Second World War the
church was restored and the frescoes
were cleaned.

STON, CHURCH OF ST MICHAEL, FRESCO, KING MICHAEL

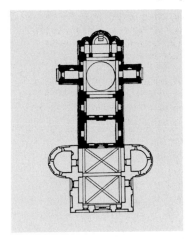

STUDENICA [H, 5]
The Church of the Virgin

The oldest church of monastery
Studenica, dedicated to the Virgin
and built between 1183 and 1196.
Its founder was Stefan Nemanja,
who took monastic orders in this
church (taking the name Simeon)
and who was buried here after his
relics had been brought from
Chilandar in 1208 or 1209. King
Stefan the First-Crowned and King
Radoslav were also buried in this
church. The church is in the form of
a single-nave building (40.80 metres
long) with a dome. On the eastern
side is a tripartite sanctuary, on the
western side is the narthex, and two
lateral vestibules are on the northern
and southern sides. The dome rests
on a cubic base. It is twelve-sided,
built of brick and decorated without
with niches and arcades supported
on semicolumns. The facades are of
blocks of polished marble. The roof
cornice is moulded, and a frieze of
small blind arcades on brackets runs
below it. Onelight, twolight and
threelight windows are harmoniously
arranged on the facade. An outer
narthex, covered with two ribbed
cross vaults, was added on the

STUDENICA, CHURCH OF THE VIRGIN

western side shortly before 1233/34. Two semicircular parekkleseions are on the lateral sides. The founder of the outer narthex was King Radoslav. The rich carved decoration emphasizes the Romanesque character of the building. It is the most important ensemble of stonework in medieval Serbia. The sculptured decoration has been preserved on the brackets, portals and windows. The western portal has the richest decoration. In the lunette is the Virgin with Christ flanked by angels. The inner sides of the door-posts show the Apostles, and enthroned Christ is above them. Mazes of tendrils and vines with representations of real and fantastic animals are carved on the archivolts and pilasters. On the front archivolt is a gryphon resting on a pillar, the base of which is in the form of a lion. The threelight window in the altar apse is also an example of excellent stoneworking. In its tympanum is a maze of tendrils and leaves with a winged dragon holding a small human figure in its claws, and a basilisk with the

STUDENICA, CHURCH OF THE VIRGIN, FRESCO, CRUCIFIXION

serpent's tail. The rich frame shows tendrils issuing from the mouth of a snake and a dragon. The frescoes were painted in several phases. The earliest layer dates from 1208/1209, and it was commissioned by Nemanja's sons Sava, Stefan and Vukan, as shown by an inscription in the drum of the dome. Some of these frescoes — the Virgin, the Eucharist, the Annunciation, and the Visitation — were painted on a yellow background covered with gold foil with drawings imitating the mosaic. Other frescoes — the deacons and bishops, remains of scenes of the Great Feasts and the standing saints in the lower zone — were painted on a blue background, with inscriptions written in white paint or gold, depending on the importance of the scene or its position. Outstanding among the paintings from this group is the monumental Crucifixion, a fresco which incorporates all the elements of the early 13th century style. The frescoes in the outer narthex and in the lateral parekkleseions date from the second stage, c. 1235. Especially

STUDENICA, CHURCH OF THE VIRGIN, FRESCO, CRUCIFIXION (DETAIL)

STUDENICA, CHURCH OF THE VIRGIN FRESCO, TRANSLATION OF THE RELICS OF
ST SIMEON

important are the frescoes illustrating
the life of Nemanja. The best
preserved among them is the
composition showing the translation
of the relics of St Stefan Nemanja,
with the portraits of the participants.
The latest layer dates from 1568.

Some frescoes in the sanctuary and
the nave, and all the paintings in the
narthex belong to this layer. An old
refectory from Nemanja's time has
been preserved in the monastic range.
The church and the entire monastery
were restored after the Second World
War.

STUDENICA, CHURCH OF THE VIRGIN,
WINDOW

STUDENICA, CHURCH OF SS JOACHIM AND ANNE, FRESCO, KING MILUTIN

CHURCH OF SS JOACHIM AND ANNE

STUDENICA [H, 5]
The Church of SS Joachim and Anne

Also known as the King's Church. It is in the courtyard of the monastery, near the Church of the Virgin. It was built and painted in 1314, in the reign of King Milutin and under the auspices of heugomenos Jovan, as recorded in an inscription chiselled on the exterior of the apse. The church is a small building (9.90 metres long) in the form of a compressed cross with an apse and a dome. The facades are enlivened by onelight and twolight windows. The frescoes are in a good state of preservation and of a high artistic quality. In addition to the usual scenes in the dome and the sanctuary, only two cycles are illustrated in the nave: the Great Feasts and the life of the Virgin. The presentation of space, the physiognomies, clothing and bearing of the figures, the modelling and the bright colours are typical of the court style of the "Palaeologue Revival".

STUDENICA [H, 5]
The Church of St Nicholas

The church is a part of the monastic complex of Studenica. It was built at the beginning of the 13th century. It is a simple single-nave building with tunnel vaulting and a semicircular apse on the eastern side. Of the original frescoes only a few have been preserved: two compositions — the Entry into Jerusalem and the Three Marys at Christ's Grave — and the individual figures of Archdeacon Stefan, two warrior saints and three bishops. In the apse is the Virgin with a medallion showing Christ on her breast.

SUBOTICA [G, 2]
The Synagogue

The synagogue was built in 1902 in the Secession style, according to the designs of Deža Jakob and Marcel Komor. It is a central design, with an imposing dome resting on iron piers. The building incorporates Oriental elements. The portals, windows and the attic are decorated with ceramic ornaments.

SUBOTICA [G, 2]
The Municipal Library

The library was built in 1896 for the Gradjanska kasina (an early form of modern centres of culture).

STUDENICA, CHURCH OF ST NICHOLAS

It was designed by Ferencz J. Reichel in an eclectic style, but the prominent elements are those of the Secession. After the Second World War it was used for other purposes: it was the Officers' Club for some time, and then it was converted into the Municipal Library.

SUBOTICA [G, 2]
The Raichle Palace

The building was designed as a family house by Ferenc Raichle and built in 1904. It is an example of the Secession style of the Gaudian type, with the facades featuring plastic elements, wavy lines and rich decoration. It was used for a variety of purposes, and today it houses the offices of the Likovni susret (Meeting of Artists).

SUBOTICA [G, 2]
The Leonović Palace

It was designed by Ödön Lechner and built in 1893. It is one of the oldest buildings of Hungarian Secession. The facade is faced with ceramic tiles, and similar decorative elements were used later on the building of the Museum of Applied Arts in Budapest.

SUBOTICA [G, 2]
The Town Hall

The building was designed as an administrative centre in 1907 and constructed from 1908 to 1910. The architects were Dezsö Jakob and Marcell Komor, close collaborators of Ödön Lechner. The building belongs to the Hungarian variant of the Secession. It has the ground floor with shops and a restaurant, two upper storeys with administrative offices and an attic floor. The exterior is lavishly decorated with typical Secession ornaments. The ceramic produced by the Zsolnai factory in Pečuj was used for the decoration of the interior and the facades.

SUBOTICA, TOWN HALL

SUBOTICA, MUNICIPAL LIBRARY

SUHA [B, 1]
The Church of St John the Baptist

The church is in the vicinity of
Škofja Loka. It was built at the
beginning of the 15th century as a
single-nave Gothic building with a
presbytery and stellar vaulting. The
architecture is modest, but the
frescoes in the presbytery are of
great artistic worth. It is the finest
example of the "painted Kranj
presbytery", a specific iconographic
arrangement typical of Gothic

art in Slovenia. Christ in the
mandorla is painted on the top of
the vault, angels are in the star-like
panels behind him, and the symbols
of the four Evangelists are round
him. The frescoes on the walls are
divided into three zones. Those in
the upper zone show the
Circumcision, the Coronation of the
Virgin and the Entry into the Temple.
In the middle zone, under painted
Gothic arcading, are the twelve
Apostles. Male and female martyrs
and the Wise and the Foolish
Virgins are shown in the lower zone.
The Last Judgment is depicted on
the western side of the arch. This
arrangement is reproduced, with
minor modifications, in the
presbytery of many other Gothic
churches. The frescoes were painted
in the in the middle of the 15th
century. They were begun by one of
the "Furlanian masters" (the
Coronation of the Virgin) and
completed by some of his disciples.
About 1530 Jernej from Loka painted
the martyrs and virgins in the lower
zone and the frescoes on the
western facade. The main altar, a
typical example of the "golden
altar", is the work of J. Janišek and
dates from 1672.

SUHA, CHURCH OF ST JOHN THE BAPTIST

SUHA, CHURCH OF ST JOHN THE BAPTIST
FRESCO, THE TWELVE APOSTLE

SVETIVINČENT [A, 3]
The Church of St Vincent

The church was built at the end of the 12th and the beginning of the 13th century. It is a single-nave building of irregular shape with three semicircular apses on the eastern side, which are submerged in the mass of the wall. The frescoes date from the end of the 13th century and show traces of Byzantine influence. The enthroned Christ is represented in the central apse; the Baptism is in the northern apse and the Madonna of Majesty is in the southern apse. Scenes from Christ's life, an iconographically interesting composition of the Last Judgment and the legend of St Vincent are on the walls of the nave. The signature of the painter — Ognobenus Trivisanus — dating from the end of the 13th century, has been preserved in the southern apse. Some frescoes were restored at the end of the 14th and the beginning of the 15th century.

ŠEMPETER [C, 1]
The Vindonius Tomb

An important cemetery with grave monuments of Romanized Celtic nobility was discovered and restored in Šempeter in 1952. The monuments were made predominantly of Pohorje marble and date from the period from the 1st century to 268 A. D., when the Savinja river flooded the site and covered it with gravel. The Vindonius tomb, the oldest in the cemetery, was raised in the 1st century by Vindonius, the governor of Celea, in memory of his wife Julia. The monument consists of two parts. The upper part has the inscription: C. VINDONIUS SUCCESSEUS, AEDILIS CLAUDIAE CELEIAE, FECIT SIBI ET IULIAE, SEXTI FILIAE INGENNUAE, UXORI FIDELISSIMAE ANNORUM QUINQUAGINTA. The lateral sides have stone reliefs showing Julia and Vindonius, making a draft on a diptych. The lower portion of the monument is a stone casket for the keeping of ashes, decorated with reliefs: on the left side is a hunter carrying a rabit, on the right side is a hunter with a net containing a bird's nest, and on the front side is a representation of Heracles leading Alceste out of the nether world.

ŠEMPETER [C, 1]
The Ennius Tomb

This is the finest and most ornate monument in the cemetery in Šempeter. Dimensions: 2.42 × 1.80 at the base, and the height is 6.60 metres. It was erected in the first half of the 2nd century for the aristocratic Ennius family. The lower part is decorated with reliefs: Europe on the bull on the front side, the Ganymede myth and a satyr with a nymph on the lateral sides. The upper part of the monument shows the portraits of the deceased (husband, wife and daughter) under an elaborately decorated canopy. The husband and wife are in the upper zone (Liberalis and Oppidana) and below them is their daughter Kalendina, flanked by the genii of death with extinguished flames. The portraits, especially that of Kalendina, rank among the finest

Roman portraits found in the territory of Yugoslavia. At the base of the upper portion is the inscription: QUINTUS. ENNIUS LIBERALIS ET ENNIA OPPIDANA FECIT.SIBI.ET KALENDINAE FILIAE.ANNORUM XVII ET. VITULO.FILIO.ANNORUM XXX.

ŠEMPETER [C, 1]
The Priscianus Tomb

The largest monument in the cemetery in Šempeter.
Dimensions: 4.82 × 3.07 metres at the base, and 8.28 metres high. It was built in the 2nd century for the Priscianus family. It consists of two parts separated by a richly moulded tablet. The upper part shows three seated figures — father, mother and son — under a canopy surmounted by a gabled roof. Their heads were damaged later. The following inscription has been preserved in the first zone of the lower part, which is a stone casket for ashes:
CAIO.CPECTATIO.CAII.FILIO…
PRISCIANO.DVVMVIRO IVRE, DICUNDO… CAIUS, SPECTATIUS FINITIMUS.DVVMVIR…
IVRE.DICUNDO.CLAUDIAE. PATER… INFELICISSIMUS FECIT… Round the inscription and on the lateral sides are reliefs showing nymphs, satyrs, Castor and Pollux. In the lower zone are relief representatitions of the four seasons of the year and of scenes from the legend of Iphigenia: Iphigenia and Orestes at the altar, Iphigenia sending word of her flight and the flight from Tauris to the ship.

ŠIBENIK [C, 5]
The Saint Anne Fortress

The town of Šibenik is first mentioned in 1066, in the time of King Petar Krešimir. It was granted municipal autonomy by Hungarian-Croatian King Stjepan IV in 1167. After that it was under the rule of Venice, King Tvrtko of Bosnia and Herceg Hrvoje Vukčić. From 1412 to 1797 it belonged to Venice, and then it passed under the rule of Austria until 1918. The Saint Anne Fortress represents the earliest part of its medieval fortifications. It has a commanding strategic position on the top of a hill above the town. Its ground plan is irregular and it is reinforced by towers. The fortress was further strengthened in the 16th and 17th centuries. Walls reinforced by towers ran from the fortress and encircled the entire suburb. The walls were for the most part pulled down in the 19th century. The town had seven gates, only one of which has been preserved. Above the town are two more fortresses: Sveti Ivan (the Saint John Fortress) and Šubićevac.

ŠIBENIK [C, 5]
The Church of St Francis

The church is in the Franciscan monastery. It is a single-nave Gothic building constructed at the end of the 14th century and radically remodelled in the age of the Baroque. It has a flat, richly carved coffered ceiling from the 18th century with paintings by Marco Capogrosso. Baroque altars carved in Venice by Giuseppe Ridolfi in 1635 according to the designs of master Girolamo Mondella from Verona have been preserved in the church.

ŠIBENIK [C, 5]
The Church of St James

The cathedral church of Šibenik. It was built on the foundations of an earlier Romanesque building. It is in the form of a triple-nave basilica (41.5 metres long), with a wide transept, a dome and three altar apses on the eastern side. The

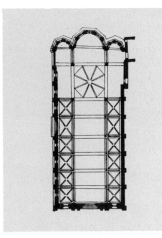

aisles have cross vaulting and galleries. The baptistry and the sacristy are below the floor of the eastern side. The church was built in three phases, from 1431 to 1555. In the first phase (1431—1441) local and Italian masters built the lateral walls and both portals. The decoration for the portals was carved by Bonino da Milano. The second phase (1441—1473) is marked by the work of Juraj Dalmatinac, who become the chief architect and gave the basic form to the church. He added the transept, prepared the structure for the dome surmounting

ŠIBENIK, CHURCH OF ST JAMES, FRIEZE

ŠIBENIK, CHURCH OF ST JAMES

ŠIBENIK, CHURCH OF ST JAMES, FRONT SII

the intersection of the transept and the nave, and built the apses, on the facades of which he placed a series of heads (74) of exceptional artistic value. He showed particular skill in the decoration of the eastern part with the choir and the richly carved stone baptistry. The third phase of construction is associated with Nikola Firentinac, who was in charge of the building from 1477 to 1505. He built the Renaissance ribbed cupola (32 metres high inside), the galleries above the aisles and the vault, which is also the roof, made of dovetailed stone slabs reinforced by joints in the form of slender ribs. The cathedral has a rich treasury.

ŠIBENIK [C, 5]
The Church of St Barbara

The church was built in Renaissance style from 1457 to 1461. The semicircular gable on the front side contains a sculptured rosette and the roof structure is surmounted by a bell-tower. Bonino da Milano and Ivan Pribislavić took part in the building of the church. Two polyptychs by Nikola Vladanov, a Renaissance painter from Šibenik, have been preserved in the church.

ŠIBENIK [C, 5]
The Orisini Palace

The palace was built in the first half of the 15th century. Especially remarkable is the decorative portal. Juraj Dalmatinac lived in it from 1455.

ŠIBENIK [C, 5]
The Foscolo Palace

A Gothic palace built at the beginning of the 15th century. It has the ground floor and two upper storeys. The windows on the front facade are especially richly decorated.

ŠIBENIK [C, 5]
The Town Loggia

The loggia is located on the square opposite the cathedral. A renaissance edifice built between 1532 and 1542 as the town hall. A porch with nine round arches is on the ground floor, and a closed loggia with a large hall behind it is on the upper storey. It was badly damaged by bombing in the Second World War, but it was restored afterwards.

ŠIBENIK [C, 5]
The New Church (Nova crkva)

A Gothic-Renaissance church built towards the end of the 15th century. The bell-tower was designed by Ivan Skok and built between 1742 and 1759. Above the passageway in the courtyard is a relief showing the Entombment, carved by Nikola Firentinac in 1502. The Baroque frescoes in the church were painted by M. Parkić (1619) and A. Monegin (1628), and the paintings on the coffered ceiling are by Dj. Mondela, I. Bojković and A. Sisanović.

ŠIŠATOVAC [G, 3]
The Church of the Nativity of the Virgin

The church is mentioned as early as the 16th century, when the monks from Žiča, oppressed by the Turks, took refuge in the territory across the Sava, founded a new monastery there and built a church for it in 1520. The present church was built on its site between 1758 and 1778. It is a domed building trefoil in plan, with a Baroque bell-tower on the western side. It had an iconostasis (1793) and wall paintings made by Grigorije Davidović Obšić. The monastery and the church were badly damaged during the Second World War.

ŠKOFJA LOKA [B, 1]
The Church of St James

The church was built in two stages. In the first stage, before 1471, a

CHURCH OF ST JAMES, INTERIOR

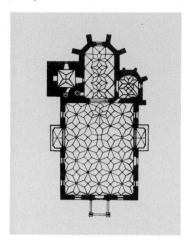

rectangular building, divided by
three pairs of piers into three equally
high and equally wide naves (the
hall-type of church — *Hollenkirche*)
was constructed. In the second
phase, c. 1524, a long choir was
added on the eastern side, and the
Chapel of St Catherine was built next
to it. In 1631 the bell-tower on the
northern side was begun, but it
was completed only a decade later.
The church has exquisite stellar
vaulting with partly preserved 15th
century frescoes. Above the main
portal is a relief showing the Agony
in the Garden (c. 1470).

ŠKOFJA LOKA, CHURCH OF ST JAMES

ŠMARJE PRI JELŠAN [C, 1]
The Church of St Roch

The church was built in the latter
half of the 17th century. It is a
simple, vaulted rectangular building
with a low presbytery. The interior
is lavishly decorated with
stuccowork, frescoes, altars and
church furniture, so that it
represents a very good example of
the Baroque illusionistic space. The
stuccowork dates from 1738 and it
is the finest interior stucco decoration
in Steiermark. The church is
approached by the Way of the Cross
with chapels of the Passion, which
contain frescoes and strikingly
expressive Baroque sculptures
showing the sufferings of Christ.

ŠPITALIČ, CHURCH OF THE VIRGIN

ŠTIP, CHURCH OF THE HOLY ARCHANGEL

ŠPITALIČ [B, 1]
The Church of the Virgin

A parish church built c. 1190. It is
supposed to have been built by
masters who had come from the
Carthusian monastery in Grenoble.
It was the "ecclesia minor" of the
Carthusian monastery at nearby
Žiče. It belongs to the transitional
Romanesque-Gothic style. It is a
single-nave building with ribbed
vaulting supported on attached
columns with floral capitals.
On the eastern side is a presbytery
with a rectangular termination. It
is built of stone blocks and the walls
are reinforced without by
countreforts. Carved decoration has
been preserved on the triumphal
arch and on the two portals. A
representation of the Agnus Dei
with the cross is in the lunette of the
main portal. The bell-tower and
the sacristy were added in the 19th
century.

ŠTAMBERG [C, 1]
The Palace

A representative palace built for
the count Attems between 1720
and 1740. A double stairway leads
to the reception hall on the first
floor. The facades are richly
decorated with stucco ornaments.
Almost all the rooms are decorated
with stuccowork and frescoes.

ŠTIP [J, 7]
The Church of the Holy Archangel

The church was commissioned by
protosebast Hrelja in 1334 and
donated to the monastery Chilandar.
It is in the form of an inscribed cross
with a dome and apse, six-sided
without, on the eastern side. It is
built of alternate courses of dressed
stone and brick, and the facades are
enlivened by shallow niches. The

TETOVO, MULTI-COLOURED MOSQUE

octagonal drum of the dome is
built of brick. A parekkleseion was
added on the southern side, but it
was pulled down later. The original
frescoes have not been preserved.

TETOVO [H, 7]
*The Multi-Coloured Mosque (Šarena
džamija)*

The mosque was built in 1495 in
early Constantinopolitan style. Its
ground plan is square (16 × 16
metres) and it was domed. The
minaret is placed laterally and it is
embedded into the mass of the wall.

In front of the mosque is a porch
supported on eight pillars. When
the mosque was restored in 1785,
the roof structure was altered and a
pavilion roof was built above the
wooden cupola. The new minber
and mihrab were also built at that
time. Especially interesting are the
painted ornaments on the facade and
on the interior walls of the space
for worship, which exhibit some
Baroque elements. There is evidence
that the paintings were restored
in the 19th century, when masters
from Debar worked in the mosque.
A 16th century turbeh and a richly
decorated fountain belong to the
complex of the mosque.

TETOVO [H, 7]
The Turkish Baths

The baths were built in 1496 for
Isak Bey Ishaković. They
underwent several reconstructions

TETOVO, TURKISH BATHS

later. The interior is typical of the buildings of this type, and the walls are built of courses of stone and brick. Today the baths are a part of the complex of the Multi-Coloured Mosque. The baths have been restored and now accommodate an art gallery.

TETOVO [H, 7]
The Arabat Baba Monastery

It was built at the end of the 18th century to serve as the monastery of the dervish sect Bektasi. It was founded by Redžep Pasha, who endowed it with large estates. The courtyard is encompassed with a high wall and has trees, flowers and a fountain in its centre. Round it are buildings of various use: a place for worship, the dining-room, residences, a turbeh and a tower with a fountain which was built, according to tradition, by Aduraman Pasha for his

ill daughter. The entire range has been restored and now houses the National Museum.

TRAKOŠĆAN [C, 1]
The Castle

It was a rather small burg in the Middle Ages, held by the counts of Celje. Later it changed hands several times and finally came into the possession of the Drašković family in 1568. The new owners strengthened it with lateral defensive towers. In the middle of the 19th century it was completely remodelled in the Romantic neo-Gothic style according to the designs of architects from Graz. It has retained that appearance to the present day. It houses a collection of arms, portraits, and furniture, the archives and a library.

TRAVNIK [E, 4]
The Fortress

It is first mentioned in historical sources in 1463, in connection with the passage of Sultan Mohamed with his army, but it is very likely that it was built at the beginning of the 15th century. It was constructed to resist cannon warfare. It has a characteristic polygonal corner tower, which also served as a dungeon, and, below it, a high hexagonal tower for the storage of ammunition and gun-power. The suburb below the fortress began to develop very early, but it achieved its greatest prosperity in the 18th and 19th centuries, when Travnik was the seat of the Viziers of Bosnia.

TRAVNIK [E, 4]
The Multi-Coloured Mosque
(Šarena džamija)

The mosque was built in 1816 and
it is one of the last Islamic
monuments in Bosnia. It has two
upper storeys and the ground floor
with a porch and shops. The place
for worship is on the first floor. The
facades have painted decoration in
the form of stylized plants. It is
popularly called the Sulejmanija.

TRAVNIK, MULTI-COLOURED MOSQUE

TREBINJE [F, 6]
The Arslanagić Bridge

The bridge was constructed in the
16th or 17th century and it spans
the Trebišnjica, on the Trebinje-
-Nikšić road. The bridge is 80 metres
long; it has two large and two small
arches. Above the larger arches the
bridge is level, and above the smaller
ones it slopes gently. It is built of
white stone, and the railing is also
made of stone slabs. At the end of
the 19th century a tower protecting
the traffic was built in the middle of
the bridge, but it was pulled down
later.

TRESKAVAC [I, 7]
The Monastery and the Church of
the Dormition of the Virgin

The monastery is on a hill above
Prizren. Its history is not sufficiently
known. It was a cult place as early
as the classical times. Five
chronological stages of construction
can be distinguished in the present
building. The earliest probably dates
from the 12th or 13th century. The
first founders were the emperors of
Byzantium, as testified by an
inscription above the interior door.
The later founders were the Serbian
kings Milutin and Dušan. The church
is a domed single-nave building
(20 metres long). A bay with a blind
dome and a narthex with two lateral
domes are on the western side.

TREBINJE, THE ARSLANAGIĆ BRIDGE

Frescoes showing scenes of the Calendar and warrior saints are in this space. A porch runs along the western and southern sides of the church. A wooden door is at the entrance. The earliest layer of frescoes, the work of Greek artists, is in the narthex and dates from c. 1340. It includes standing figures, scenes from the Calendar, Christ Emmanuel in the southern dome, and, in the northern dome, a representation of the Celestial Court, which also shows warrior saints in the costume of Byzantine nobility, with high caps and staves in their hands. The frescoes in the porch were painted c. 1360, and those in the nave of the church date from the end of the 15th century. The church underwent extensive reconstructions in 1570 and 1871.

TRESKAVAC, CHURCH OF THE DORMITION OF THE VIRGIN, FRESCO

TROGIR, MARKO'S TOWER

TROGIR [C, 5]
The Kamerlengo Fortress

The settlement of Tragurion was founded by the Greeks in the 3rd century B.C. on a small island which is today joined to the mainland by a bridge. During the Roman times it grew into an important port. After the fall of the Western Roman Empire, Trogir

became a part of Byzantium. In the 11th century it became an episcopal seat, and in 1107 Hungarian--Croatian King Koloman recognized its right to civic autonomy. It developed into a strong economic and cultural centre. From 1420 to 1797 it was in the possession of Venice, and then it was taken by the Austrians, who held it until 1918.

The inner core of the town was formed between the 13th and the 15th century within the town walls, which the Venetians restored in the 15th century. It was then that two large fortifications, the Tower of St Mark and the Kamerlengo fortress were built. The Kamerlengo fortress was added to an earlier tower constructed by the Genoese in 1380, when they used Trogir as a stronghold in their struggle against Venice. The major part of the town walls was pulled down in the 19th century. There are some surviving parts on the southern side, with a Renaissance gate (16th century) and, next to it, a small loggia for the accommodation and inspection of travellers before they were allowed to enter the town.

TROGIR, THE KAMERLENGO FORTRESS

TROGIR [C, 5]
The Church of St Barbara

The church was probably built in
the 10th century. Its founders were
a certain Majus and his wife Petra,
about whom there is no other
evidence apart from an inscription
chiselled into the portal. It is a
pre-Romanesque basilica with a nave
and two aisles. The nave is higher
and ends in a deep semicircular
apse, while the aisles terminate in
shallow semicircular niches. The nave
and the aisles have cross vaulting
and are partitioned by round arches
resting on three pairs of clasical
columns. The walls of the church
incorporate fragments of classical
sculptures and pre-Romanesque
plaitwork reliefs.

TROGIR, CHURCH OF ST LAWRENCE

TROGIR [C, 5]
*The Church of St Lawrence (Crkva
sv. Lovrenca)*

The cathedral church of Trogir.
Its core was built during the 13th
century. It is in the form of a
Romanesque triple-nave basilica
(45 metres long). Three semicircular
apses are on the eastern side, and a
porch is on the western side. Gothic
cross vaulting was added in the 14th
century. The facades are enlivened
by pillars, high windows and a frieze
of small blind arcades below the
roof cornice. The apse is also
decorated with slender colonnettes
in the form of a torded rope. A
baptistry and a chapel dedicated to
Ivan Ursini were added on the
northern side in the 15th century.
Above the porch on the southern
side rises a bell-tower, built in

several stages: the first storey is
Gothic (Matej Gojković, 1422); the
second floor has elements of the
florid Venetian Gothic, and the
third was designed by Trifun Bokanić
in late Renaissance style towards
the end of the 16th century. At the
western entrance is a portal, the
finest example of Romanesque

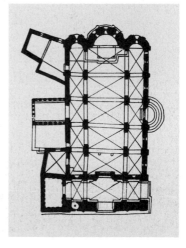

sculpture in Dalmatia. A chiselled Latin inscription says that it was carved by master Radovan in 1240. Scenes from Christ's life and the Passion are represented in the archivolts, and the Nativity, with a number of lively details, is depicted in the lunette. The lower portion contains a representation of Adam and Eve on lions, and, on the colonnettes behind them, are scenes from everyday life and illustrations of the months of the year amidst tendrils and leaves. A triangular gable with a statue of St Lawrence was added to the portal in the 14th century. Rich carved decoration has been preserved in the interior of the church, too. The octogonal Romanesque pulpit is from the 13th century, and the ciborium with a representation of the Annunciation, the work of master Mauro, dates from the first half of the 14th century. The church also contains Gothic choir stalls (Ivan Budislavić,

1449), a stone plyptich in the Chapel of St Jerome (Blaž Trogiranin, 1438), a number of paintings by native and foreign masters, and a rich treasury.

TROGIR [C, 5]
The Church of St John the Baptist

A Benedictine church built in 1270. It is a single-nave Gothic building. Its front facade is surmounted by a bell-tower and it has a typical Romanesque portal. The windows have semicircular tops and the upper parts of the facades are enlivened by small blind arcades. Traces of Gothic frescoes have been found in the interior. The church contains a relief of the Lamentation, carved by Nikola Firentinac about 1470.

TROGIR, DOMINICAN MONASTERY (DETAIL)

TROGIR [C, 5]
The Church of St Dominicus

The church is a single-nave Gothic building constructed in the 14th century. The portal dates from 1372 and is the work of the Venetian master Niccolò Dente. The lunette shows the Virgin, Bishop Augustinus, who consecrated the church and, next to him, a small figure representing his sister Bitkula. The church contains two Baroque altars and the coat-of-arms of the Sobota Family, made by Nikola Firentinac in 1469. The monastery has a Renaissance cloister, which was damaged by bombing in the Second World War. It has been restored and now it houses the Town Lapidarium.

TROGIR [C, 5]
The Cathedral. The Baptistry

The baptistry was constructed in 1467 on the northern side of the vestibule of the cathedral. It is a masterpiece of master Andrija Aleši. It is a small chamber (8 × 4.5 metres) with a longitudinal coffered vault and it has carved decoration from the floor to the top of the vault. A relief representing the Baptism of Christ is above the entrance door. Leaves with flowers and laurel leaves are carved on the door posts. The interior decoration consists of coffered vaulting, fluted half-pilasters, rosettes, shells, acanthus leaves, a frieze with leaves and a frieze with rerepesentations of boys. The baptistry contains two sculptures of exceptional value: a relief of St Jerome and a statue of

TROGIR, DOMINICAN MONASTERY

TROGIR, TOWN HALL

St John the Baptist. The entire building expresses fully the merging of Gothic and Renaissance styles, which is a characteristic feature of the Dalmatian art of that time.

TROGIR [C, 5]
The Town Hall

It was built on the old square at the end of the 15th century. It consists of the ground floor and two upper storeys. It is built of dressed stone, but the original appearance of the main facade was altered in the reconstructions in 1890 and 1943. A well-preserved Gothic courtyard is behind the building.

TROGIR [C, 5]
The Church of St Nicholes

The church is in the Benedictine convent. It was built in the 16th century on the foundations of a considerably older church. It has undergone several reconstructions, so that it exhibits elements of various styles. The bell-tower was built in 1598. A relief representing Kairos (1st century A. D.), ascribed to the school of Lysippus, is preserved in the monastery, and a Greek inscription, from the 4th century B. C., containing the earliest reference to Trogir, is incorporated into its walls.

TROGIR [C, 5]
The Large Ćipiko Palace

The palace was built towards the end of the 15th century for the wealthy and distinguished Trogir general and humanist Koriolan Ćipiko. It has the ground floor and two upper storeys, marked on the front facade by two monumental threelight windows in florid Gothic style. In front of the middle window is a terrace supported on richly moulded brackets. It is supposed that the building was designed by master Andrija Aleši. Opposite it is the "small" palace, and formerly both building were connected by a passageway at the first floor level.

TROGIR, THE LARGE ĆIPIKO PALACE

TROGIR [C, 5]
The Cathedral. The Chapel of Ivan Ursini

The chapel adjoins the northern wall of the cathedral and it was built between 1468 and 1497 according to the designs of Nikola Firentinac, who also carved most of its decoration. It represents a masterpiece of Renaissance art in Dalmatia. The chapel is rectangular (9.5 × 5.5 metres) and represents a full synthesis of architecture and sculpture. A relief representing the Coronation of the Virgin is in the lunette. The entire interior is decorated with sculptures. A series of small winged angels with torches, executed in deep relief, is in the lower zone, and the niches in the walls contain twelve statues, including Christ, the Virgin, St Peter and St Paul. The statue of St Jerome in one of the niches was made by Andrija Aleši, and the statue of St John, sculptured by Ivan Duknović, was brought here and placed into one of the niches in 1503. The windows are small and round, and the ceiling is coffered. In the centre of the chapel is a 14th century sarcophagus, with the carved image of Bishop Ivan Ursini of Trogir.

TROGIR [C, 5]
The Loggia

The loggia was built on the old square, opposite the cathedral, in the 15th century. Its structure is typical of this kind of building in Dalmatia. The Renaissance columns have richly decorated capitals. The original judge's desk and a large relief, made by Nikola Firentinac in 1471, have been preserved in the loggia. The relief represents the patron of the town Ivan Ursini, the symbol of justice and the lion of St Mark, symbol of Venice. Next to the loggia is the town clock-tower and a small church dedicated to St Sebastian.

TUNJICE [B, 1]
The Church of St Anne

The church is situated in the vicinity of Kamnik. It was built between 1761 and 1766 on the foundations of an earlier building. Strong influence of Austrian Baroque is apparent in its design. It belongs to the type of church with the central design surmounted by a wide dome. The presbytery on the eastern side

TROGIR, THE LOGGIA

has a semicircular termination, Two bell-towers adjoin the facade on the western side. Four massive piers support a semicircular gable and flank the main entrance. The squinches supporting the dome are pierced by circular windows. In addition to the main altar (1782), the church has four lateral altars and a large Gothic Crucifixion from c. 1500. The altar frescoes representing St Luke and St Catherine were painted by Janez Potočnik in 1775.

TURNIŠČE [D, 1]
The Church of the Virgin

The church is a single-nave Romanesque building with an apse

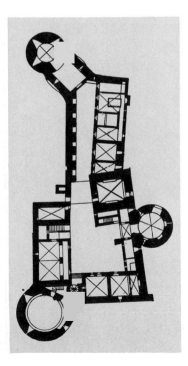

(8.10 × 5.30 metres), built in the first half of the 13th century. A radical reconstruction was undertaken c. 1380: a Gothic church with a bell-tower was added on the western side, and the Romanesque church was converted into a presbytery with Gothic vaulting. It is supposed that the church was reconstructed by Janez Akvila (Johannes Aquila). Especially valuable are the frescoes in the church. They were painted in several stages. The earliest ones are on the vaults of the presbytery (the symbols of the Evangelists, angels, the Adoration of the Kings, the Nativity), and they date from c. 1380. Another painter completed, in 1383, the work of the first master in the presbytery (the Apostles), and a third artist, commissioned by Hungarian nobles, painted the frescoes on the walls of the nave in 1389. Outstanding among the frescoes is the legend of King Ladislav I with eleven scenes depicting the battles of the Hungarians with the Polovtsy. Janez Akvila painted the Majestas Domini in the half-dome of the apse in 1393, thus completing the work done by himself, his disciples and his assistants in this church.

ULCINJ [F, 7]
The Medieval Town

A Roman town in this area is mentioned by Pliny, but the medieval town grew up on another site in the 9th century. At that time it was incorporated into the Byzantine thema Dalmatia. In the 11th and 12th centuries it belonged to the Zeta principalities, until Stefan Nemanja incorporated it into the Serbian state some time after 1181. From 1396 it was held by the members of the Balšić family. In

ULCINJ, MEDIEVAL TOWN

1421 it was captured by the Venetians, and in 1571 by the Turks. The town was a stronghold of Algerian pirates in the 18th century. In 1878 it was incorporated into the Montenegrian state. Traces of three phases of building are visible on the fortifications — early medieval, Venetian and Turkish. The most conspicuous part of the fortress is the massive and imposing "Balšić Tower". Foundations of two medieval churches, dating from the 11th and 13th century, have been preserved in the settlement. A tablet belonging to a ciborium was found in the ruins (today in the National Museum in Belgrade). It has a Latin inscription, plaitwork decoration and a relief showing two lions. The tablet dates from the 11th century and was part of the stone furniture in one of the ruined churches.

VARAŽDIN [D, 1]
The Old Fortress

The fortress was built at the end of the 14th century, when the town was held by the counts of Celje. The quadrangular tower with a Gothic portal dates from that time. The fortress changed hands several times until the middle of the 16th century, when I. Ungand, a baron from Steiermark, enlarged it and reconstructed it as a Renaissance castle. These extensive works were carried out by Domenico dell'Allio

VARAŽDIN, OLD FORTRESS

from Graz. It was then that the three imposing round towers and the inner yard with porches supported on arcades were added. The fortress was encircled by moats and ramparts. It was converted into a museum in 1925.

VARAŽDIN [D, 1]
The Church of the Dormition of the Virgin

The church was built for the Jesuit order in Varaždin and modelled on Vignola's church Il Gesù in Rome. The donator was Count Gašpar Drašković. It was built according to the design of Juraj Mattota, a Jesuit, from 1642 to 1646. It is a single-nave Baroque building of the longitudinal type, with four lateral chapels on either side, as in the Church of St Catherine in Zagreb. On the eastern side is the rectangular sanctuary, against which a high bell-tower was built. The front facade is enlivened by lesenes. The Baroque portal, consisting of two columns surmounted by a gable, features the arms of Count Drašković. The stucco decoration was made by A. J. Quadria. The main altar was made in Maribor in 1737.

VARAŽDIN [D, 1]
The Church of St John the Baptist

The church belongs to the
Franciscan order and was built
under the auspices of Abbot Matija
Jantolković c. 1650. The architect is
not known, but he is supposed to
have come from Graz. It is a
single-nave building with four lateral
chapels on either side, in imitation
of Jesuit churches. The sanctuary is
elongated and has a straight
termination. A late Renaissance
portal with an open triangle on the
gable is on the front facade. The
slender and soaring Renaissance
bell-tower (54,5 metres) was built
between 1634 and 1641. Outstanding
among the rich furniture is the main
altar, designed by Krištifor Zipl in
1715 and made by masters M. Simon
and H. Sulc from Maribor.

VARAŽDINSKE TOPLICE [D, 1]
Aquae Iasae

A spa from the Illyrian times. It was
devastated by a disastrous
conflagration in the 4th century,
but it was restored by Emperor
Constantine. Several altars
consecrated to various deities, have
been preserved. Especially
remarkable are the reliefs showing
nymphs. An inscription mentions
that a shrine dedicated to them
existed on this site in the 2nd century.
Apart from the baths and their
installations, other structures have
been preserved, including a basilical
hall with frescoes, a forum, porches
and a colonnade.

VELESOVO [B, 2]
The Dominican Convent

The Dominican convent was
founded in 1238 on the orders of the
Patriarch of Aquileia Berthold.
The original church and some other
buildings were constructed at that
time. The convent was heavily
damaged during an irruption of the
Turks in 1471. A new nunnery,
designed in pure Baroque style, was
constructed from 1732 to 1771. It
is partly modelled on the Ursuline
church in Ljubljana. The paintings
on the altars were made by
M. J. Kremser-Schmidt in 1771, and
those in the choir were painted by
Valentin Metzinger. The finest
Romanesque sculpture in the round
in Slovenia — the Virgin with
Christ — has been preserved in this
church. It combines late
Romanesque influences with elements
of French sculpture and of north
Italian art from the circle of
Benedetto Antelami. It is supposed
that it was made in northern Italy
c. 1200, and that it reached Velesovo
as a present of the Patriarch of
Aquileia on the occasion of the
foundation of the monastery.

VELIKI TABOR [C, 2]
The Palace

The palace is situated on a lonely
plateau west of Desinić in Hrvatsko
Zagorje. It was in the possession of
I. Corvinus, the Ratkaj family,
I. Thugutt, brothers Grünewald and
the painter O. Iveković. It was built
in the Middle Ages, but it got its
present appearance in the
Renaissance. Its ground plan is an

VELIKI TABOR, THE PALACE

irregular pentagon with four semicircular bastion towers. The upper storeys are marked on the facade by a course of brackets running the entire length of the building. A two-storeyed porch with arcading is in the courtyard. The palace is still in a good state of preservation and suitable for dwelling.

VELUĆE [I, 5]
The Church Dedicated to the Presentation of the Virgin

The church was built at the end of the 14th century and its founders were noblemen Oliver, Dejan, Bratan and Konstantin. It is modelled on the Lazarica and it is in the form of a compressed trefoil (16 metres long) with a dome. The facades are built of dressed stone and enlivened by cordon cornices and colonnettes. The church does not have so rich ceramic decoration as the other buildings of the Morava School. The sculptured decoration is modelled on that of Lazarica and adorns the portals, windows, archivolts and rosettes.

VELJUSA [J, 7]
The Church of the Virgin of Tenderness

The church is in the vicinity of Strumica. It was founded in 1080 by monk Manojlo, who became the Bishop of Strumica later. This is attested by an inscription in stone above the door leading to the narthex. It is quatrefoil in plan (9 metres long) and has a dome on a tall drum, which is octagonal without. On the western side is a domed narthex, and a small Church of the Holy Saviour, also domed, was added on the southern side. During Turkish rule the outer narthex was built, a porch was added and the roof structure was repaired. The church is built of stone and brick. The eastern, northern and southern conchs are five-sided without and their walls are enlivened by two rows of shallow niches. The mosaic floor and parts of the original altar screen made of stone and ornamented in a way typical of the 11th century Byzantine sculpture have been preserved in the interior of the church. The

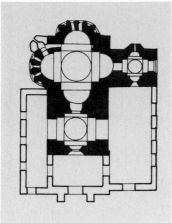

surviving frescoes are few: the
Harrowing of Hell in the northern
conch, the Presentation into the
Temple in the western conch, and
the enthroned Virgin and the
Adoration of the Lamb in the
sanctuary (which is an unusual
subject in the Byzantine iconography
of the time). Christ is represented in
the dome, and the Virgin, St John
and two angels are depicted on the
drum. In the dome of the Church
of the Holy Saviour is Christ
Emmanuel, in the apse is the Council
of the Archangels, and in the
passages are three saints, among
whom St Panteleimon is especially
remarkable. The entire ensemble of
frescoes is very important for the
study of the Byzantine art of the
11th century. Veljusa was neglected
later and its frescoes were covered
with whitewash. It was restored in
1958.

VISOKO POD KUREŠČKOM [E, 4]
The Church of St Nicholas

The church is a single-nave building
with a presbytery and it dates from
the beginning of the 15th century.
The nave has a flat timber ceiling,
and the presbytery has ribbed
vaulting. The architectural value of
the building is very modest, but the
frescoes are of a high artistic quality.
As two inscriptions show, they
were painted in 1443 by Janez of
Ljubljana, and they conform to the
iconographic programme of the
"painted Kranj presbytery". Angels
and the symbols of the Evangelists
are painted on the vaults. The walls
are divided into three zones: in the
centre of the upper zone is Christ
the Ruler surrounded by saints. In
the second zone are the Apostles,
with scenes from the life of
St Nicholas, the patron of the church.
The Annunciation and St George
slaying the dragon are depicted on
the eastern side of the triumphal
arch, and Cain and Abel, the
Crucifixion and St Nicholas
succouring sailors are on the
western side. There are some
frescoes on the facade, too, but they
are considerably damaged.

VIŠEGRAD [G, 5]
The Mehmed Pasha Sokolović Bridge

The bridge spanning the Drina was
built between 1571 and 1577 on the
orders of Mehmed Pasha Sokolović,
the Grand Vizier of Turkey. It was
designed by the imperial architect
Kodža Sinan. The length of the
bridge is 179.5 metres, and it has
11 pointed arches rising gently

VIŠEGRAD, THE MEHMED PASHA SOKOLOVIĆ BRIDGE

towards the middle. The supporting piers are specially reinforced. There is a descending ramp on the left bank of the river. The height of the bridge is 14.5 metres when the water level is normal, and the width is 6 metres. It is built of dressed and roughly hewn stone and the blocks of stone were joined together not only by mortar, but also by iron clamps soldered with lead. The external surfaces are enlivened by shallow decorative niches. The middle part of the bridge was damaged in the First and Second World Wars, but it has been restored.

VODOČA [J, 7]
The Church of St Leo

The church is near Strumica. It was the cathedral church of the bishops of Strumica. It was built in the middle of the 11th century as a basilica with a nave, two aisles and a transept. A narthex was added on the western side later. The facades are built of alternate courses of stone and brick. Only two frescoes of high artistic value have been preserved:

VODOČA, CHURCH OF ST LEO

St Panteleimon and Deacon
Isaurius. The stylistic features of
the latter resemble closely those of
the frescoes in the Church of
St Sophia in Ohrid. The church was
completely restored after the Second
World War.

VRAĆEVŠNICA [H, 4]
The Church of St George

It is in the vicinity of Gornji
Milanovac. It was built in 1428 and
its founder was Radič Postupović,
a high state dignitary. The church is
a single-nave building with tunnel
vaulting (20 metres long). The altar
apse (five-sided without) is on the
eastern side, and a domed narthex
is on the western side. The facades
are built of dressed stone, and are
enlivened by two rows of blind
arcading. The lower frieze of arcades
rests on thin pilaster-strips. The
original layer of frescoes in the
church was painted over in 1737.
The monastery was twice damaged
and restored (in the 16th and 18th
centuries). It was here that
Karadjordje convened the National
Assembly and read the conclusions
of the Peace of Bucharest in 1812.

VRDNIK [G, 3]
The Church of the Ascension

The church is situated in Fruška
Gora. A monastery existed on this
site as early as the beginning of the
16th century. At the end of the 17th
century (1697) the monks who had
fled from Ravanica settled here.
Therefore Vrdnik is also called
Ravanica. The present church was

VRŠAC, THE TOWER

built from 1801 to 1811 according to the designs of Kosta Zmijanović, and the chief builder was Kornelije from Novi Sad. It is a single-nave building with a small dome, a semicircular apse on the eastern side and a Baroque bell-tower on the western side. The facades are divided by pilasters and show traces of the influence of classicism and Biedermeier. The iconostasis was painted by Dimitrije Avramović in 1853. Amvrozije Janković painted the frescoes in the monastic refectory in 1776. The monastery has a rich treasury.

VRŠAC [H, 3]
The Tower

The old fortress stood on the top of Vršački breg and the only surviving part of it is a tower about 20 metres high. It was built in the middle of the 15th century. It has three storeys and was entered by a draw-bridge. The Turks captured the fortress in 1525 and held it until 1717, when it was surrendered to Austria. The demolishing of the old walls began after 1699, since the Treaty of Karlovci prescribed that the Vršac fortress should no longer be a military stronghold.

VRŠAC [H, 3]
The Church of St Nicholas

It is the Orthodox cathedral church of Vršac. It was built from 1783 to 1785 on the site of an earlier church. It has a Baroque bell-tower. The original iconostasis of Pavel Djurković was painted over in the

1870s, during the restoration of the church. The earlier frescoes were painted by Simeon Jakšić and Mihail Popović in 1808, and the later ones by Paja Jovanović at the end of the 19th century.

VRŠAC [H, 3]
The Cathedral

The cathedral is a neo-Gothic building constructed between 1860 and 1863. It was designed by F. Brandeis.

VRŠAC [H, 3]
The Bishop's Palace (Vladičanski dvor

The palace was built in Baroque style in 1759. Within the building is a Chapel of the Holy Archangels, with an iconostasis painted by Nikola Nešković. The building underwent considerable reconstruction in 1904.

VRŠAC, THE BISHOP'S PALACE

VRŠAC [H, 3]
The Town Hall

The Town Hall is situated next to
the building of the old 18th century
administrative centre. It was built in
1860 in neo-Gothic style, according
to the designs of V. Biher.

VUZENICA [C, 1]
The Church of St Nicholas

The church was built in the second
half of the 12th century as a parish
church. It is a typical single-nave
Romanesque church with a flat
ceiling and a bell-tower at the eastern
end. The bell-tower was massive and
6 metres high, but the only survivng
parts of the original cross vaulting
on its ground floor are a few Gothic
brackets of geometric shape with
stylized leaves. In the second phase
of building, in the 13 th century, a
Romanesque portal was added and
the bell-tower was reconstructed. In
the third phase, in the 14th century,
the church underwent extensive
reconstruction: it was then that the
late Gothic ribbed cross vaulting
and the elongated choir were added.
The Chapel of the Holy Cross, built
against its northern side, contains
frescoes from the second half of the
15th century, interesting because of
their iconographic content. The
entire church got a Baroque
appearance in the 17th and 18th
centuries, when the new Baroque
furniture was also made. The main

VRŠAC, TOWN HALL

altar is the work of the Baroque master Christoph Rudolf and dates from 1739.

ZADAR [B, 4]
The Town Fortifications

The historical core of the town is located on a natural peninsula which lies at the entrance to a deep port. It is first mentioned as early as the 4th century B. C. Roman historians call it Jader, and Constantine Porphyrogenitus refers to it as Diadora in the 10th century. It was a municipium and a colony, and, in Byzantine times, the capital of the thema of Dalmatia. In the 10th and 11th centuries it was under Croatian rulers and it retained its autonomy throughout the Middle Ages. On several occasions it waged war with the Venetians. In 1358 it fell into the hands of King Lodovik I of Croatia-Hungary, then it passed under the rule of King Sigismund and finally of Ladislaus of Naples, who surrendered it to Venice in 1409. The town was fortified with massive walls with towers already in the time of Caesar and Emperor Agustus, and its urban core had all the features of a Roman town layout. A new system of fortifications, encompassing the entire town area, was built on the foundations of the classical walls in the Middle Ages. A large castle, separated from the town by a canal, was built at the entrance to the port on the northern side. The further work on the fortification of Zadar was done mostly by the Venetians, for the town protected their commerce in the Adriatic and represented a bulwark against the Turks, who had captured the entire hinterland. The fortifications were

given their final form in the 16th century, when a large fortress and six pentagonal bastions on the eastern, landward side were built. Three public cisterns existed in the town. After the fall of Venice in 1797 Zadar passed under Austrian rule and in 1920 it was ceded to Italy by the Treaty of Rapallo, as an enclave of the Yugoslav mainland. It was heavily bombed in the Second World War, so that many of its old buildings and monuments were destroyed.

ZADAR [B, 4]
The Church of St Donatus

The church was built in the first half of the 9th century, on the site of the former Roman forum, the stone remains of which are incorporated into the foundations and walls of the church. According to the legend, its founder was Bishop Donatus (he lived in the time of Charlemagne), after whom the church was named in the 15th century. It was originally dedicated to the Holy Trinity and it is referred to by that name in Constantine Porphyrogenitus's work *De Administrando Imperio* (949). It is a

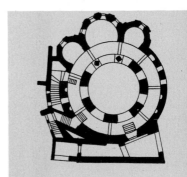

ZADAR, CHURCH OF ST DONATUS

pre-Romanesque building with the central design (diameter 21 metres, height 26 metres). The circular central part comprises the entire height of the building and was probably domed. Six massive piers and two pillars with arches are on the ground floor. Round this space is a ring-like nave, which has a vaulted ground floor and an upper storey which serves as a gallery and is reached by a staircase. On the eastern side is the altar space with three semicircular apses, while a narthex, irregular in form, is on the western side. The church is built of broken stone and classical bricks, which were used for arches. The drum is made of travertine. The facades are enlivened by lesenes and shallow niches, which have semicircular tops on the apses. The altar apses and the drum are pierced by windows. The church underwent considerable reconstruction in the 18th century and was converted into a storehouse.

The first archaeological explorations were made in the 1870s. Extensive restoration work has been in progress since 1954. Stone sculptures dating from the 9th century and, on the upper floor, beams with pre-Romanesque motifs have been preserved in the church.

ZADAR [B, 4]
The Church of St Lawrence

The church was built in the 11th century, but there is no historical evidence on its founder. It is a pre-Romanesque domed basilica with a nave and two aisles. The eastern and western bays have cross vaulting, and the northern and southern bays are surmounted by semi-cupolas resting on squinches. The sanctuary was square in plan and a vestibule with a bell-tower was

ZADAR, CHURCH OF THE VIRGIN

added on the western side. The columns have capitals and moulded bases. The church had rich sculptured decoration. The pluteus (now in the Archaeological Museum) has been partly preserved. It shows, in addition to the pre-Romanesque plaitwork, the Annunciation, the Visitation, the Nativity, the Journey of the Three Magi and the Three Magi before Herod. The sides of the southern portal are decorated with carved tendrils, and Christ surrounded by angels, gryphons and trees (the Majestas Domini) was carved on the lintel. This relief is now in the Archaeological Museum. The church is considerably damaged and its dome is destroyed.

ZADAR [B, 4]
The Church of the Virgin

The church was built in 1091 on the foundations of an earlier building as the church of the Benedictine convent founded by Čika, a noblewoman from the well-known Madia famils. It was an important religious and cultural centre in the Middle Ages. It is in the form of a Romanesque basilica with a nave, two aisles and three apses. The bell-tower with the chapter house was added between 1105 and 1111. The chapter house has a vault with two arches placed one across the other and supported on four pillars. This is the only example of such a vault in Dalmatian architecture. This house also contains capitals with the inscription REX

ZADAR, CHURCH OF ST CHRYSOGONUS

COLLOMANUS and early Romanesque frescoes dating from the beginning of the 12th century. Four busts of saints were on the vault, and the Majestas Domini and scenes from Crhist's life were on the walls. The entire complex underwent reconstructions in the Gothic, Renaissance and Baroque ages, and was heavily damaged by bombing in the Second World War. Restoration is in progress. The church houses a very fine collection of objects of sacred art which is on permanent display in the church.

ZADAR [B, 4]
The Church of St Dominica (Crkva sv. Nedelje)

There is no historical evidence on this church. It is a pre-Romanesque basilica with cross vaulting and the apse submerged in the mass of the wall. It was pulled down in 1890, but two sreen tablets with high quality carved decoration have been preserved. One of them shows two scenes from Christ's childhood: the Massacre of the Innocents and the Flight into Egypt. The upper part is moulded and decorated with plaitwork ornaments and representations of birds and stylized plants. The figures and scenes are placed in a frieze of arcades, which are, like all the figures, transformed into linear arabesques. The relief dates from the 11th century and is now on display in the Archaeological Museum.

ZADAR [B, 4]
The Church of St Chrysogonus (Crkva sv. Krševana)

The old Benedictine monastery is mentioned in historical sources as early as the 10th century, although the church was thoroughly reconstructed and consecrated in 1175. It is in the form of a Romanesque basilica with a nave, two aisles and three apses on the eastern side. It is built of dressed stone, and the facades are enlivened by blind arcades and lesenes. Especially decorative is the middle apse, which has blind arcades in the lower zone and a gallery of arches on slender colonnettes in the upper zone. Two layers of frescoes have been preserved in the northern aisle and in the apse: the earlier was painted at the end of the 12th century (several figures of saints), and

ZADAR, CHURCH OF ST ANASTASIA

the later dates from the beginning of the 13th century. In the lower zone is Archangel Michail with a white disc and two small figures on it, in the middle zone is the Deesis, and the Nativity, with unconventional and expressive heads of shepherds. Parts of 15th century frescoes painted in Gothic style have been preserved in the southern apse. The middle apse was faced with a mosaic, but it is completely destroyed now.

ZADAR [B, 4]
The Church of St Anastasia
(Crkva sv. Stošije)

The cathedral church of Zadar. It was built on the foundations of an earlier building in the 13th century (consecrated in 1285), but some work was done on it in later years, too. It is in the form of a basilica with a nave, two aisles and three apses. The front facade is richly decorated with horizontal rows of blind arcades, two rosettes and three Romanesque portals. The lunette of the main portal contains a Gothic relief (1324) showing the Virgin with Christ between St Zoilus and St Anastasia. The northern facade has a decorative gallery with arcades on slender colonnettes. The colonnades in the interior which separate the aisles from the nave consist of masonry pillars and classical columns with Corinthian capitals. The ground floor and the upper storey of the bell-tower were built in the 14th century, and the upper portions were added in the 19th century. A triple-nave baptistry stood in the churchyard, but it was demolished in the Second World War. Frescoes painted in Romanesque-Gothic style and dating from the end of the 13th century have been preserved in the two lateral apses. Christ with saints is represented in the northern apse, while the Deesis and, on the upper part of the wall, St Cosmas and Damyan, are shown in the southern apse. The noteworthy items of church furniture include Romanesque pews, a ciborium dating from 1332 and choir stalls carved by Matej Moronzon in 1418.

ZADAR [B, 4]
The Church of St Simeon

The church was built in the 12th century, but it underwent reconstructions in the Gothic, Renaissance and Baroque eras. It contains a masterpiece of Zadar goldworking — the sarcophagus of St Simeon. It weighs 250 kilograms. It is made of gilt silver and it was commissioned by Queen Jelisaveta, the wife of Lodowick I and daughter of the Ban of Bosnia Stjepan Kotromanić. The sarcophagus was made between 1377 and 1380 by goldsmiths Francesco da Milano, Andrija Markov from Zagreb, Petar, the son of Bal from Rača, Stipan Pribičev and Mihovil Damjanov. The image of St Simeon is on the lid, and thirteen compositions are round it. They illustrate the legend of St Simeon and show the entry of King Lodowick into Zadar, Ban Pavle Šubić with his wife, Queen Jelisaveta and the death of Stjepan Kotromanić.

ZAGREB [C, 2]
The Cathedral

A small cathedral church, the foundations of which have been partly preserved, stood on the site of the present cathedral in the 11th century. In the 12th century the larger cathedral was built (consecrated in 1217), but it was burnt down already in 1220. The new church was torn down by the Mongolians in 1242. The present cathedral was built in several successive stages on these remains. The sanctuary on the eastern side with the two lateral chapels was built in the second half of the 13th century, in the time of Bishop Timotheus, and in the 14th and 15th centuries the entire western part was added, so that the building got the appearance of a representative Gothic basilica with a nave and two aisles. The church was badly damaged in a great fire in 1624, but it was restored in 1632 and 1647, when master Hans Albertal

ZAGREB, CATHEDRAL

constructed new Gothic vaulting and completed, in 1641, the big Renaissance bell-tower. The cathedral was heavily damaged again in an earthquake in 1880. It was thoroughly restored by H. Bollé, who raised the two high neo-Gothic bell-towers on the front facade, built new vaults and dismantled the old portal. The work was completed in 1902. The cathedral contains Renaissance wooden stalls from 1520, a number of important works of art on the altars and a very rich treasury with some objects dating from as early as the 11th century. Between 1513 and 1521 the complex of the cathedral was fortified in the typical Renaissance style. The builders were Juraj from Ivanić, Jurko Kranjec, Petrić Palir and Petar Alemanus. A monumental archiepiscopal palace was built on the fortification walls in 1730, during the incumbency of Bishop Branjug. It incorporates the Gothic chapel of St Stephen with frescoes from the middle of the 14th century.

ZAGREB, CATHEDRAL

ZAGREB, CHURCH OF ST CATHERINE

ZAGREB [C, 2]
The Church of St Catherine

The church was built between 1620 and 1632 as the church of the Jesuit order and it is modelled on Vignola's church Il Gesù in Rome. It is the finest Baroque church in Croatia. It is supposed that it was designed by Juraj Jaszi, a Jesuit, and there is documentary evidence of numerous native masters who took part in its construction. It is a single-nave building of a longitudinal type, with four chapels on either side. On the eastern end is the elongated sanctuary surmounted by a small spire. The front facade is enlivened by lesenes and niches with statues (5), but its original appearance was altered in the restoration carried out by H. Bollé after an earthquake in 1880. The vaults are decorated by illusionistic paintings, made by Giulio Quaqlio in 1721. Two of the altars are particularly important: one was made by Francesco Robba in 1729, and the other, the Altar of the Holy Ghost, is the work of Toma Dervant and Ivan Jakov Altenbacher from Varaždin and dates from 1675—1678. The latter altar is adorned by a painting by Bernard Bobić. The representative building of the Jesuit College, designed by Antun Moketi, was built next to the church in the middle of the 17th century.

ZAGREB [C, 2]
The Church of St Mark

The church was built at the end of the 14th century as the parish church of the medieval settlement Gradec (modern Gornji Grad). It is a late Gothic triple-nave basilica of the hall type. The surviving parts of the original building include the rib vaulting resting on masonry pillars and the southern portal, the most ornate Gothic portal in Yugoslavia, which was made c. 1400 under the influence of Parler's Prague workshop. Statues of Christ, the Virgin, St Mark and the Apostles are in the niches. The Baroque bell-tower, by Mazeti and Donati, was added on the northern side in the second half of the 17th century (c. 1660). The church and the bell-tower underwent several reconstructions, the most extensive being the one carried out towards the end of the 19th century, when H. Bollé made a pseudo-Gothic restoration and built a roof of

ZAGREB, CHURCH OF ST MARK

multi-coloured tiles with the
coats-of-arms of Croatia, Slavonia,
Dalmatia and the city of Zagreb.
In 1937 the church was adorned
with frescoes by Joza Kljaković
and sculptures (Pietà, the Crucifision,
the Virgin with Christ and a relief of
St Mark) by Ivan Meštrović. Many
precious objects of old gold-working
art have been preserved in the
treasury.

ZAGREB [C, 2]
*The Yugoslav Academy of Science
and Arts*

The building was constructed
between 1876 and 1884. It was
designed by Friedrich Schmidt in
Italian neo-Renaissance style and
represents an example of historicism
in the architecture of the second
half of the 19th century. It belongs
to the type of the quadrangular
closed palace. The facades are
divided into three zones. The corners
of the ground floor and the first
storey have rusticated decoration.
The front facade is given special
emphasis. In front of it is a porch

ZAGREB

1. Cathedral
2. Church of St Mark
3. Church of St Catherine
4. Lotršćak Tower

ZAGREB, YUGOSLAV ACADEMY OF SCIENCE AND ARTS

supported on four pillars. The buildng houses a rich library, the archives and Strossmeyer's Gallery, with a fine collection of West European paintings.

ZAGREB [C, 2]
The Lotrošćak Tower

It is one of the few remains of the defence walls and towers which encompassed Gradec, the original core of old Zagreb (modern Gornji Grad) in the 13th century. The Lotrošćak or Habernik Tower controlled the entrance to the town from the southern side, but later it changed its function. For some time it housed the bell which sounded alarm and the closing of the town gates. In front of the tower is Strossmeyer's promenade with a belvedere.

ZAGREB [C, 2]
The Archaeological Museum

The building was constructed in 1879 as the family palace of the Vranicani family. It was designed by F. Kondrat in neo-Renaissance style. Now it houses the Archaeological Museum, which was formerly a part of the old National Museum, established as early as 1846.

ZAGREB [C, 2]
The Museum of Arts and Crafts

It was built between 1888 and 1892 according to the design of H. Bollé in an eclectic combination of various styles.

ZAGREB, CROATIAN NATIONAL THEATRE

ZAGREB [C, 2]
The Croatian National Theatre

The construction of the theatre was completed in 1895. It is a neo-Baroque edifice designed by Hermann Helmer and Ferdinand Fellner, architects from Vienna. In front of the front facade, which is emphasized by two low cupolas, is a porch supported on columns. It was thorughly reconstructed in the 1970s. In front of the building is the Well of Life, a work by Ivan Meštrović.

ZAGREB [C, 2]
The Oršić-Rauch Palace

The palace is located in Gornji Grad. It was built between 1740 and 1780 for the distinguished Zagreb family Vojković-Kulmer--Oršić-Rauch. It is the finest Baroque family mansion in Zagreb. It has the ground floor and an upper storey. Especially impressive is the front facade. It is divided into three zones: in the first zone is the door flanked by pillars, in the second zone are three high windows between thin pilasters, and in the third zone is a pediment with volutes and stucco decoration. Since the end of the Second World War the palace houses the Historical Museum of Croatia.

ZAGREB [C, 2]
The Ban's Residence

The building of this late Baroque palace was completed in 1808. It was the seat of the National Assembly and it housed the Croatian State Archives. Today it is a representative building of the Presidium of the National Assembly of the Socialist Republic of Croatia.

ZAGREB, THE VRANICANI PALACE

ZAGREB [C, 2]
The Vranicani Palace

A neo-Baroque building designed by O. Hoffer and built in 1883. It belongs to the type of the closed palace with an inner courtyard. The building houses the Modern Gallery and the Cabinet of the Graphic Arts of the Yugoslav Academy of Science and Arts.

ZAGREB [C, 2]
The Main Railway Station

The construction was completed in 1892 according to the designs of E. Faf in neo-Classical style. In front of the station is the spacious King Tomislav Square with the Zrinjevac Park. The statue of King Tomislav on horseback is the work of Robert Frangeš-Mihanović. The monument was cast in 1931, and put into place in 1947.

ZAGREB [C, 2]
The Pejačević Palace

The palace is situated in Gornji Grad. It was built in late Baroque style in 1797. The first theatre in Zagreb was in this building. Subsequently it was used for various purposes.

ZAGREB [C, 2]
The Arts Pavilion

It was built in 1896 in Secession style as an exhibition pavilion for the Hungarian Millennium Exhibition in Pest. It was transferred to Zagreb in 1898 and from that time onwards it has been used for

ZAGREB, ARTS PAVILION

occasional exhibitions. In front of
the building is a monument to the
painter Andrija Medulić, a work
of Ivan Meštrović.

ZAGREB [C, 2]
The Exchange

The building was designed by
Viktor Kovačić and it was built
between 1923 and 1927 on the site
of the old fair ground. After
Kovačić's death in 1924 the
construction was completed by
H. Ehrlich. The main facade is
neo-Classical, with four Ionic
columns. The building houses the
National Bank of Croatia today.

ZAVALA [E, 6]
*The Church of the Presentation into
the Temple*

The church is in Popovo Polje, in
Herzegovina. It is first mentioned in
historical sources in 1514, but it is
probably a little older. It is a small
single-nave building, partly cut
into the rock. The frescoes were
painted in 1618/19, in the time of
Patriarch Pajsije, by the well-known
painter Djordje Mitrofanović from
Chilandar. These wall paintings
stand out among the contemporary
frescoes because of their interesting
iconography and fine artistic
quality.

ZEMUN, CHURCH OF ST NICHOLAS

ZEMUN [H, 3]
The Church of St Nicholas
(Nikolajevska crkva)

A Baroque church built between
1725 and 1731. It was damaged by
fire in 1867, but it was restored in
1870. It is a single-nave building
with a semicircular apse on the
eastern end and a two-storeyed
bell-tower on the western side. The
icons on the richly carved
iconostasis were painted by Dimitrije
Bačević in 1762. The lower part of
the iconostasis was re-painted in
the middle of the 19th century. The
frescoes in the Nazarene style were
painted by Živko Petrović in 1848.

ZEMUN [H, 3]
The Church of the Virgin

The church was built between 1776
and 1780. It is a single-nave edifice
with a semicircular apse on the
eastern side and a tripartite
narthex on the western side. A
two-storeyed bell-tower was built
above the narthex at the end of the
18th century. Originally, the facade
had elements of old architecture
which were lost in the reconstruction
carried out in 1880. The iconostasis
was carved by Aksentije Marković,
and the icons were painted by Arsa
Teodorović in 1815.

ZEMUN [H, 3]
The Špirta House

A pseudo-Gothic building
constructed in 1853 for the wealthy
Zemun family Špirta. It is a
one-storey building with a courtyard.
The dominating features on the
facade are the high neo-Gothic
windows and a large gate for coaches.
The house was converted to a
hotel, and today it houses the Town
Museum.

ZEMUN, THE ŠPIRTA HOUSE

ZGOŠĆA, STEĆAK

ZGORNJA DRAGA [B, 2]
The Church of St Martin

The church is close to Stična. It was built in the second half of the 12th century. It is a typical Romanesque single-nave building with a semicircular apse (12.40 × 7 metres). The nave is covered with two cross vaults. It is built of stone and covered with plaster. An indented cornice and the original Romanesque window are on the facade of the apse. It is supposed that the church was built by master Mihael, who also constructed the monastery at Stična. A bell-tower and a vestibule were added on the western side in the Baroque era.

ZGOŠĆA [E, 4]
The stećak from Donja Zgošća

The *stećak* was found at Donja Zgošća near Kakanj, in the neighbourhood of which there were several cemeteries. It is considered the finest *stećak* in the territory of Bosnia. It is in the form of a sarcophagus and it is richly ornamented on all four sides. The front part shows, in the upper zone, a lord, a castle with the figures of the lord, women and courtiers, and, in the lower zone, two sadled steeds. One of the lateral sides contains scenes of boar and deer hunting, and the other has a representation of a tournament with five mounted knights. The

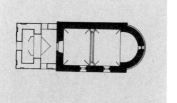

ZGOŠĆA, STEĆAK

back side is filled with exuberant vegetable ornaments. It belonged to some eminent nobleman. It was formerly supposed that it was the sepulchral monument of Ban Kulin, but this hypothesis has been discarded, for the Gothic elements on it show that it was made in the middle of the 15th century. The monument is now exhibited in the courtyard of the National Museum in Sarajevo.

ZRENJANIN [H, 2]
The Church of the Dormition of the Virgin

The church was constructed, with interruptions, from 1744 to 1787. It contains an iconostasis, carved by Arsenije Petrović between 1785 and 1790. The icons on it were painted by Georgije Popović in 1815.

ZRENJANIN [H, 2]
The Church of the Presentation to the Temple

The construction was completed in 1777 in classical style. The icons on the richly carved iconostasis were painted by Arsa Jovanović in 1816/17. The frescoes on the vaults were painted by Stevan Aleksić in 1913.

ZRENJANIN [H, 2]
The Town Hall

The Town Hall was designed by Josip Fischer as the centre of the regional administration and it was built on 1820. Later, in 1887, it

ZRENJANIN, CHURCH OF THE DORMITION OF THE VIRGIN

was radically reconstructed according to the design of Djula Bartoš and Eden Lehner. Another storey and a spire were added, the wings were extended, and the entire building was remodelled in neo-Baroque style, with elements of the Secession.

ZRZE [I, 7]
The Church of the Transfiguration

The church was built during the reign of Emperor Dušan, about the middle of the 14th century. Its founder was monk German. It is a single-nave building to which a bay was added on the western side and painted with frescoes in 1368/69. These paintings were commissioned by a certain Hajko (probably German's son) and his sons Pribil and Prijezda. The Communion of the Apostles is shown on the western wall of the bay, above it is Abraham's Hospitality, and the Passion is illustrated on the southern and northern walls. The frescoes are expressive and have a rustic quality. They are supposed to be the work of a master Dimitrije. Two grandsons of monk German lived in the monastery: painters Metropolitan

Jovan and Makarije. Threatened by the Turks, they handed over the monastery to their serf Konstantin and his family, who restored it. Jovan went to paint frescoes in Andreaš, and Makarije took refuge in Serbia and probably worked on the wall paintings in Ljubostinja. After his return to Zrze he painted, in 1421/22, the icon of the Virgin Pelagonitissa for the iconostasis which had already been adorned by an icon of Christ, painted by his brother Jovan in 1393/94. These two icons are today in the Art Gallery in Skopje. The frescoes were painted over in the 17th century. They were cleaned and restored in 1963.

ZVEČAN [H, 6]
The Fortress

The fortress is mentioned in historical sources at the end of the 11th century as a frontier stronghold, and there is also a reference to it later, in 1172, when Stefan Nemanja defeated the Byzantines at Pantin. King Stefan Dečanski was imprisoned and murdered in it in 1331. In the second half of the 14th century it was held by local noblemen, and in 1399 it was captured by the

Turks. It became an important Turkish stronghold for their incursions into Bosnia. It was abandoned in the 18th century. The town consists of two parts: the fortress and the suburb, which is surrounded on the southern side by a wall with towers. It was of great strategic importance, for it controlled the Bosnian and Ibar roads to Metohija, and later it defended the adjacent mine of Trepča. The fortress is of an irregular shape, adapted to the cliff, and it has five towers. It is built on two platforms. The keep and the foundations of the Church of St George are on the upper level, and the remains of a cistern and of dwelling houses are on the lower level. An underground corridor led from the northern side to the foot of the hill; it served for the supply of water from the Ibar river.

ZVORNIK [F, 4]
The Fortress

The fortress is situated on the left bank of the Drina in eastern Bosnia. It consists of three parts. The middle part is the largest and it was built as early as the 14th century for the feudal lords of the Zlatonosović family. At the beginning of the 15th century (1433) it came into the possession of Despot Djurdje Branković, who built the upper fortress with the keep. About 1462 the Turks captured it and built the lower fortress with strong walls and three towers on the bank of the river. The town was considerably damaged in the fights between the Turks and the joint forces of the Hungarians and the Austrians. Foundations of a Franciscan church, later turned into a mosque, have been preserved within the walls.

ZVORNIK, FORTRESS

ŽIČA, CHURCH OF THE ASCENSION

ŽIČA [H, 5]
The Monastery

The main church is dedicated to the Ascension. It was founded by Stefan the First-Crowned and built in 1208. After the Serbian Church attained independence, the church became the seat of the autonomous Serbian Archbishopric. It played an important role in the religious, political and cultural life of Serbia in the Middle Ages. The church is in the form of a domed single-nave building (44 metres long). A spacious apse is on the eastern side, and the choirs on the northern and southern sides form a low transept.

Two parekkleseions were added to the western bay: the northern one is dedicated to St Sabas of Jerusalem, and the southern one to Stephen Protomartyr. A spacious narthex, with ribbed cross vaulting and a high tower at the entrance, stands on the western side. The facade is whitewashed and painted red, in imitation of the churches on Mount Athos. The monastery was damaged at the end of the 13th century, during an incursion of the Polovtsy, but it was restored in the time of Archbishop Danilo II and King Milutin. The frescoes are considerably damaged, and many are destroyed. What has been preserved can be divided into two chronological groups. The earlier ones (dating from about 1220) are in the lateral choirs (The Crucifixion,

ŽIČA, CHURCH OF THE ASCENSION, FRESCO, ST MATTHEW

the Deposition, the Apostles) and
in the bell-tower (c. 1230). The
later ones date from between 1309
and 1316 and are in the area below
the dome, in the lower zone of the
sanctuary (the standing figures) and
on the western wall (a monumental
Dormition of the Virgin). It is
thought that the same painters were
the authors of the murals in the
lateral parekkleseions and in the
passage below the bell-tower: the
Christmas Hymn, the Forty Martyrs
of Sebast, SS Peter and Paul, and a
painted charter granted to the
monastery by Stefan the
First-Crowned. It is supposed that
these frescoes were painted by the
fellow-workers and assistants of
Mihail and Evtihije. Major
restoration work was carried out in
the monastery in 1928.

ŽUŽEMBERK [B, 2]
The Renaissance Burg

It is situated in the upper reaches
of the Krka river. It is first mentioned
in historical sources in 1293, but it
got the present form in the 1530s.
It has all the features of Renaissance
fortification architecture: circular
towers, slanting walls and a wall
cornice, semicircular in section,
between the storeys. The courtyard
has corridors with arcading. In
the centre is a high tower, square in
plan, which belongs to the oldest
medieval core. It underwent
reconstructions in the 17th and 18th
centuries.

CHRONOLOGY OF THE MONUMENTS DESCRIBED IN THIS BOOK

PREHISTORY

Lepenski Vir, the settlement: sixth millenium B.C.

THE CLASSICAL PERIOD

Pula, Temple of Augustus: 1st century A.D.
Pula, Amphitheatre: 1st century A.D.
Djerdap, Roman road: 1st century A.D.
Šempeter, Vindonius tomb: 1st century A.D.
Djerdap, Tabula Traiana: 100 A.D.
Nin, Classical temple: 1st century A.D.
Bitolj, Heraclea Lyncestis; 1st-5th century
Sremska Mitrovica, Sirmium: 1st-6th century
Stobi, Classical town: 1st-6th century
Šempeter, Priscianus tomb: 2nd century A.D.
Šempeter, Ennius tomb; 2nd century A.D.
Pula, Twin gate: 2nd century A.D.
Solin, Salona: 2nd-6th century
Skopje, Kale: classical period-Middle Ages
Niš, Mediana: 3rd—6th century
Split, Diocletian's palace: c. 300 A.D.
Niš, tomb: 6th century
Varaždinske Toplice, Aquae Iasae: 4th century
Gamzigrad, Romuliana, late classical stronghold: 4th century
Split, Baptistry (Roman temple): 4th—11th century
Beograd, Kalemegdan, fortress: Roman period-18th century
Blagaj on the Buna river, Šćepan grad: Roman period-Middle Ages
Lebane, Caričin grad: 6th century
Pula, Funeral chapel: 6th century
Poreč, Cathedral of the Euphrasiana: 535-550

PRE-ROMANESQUE AND ROMANESQUE

Zadar, Church of St Donatus: 9th century
Ulcinj, Medieval town: 9th—16th century
Trogir, Church of St Barbara: 10th century
Omiš, Church of St Peter at Priko: 10th century
Bled, Castle: end of the 10th century
Nin, Church of the Holy Cross: 11th century
Kuti, Church of St Thomas: 11th century
Kotor, Church of St Luke: 11th century
Bar, Medieval town: 11th century
Split, Church of the Holy Trinity: 11th century
Split, Church of Our Lady of the Belfry: 11th century
Split, Church of St Martin: 11th century
Zadar, Church of St Lawrence: 11th century
Zadar, Church of St Dominica: 11th century
Rab, Supetarska Draga, Church of St Peter: 1066
Ston, Church of St Michael: c. 1080
Zadar, Church of the Virgin: 1091
Kotor, Church of St Triphon: 1166
Zadar, Church of St Chrysogonus: 1176
Rab, Church of St Mary Major: 1177
Dravograd, Church of St Vitus: 1177
Rab, Bell-tower: 1181
Špitalič, Church of the Virgin: 1190
Mljet, Church of the Virgin: 12th century
Vuzenica, Church of St Nicholas: 12th century
Kamnik, Mali grad, Double chapel: 12th century
Kanfanar, Church of St Agatha: 12th century
Krk, Cathedral: 12th century
Split, Church of St Nicholas: 12th century
Zgornja Draga, Church of St Martin: 12th century
Stična, Cistercian abbey: 12th century
Zadar, Church of St Simeon: 12th—17th century
Svetivinčent, Church of St Vincent: 12th——13th century

Selo in Prekomurje, Church of St Nicholas: 13th century
Turnišće, Church of the Virgin: 13th century
Velesovo, Virgin with Christ: 13th century
Split, Cathedral, Buvina's doors: 1214
Kotor, Church of St Mary Collegiate: 1221
Trogir, Cathedral, Radovan's portal: 1240
Poreč, Canons' House: 1251
Kostanjevica, Church of St James: 13th century
Kostanjevica, Church of the Virgin: 13th century
Maribor, Cathedral: c. 1260 (1400)
Ptuj, Church of St George: 13th (14th) century
Trogir, Church of St John the Baptist: 1270
Zagreb, Lotrošćak Tower: 13th century
Zadar, Church of St Anastasia: 13th century
Rovinj, Chapel of the Holy Trinity: 13th century
Samobor, The old fortress: 13th—18th centuries
Koper, Baptistry: 1317

MEDIEVAL ART IN SERBIA, MACEDONIA, BOSNIA AND HERZEGOVINA

Novi Pazar, Church of St Peter in Ras: 9th—11th centuries
Prilep, Marko's Town: 10th-14th centuries
Ohrid, Fortifications: 11th century
Zvečan, Fortress: 11th—14th centuries
Ohrid, Church of St Sophia: 11th-14th centuries
Prizren, Medieval fortress: 11th—15th centuries
Vodoča, Church of St Leo: 11th century
Veljusa, Church of the Virgin of Tenderness: 1080
Nerezi, Church of St Panteleimon: 1164
Novi Pazar, Djurdjevi Stupovi, frescoes: 1170—1171
Kurbinovo, Church of St George: 12th century
Bijela, Church of the Virgin: 12th—13th centuries
Studenica, Church of the Virgin: 1183—1196, frescoes: 1208—1209
Bijelo Polje, Church of St Peter: 1195, frescoes: c. 1320
Novi Pazar, Ras fortress: 12th century
Prilep, Church of St Nicholas: 12th century, frescoes: 1200
Kraljevo, Žiča: 1208, frescoes: 1220 and c. 1310
Mileševa, Church of the Ascension: 1219, frescoes: before 1228
Morača, Church of the Dormition of the Virgin: 1251—1252, frescoes: c. 1260
Peć, Church of the Apostles: 13th century
Studenica, Church of St Nicholas: 13th century

Sopoćani, Church of the Holy Trinity: before 1263, frescoes: c. 1265
Manastir, Church of St Nicholas: 1266, fresoes: 1271
Gradac, Church of the Annunciation: c. 1275
Ohrid, Church of St John the Divine — Kaneo: 13th century
Koriša, Hermitage of Petar of Koriša: 13th and 14th centuries
Prilep, Church of St Demetrius: 13th century, frescoes: 1290
Ohrid, Church of the Virgin the Perilebtos, 13th century, frescoes: 1294—95
Arlije, Church of St Achilius: end of the 13th century, frescoes: 1296
Radožda, Church of Archangel Michael, frescoes: 13th—14th centuries
Prizren, Church of the Mother of God Ljeviška: 1306—1307, frescoes: 1310—1313
Skopje, Church of St Nicholas: 1307—1308, frescoes: 1316
Studenica, King's Church, frescoes: 1314
Banjska, Church of St Stephen: 1313—1315
Staro Nagoričano, Church of St George: 1313, frescoes: 1316—1318
Gračanica, Church of the Annunciation: c. 1315, frescoes: c. 1318
Peć, Church of St Demetrius: 1321—1324, frescoes: c. 1345
Peć, Church of the Virgin Hodeghetria, frescoes: 1330—1337
Kučevište, Church of the Holy Saviour: c. 1330
Peć, Patriarchate, narthex: c. 1330, frescoes: 1337, 1565
Maglič, Fortress: 14th century (first reference)
Karan, White Church, frescoes: 1332—1337
Ljuboten, Church of St Nicholas: 1337
Štip, Church of the Holy Archangel: 1334
Treskavac, Church of the Dormition of the Virgin: 13th century, frescoes: c. 1340
Dečani, Church of Christ the Pantocrator: 1327—1335, frescoes: 1335—1350
Lesnovo, Church of the Holy Archangel: 1341, frescoes: 1347—48
Prizren, Church of the Holy Archangels: 1343—1352
Ohrid, Church of St Nicholas Bolnički: 1330—1340
Ohrid, Church of SS Constantine and Helena: middle of the 14th century
Ohrid, Church of the Virgin Bolnička: middle of the 14th century
Budisavci, Church of the Transfiguration: 14th century, frescoes: 1568
Matejče, Church of the Nativity of Virgin, frescoes: 1355—1360
Ohrid, Monastery Zaum, frescoes: 1361
Psača, Church of St Nicholas: c. 1354, frescoes: 1365—1371
Konče, Church of St Stephen: 1366—1371
Zrze, Church of the Transfiguration: 14th century, frescoes: 1368—1369

Golubac, Fortress: 14th century (earliest reference)
Gornjak, Monastery: 14th century
Lešak, Monastery — Church of St Anastasia: 14th century Church of the Virgin: 14th century
Matka, Church of the Virgin: 14th century, frescoes: 1497
Peštani, Church of the Virgin: 1370
Pološko, Church of St George: c. 1370, 17th century
Prilep, Church of the Holy Archangel, frescoes: 1372
Marko's Monastery, Sušica, frescoes: 1376—1381
Skopje, Andreaš, frescoes: 1389
Nova Pavlica, frescoes: 1389
Ohrid, Church of St Naum: 14 century
Poganovo, Church of St John the Theologos, 14th century, frescoes: 1499
Lipljan, Church of the Entry into the Temple: c. 1380
Kučevište, Church of the Holy Archangel: second half of the 14th century
Kruševac, Lazarica: c. 1380
Ljubostinja, Church of the Dormition of the Virgin: c. 1390, frescoes: c. 1403
Krupa, Monastery: 14th century
Naupara, Church of the Nativity of the Virgin: end of the 14th century
Veluće, Church of the Presentation of the Virgin: end of the 14th century
Prizren, Church of St Saviour: 14th century
Ravanica, Church of the Ascension: 14th century, frescoes: c. 1385
Krka, Church of the Holy Archangel Michael: 14th century (reconstructed in the 17th and 18th centuries)
Novo Brdo, Medieval town: 14th—15th centuries
Kratovo, Medieval towers: 14th—15th centuries
Kalenić, Church Dedicated to the Entry into the Temple: beginning of the 15th century
Koporin, Church of St Stephen: beginning of the 15th century
Resava, Fortress, monastery: 1407—1418
Vraćevšnica, Church of St George: 1428
Smederevo, Fortress: 1428—1480
Stolac, Medieval fortress: 1444 (earliest reference)
Cetinje, Monastery: 1484
Zvronik, Fortress: 14th—15th centuries
Doboj, Fortress: 15th century
Maglaj, Medieval fortress: 15th century
Počitelj, Old town: 15th century (encompassed with walls again in the 17th century)
Radimlja, Medieval cemetery: 15th and 16th centuries
Bileća, Cemetery with *stećci:* 15th—16th centuries
Zgošća, *Stećak* from Donja Zgošća: 15th century

THE GOTHIC AND THE RENAISSANCE

Zagreb, Cathedral: 12th—15th centuries
Motovun, Old Town: 13th—17th centuries
Ostrožac on the Una river, Old Fortress: 13th—18th centuries
Trogir, Church of St Dominicus: 1372
Koper, Governor's Palace: 1386—1452
Martijanci, Church of St Martin, frescoes: 1392
Bač, Medieval fortress: 14th century
Celje, Old citadel: 14th century
Dubrovnik, Cloister of the Franciscan monastery: 14th century
Hvar, Bell-tower of the Church of St Mark: 14th century
Ilok, Fortress: 14th century
Šibenik, Church of St Francis: 14th century
Šibenik, Saint Anne Fortress: 14th century
Varaždin, Old Fortress: 14th century
Crngrob, Church of the Virgin, frescoes: 14th—15th centuries
Dubrovnik, Town walls: 14th—15th centuries
Hercegnovi, Town fortifications: 14th—18th centuries
Hvar, Fortress: 14th—15th centuries
Olovo, Cemetery: 14th—15th centuries
Korčula, Fortifications: 15th—16th centuries
Klis, Fortress: 14th—15th centuries
Jajce, Medieval fortress: 14th—15th centuries
Ston, Town fortifications: 14th—15th centuries
Ravanjska vrata, Cemetery: 14th—16th centuries
Zadar, Town fortifications: 14th—16th centuries
Krk, Town fortifications: 1407
Ptujska Gora, Church of the Virgin, frescoes: 1420
Celje, Church of St Daniel, frescoes: 1410—1420
Lake Bohinj, Church of St John the Baptist, frescoes: 1430
Šibenik, Church of St James: 1431—1555
Split, Town Hall: 1443
Visoko pod Kureškom, Church of St Nicholas, frescoes: 1443
Pag, Town fortifications: 1443—1470
Pag, Cathedral: 1443—1488
Dubrovnik, Onofrio's Big Fountain: 1444
Kaštel Lukšić, Tomb of Arnerius: 1446—1448
Muljava, Church of the Dormition of the Virgin, frescoes: 1456
Kameni vrh, Church of St Peter, frescoes: 1459
Kranj, Church of St Cantianus, frescoes: 1460
Koper, Loggia: 1462—1464
Mače, Church of St Nicholas, frescoes: 1467
Trogir, Baptistry: 1467

Trogir, Chapel of Ivan Ursini: 1468—1497
Škofja Loka, Church of St James: 1471
Beram, Church of the Virgin at Škriline, frescoes: 1474
Lovran, Church of St George, frescoes: 1479
Hrastovlje, Church of the Holy Trinity, frescoes: 1490
Hvar, Town loggia: 1497
Vršac, Tower, 15th century
Badija, Franciscan monastery: 15th century
Zagreb, Church of St Mark: 15th century
Trogir, Ćipiko Palace: 15th century
Šibenik, Church of St Barbara: 15th century
Trogir, Town Hall: 15th century
Dubrovnik, Church of Our Lady of Danče: 15th century
Kamnik, Church of St Primus: 15th century
Trogir, Loggia: 15th century
Pazin, Church of St Nicholas, frescoes: 15th century
Trogir, Kamerlengo Fortress: 15th century
Piran, Venetian House: 15th century
Šibenik, Orsini Palace: 15th century
Šibenik, Foscolo Palace: 15th century
Rab, Nimira Palace: 15th century
Hvar, Church of Our Lady of Mercy: 15th century
Dubrovnik, Cloister of the Dominicans: 15th century
Budva, Hektorović Palace: 15th century
Budva, Fortifications: 15th century
Šibenik, New Church:15th century
Suha, Church of St John the Baptist: 15th century
Poreč, Gothic Palace: 15th century
Split, Papalić Palace: 15th century
Lepoglava, Church of the Virgin: 15th century (remodelled in the 17th and 18th centuries)
Korčula, Church of St Nicholas: 15th century
Koper, Cathedral: 15th—16th centuries
Korčula, Church of St Mark: 15th—16th centuries
Kotor, Town fortifications: 15th—16th centuries
Rab, Church of St Francis: 1491
Dubrovnik, Rector's Palace: 15th—16th centuries
Maribor, City Castle: 15th—18th centuries
Piran, First of May Square: 15th—19th centuries
Rab, Loggia: beginning of the 16th century
Split, Church of St Roch: 1516
Dubrovnik, Sponza: 1516—1522
Dubrovnik, Church of St Saviour: 1520
Stari Grad, Tvrdalj: 1520
Dubrovnik, Villa of the Sorkočević family: 1521
Šibenik, Town Loggia: 1532—1542
Begunje, Church of St Peter, frescoes: 1530—1540
Sisak, Fortress: 1544—1550
Senj, Nehaj fortress: 1558
Trakošćan, Castle: 1568
Hvar, Arsenal: 1579—1611
Koper, Balgramoni-Tacco Palace: 16th century
Veliki Tabor, Palace: 16th century
Žužemberk, Palace: 16th century
Trogir, Church of St Nicholas: 16th century
Korčula, Gabrielis Palace: 16th century
Maribor, Town Hall: 16th century
Kotor, Pim Palace: 16th century
Ljubljana, Old town: 16th—19th centuries

ISLAMIC ARCHITECTURE

Skopje, Sultan Murat Mosque: 1436
Priština, Fatih Mosque: 1461
Skopje, Isa Bey Mosque: 1475
Skopje, Mustapha Pasha Mosque: 1492
Tetovo, Multi-Coloured Mosque: 1495
Skopje, Daut Pasha Baths: 1484—1497
Ram, Fortress: 1480—1512
Travnik, Fortress: 15th century
Tetovo, Turkish baths: 15th century
Sarajevo, Gazi Husrev Bey Mosque: 1530
Sarajevo, Gazi Husrev Bey School: 1537
Sarajevo, Gazi Husrev Bey Covered Market: 1540
Skopje, Kuršumli Inn: c. 1550
Foča, Aladža Mosque: 1550
Sarajevo, Brusa Covered Market: 1551
Mostar, Karadjoz Bey Mosque: 1557
Sarajevo, Ali Pasha Mosque: 1561
Mostar, Stone bridge: 1566
Pljevlja, Hussein Pasha Mosque: 1569
Čajniče, Sinan Bey Mosque: 1570
Višegrad, Mehmed Pasha Sokolović Bridge: 1571—1577
Banja Luka, Ferhad Pasha Mosque: 1579
Bihać, Captain's Tower: 16th century
Počitelj, Mosque: 16th century
Prizren, Sinań Pasha Mosque: 1615
Trebinje, Arslanagić Bridge: 16th—17th centuries
Niš, Fortress: 17th century
Tetovo, Arabat Baba Monastery: end of the 18th century
Travnik, Multi-Coloured Mosque: 19th century

THE PERIOD OF TURKISH RULE

Krušedol, Church of the Virgin: 1509—1914, frescoes: 1543, 1545,1750
Piva, Church of the Dormition of the Virgin: 1573—1586, frescoes: 1604—1606, 1926
Novo Hopovo, Church of St Nicholas, 1576, frescoes: 1609, 1654
Lomnica, Church of St George: 16th century, iconostasis: 1578—9, frescoes: 1580—1608

Banja near Priboj, Church of St Nicholas, frescoes: c. 1572

Plevlja, Church of the Holy Trinity: 16th century, frescoes: 1592—1595

Slepče, Church of St John the Forerunner: 16th century

Kablar, Church of the Annunciation: 1602

Zavala, Church of the Presentation to the Temple: 16th century, frescoes: 1618—19

Biogorski: Church of St John, Rastuša, 1800, wood-carving: 1830—1840

Skopje, Church of St Saviour, wood-carving: 1824

BAROQUE

Celje, Old County Hall, ceiling: 1600

Hvar, Cathedral: beginning of the 17th century

Zagreb, Church of St Catherine: 1620—1632

Varaždin, Church of the Dormition of the Virgin: 1622—1646

Ljubljana, Franciscan Church: 1646—1660

Varaždin, Church of St John the Baptist: 1650

Ljubljana, Fountain of the Kranjska rivers: 1660

Samobor, Church of St Anastasius: 1671—1675

Šmarje, Church of St Roch: 17th century

Rijeka, Castle of Trsat: 17th century

Split, Milesi Palace: 17th century

Dubrovnik, Cathedral: 1672—1713

Dubrovnik, Church of St Ignatius: 1699—1725

Poreč, Sinčić Palace: 17th century

Karlovac, Fortress: 17th century

Perast, Church of Our Lady of the Rocks: 17th century

Petrovaradin, Fortress: 17th—18th centuries

Ljubljana, Church of St Nicholas: 1700—1707

Dubrovnik, Church of St Blaise: 1706—1715

Korčula, Church of All Saints, ceiling: 1713

Ljubljana, Church of the Holy Trinity: 1716—1726

Ljubljana, Town Hall: 1718

Samobor, Church of the Virgin: 1722

Ljubljana, Portal of the Seminary: beginning of the 18th century

Bodjani, Church of the Presentation to the Temple: 1722, frescoes: 1737

Zemun, Church of St Nicholas: 1725—1731

Rovinj, Church of St Euphemia: 1736

Jazak, Church of the Holy Trinity: 1736—1758

Mala Remeta, Church of the Virgin: 1739

Belec, Church of Our Lady of the Snows: 1739—1741

Zagreb, Oršić-Rauch Palace: 1740—1780

Privina Glava, Church of SS Michael and Gabriel: 1741—1760

Zrenjanin, Church of the Dormition of the Virgin: 1744—1787

Rijeka, Town Tower: 18th century

Sladka Gora, Church of the Virgin: c. 1750

Krušedol, Church of the Virgin, wall paintings: 1750—1756

Ljubljana, Schweiger House: 1755

Novi Sad, Church of the Dormition of the Virgin: 1755

Šišatovac, Church of the Nativity of the Virgin: 1758—1778

Vršac, Bishop's Palace: 1759

Tunjice, Church of St Anne: 1761—1766

Maribor, Church of St Aloysius: 1769

Ljubljana, Gruber Palace: 1722

Zemun, Church of the Virgin: 1776—1780

Zrenjanin, Church of the Presentation to the Temple: 1777

Savina, Church of the Virgin: 1777—1799

Sremski Karlovci, Church of St Nicholas, iconostasis: 1781

Vršac, Church of St Nicholas: 1783—1784

Novi Sad, Almaška Church: end of the 18th century, iconostasis: 1810—1811

Štatemberg, Palace: 18th century

Dornava, Baroque Palace: 18th century

Kovilj, Monastery, Church of the Holy Archangel: 18th century

Osijek, Fortress: 18th century

Prčanj, Parish church: 18th—19th centuries

Zagreb, Pejačević Palace: 18th century

NINETEENTH AND TWENTIETH CENTURIES

Vrdnik, Church of the Ascension: 1801—1811

Pančevo, Church of the Dormition of the Virgin: 1807—1811

Zagreb, Ban's Residence: 1808

Belgrade, Princess Ljubica's Residence: 1829—1831

Belgrade, Secondary School: 1837

Cetinje, Biljarda: 1838

Belgrade, Cathedral: 1841

Sombor, Town Hall: 1842

Zemun, Špirta House: 1853

Vršac, Cethedral: 1860—1863

Novi Sad, Church of St Nicholas, iconostasis: 1862

Belgrade, Captain Miša's Foundation: 1863

Cetinje, Palace: 1863—1871

Osijek, Theatre: 1866

Arandjelovac, Old Edifice: 1868—1872

Pančevo, Church of the Transfiguration: 1874—1878

Zagreb, Yugoslav Academy of Science and Arts: 1876—1884

Belgrade, Old Royal Palace: 1882

Zagreb, Vranicani Palace: 1883

Belgrade, House of Aleksa Krsmanović: 1885
Zrenjanin, Town Hall: 1887
Zagreb, Museum of Arts and Crafts: 1888—1892
Belgrade, Nikola Spasić's Foundation: 1889
Belgrade, National Bank building: 1889
Sombor, Bačko-Bodroška District Hall: end of the 19th century
Ljubljana, Opera: 1892
Zagreb, Main Railway Station: 1892
Belgrade, Ministry of Justice: 1893
Osijek, Church of SS Peter and Paul: 1894—1898
Zagreb, Croatian National Theatre: 1895
Belgrade, Officers' Club: 1895
Belgrade, Old Lottery Building: 1896
Ljubljana, People's Centre: 1896
Čurug, Church of the Ascension, iconostasis: 1897
Zagreb, Arts Pavilion: 1898
Vršac, Town Hall: 19th century
Sremski Karlovci, Patriarch's Residence: 19th century
Subotica, Lenović Palace: 19th century
Subotica, Municipal Library: 19th century
Zagreb, Archaeological Museum: 19th century
Subotica, Synagogue: 1902
Belgrade, Funds Board Building: 1903
Subotica, Reichle Palace: 1904
Belgrade, Hotel „Moskva": 1906
Belgrade, Federal People's Assembly: 1906 (1937)
Belgrade, Third Belgrade Grammar School: 1906
Belgrade, Officers' Co-operative Society: 1908
Subotica, Town Hall: 1908—1910
Belgrade, Smederevo Bank: 1910
Cavtat, Mausoleum of the Račić family: 1923
Zagreb, Exchange: 1923—1927
Avala, Tomb of the Unknown Hero: 1934
Ljubljana, National and University Library: 1939

A

B

C

N

O

P

BIBLIOGRAPHY

G. Millet, L'ancien art serbe, Paris, 1917.

Gj. Szabo, Sredovječni gradovi u Hrvatskoj i Slavoniji, Zagreb, 1920.

F. Stelè, Oris zgodovine umetnosti pri Slovencih, Ljubljana, 1924.

V. Petrović — M. Kašanin, Srpska umetnost u Vojvodini, Novi Sad, 1921.

Karaman, Iz kolijevke hrvatske prošlosti, Zagreb, 1930.

Lj. Babić, Umjetnost kod Hrvata u XIX stoljeću, Zagreb, 1934.

F. Stelè, Monumenta artis Slovenicae I, Ljubljana, 1935.

F. Stelè, Monumenta artis Slovenicae II, Ljubljana, 1938.

M. Garašanin — J. Kovačević, Pregled materijalne kulture Južnih Slovena, Beograd, 1950.

Lj. Karaman, Pregled umjetnosti u Dalmaciji, Zagreb, 1952.

A. Deroko, Monumentalna i dekorativna arhitektura u srednjovekovnoj Srbiji, Beograd, 1953.

K. Prijatelj, Umjetnost 17 i 18 stoljeća u Dalmaciji, Zagreb, 1956.

M. Zadnikar, Romanska arhitektura na Slovenskem, Ljubljana, 1959.

F. Stelè, Umetnost v Primorju, Ljubljana, 1960.

V. Đurić, Ikone iz Jugoslavije, Beograd, 1961.

J. Korošec, Rimske iskopine v Šempetru, Ljubljana, 1961.

G. Subotić, Arhitektura i skulptura srednjeg veka u Primorju, Beograd, 1963.

B. Fučić, Istarske freske, Zagreb, 1963.

A. Deroko, Spomenici arhitekture IX—XVIII veka u Jugoslaviji, Beograd, 1964.

I. Zdravković, Izbor građe za proučavanje spomenika islamske arhitekture, Beograd, 1964.

Š. Bešlagić, Stećci u Jugoslaviji, Beograd, 1965.

S. Petković, Zidno slikarstvo na području Pećke patrijaršije 1557—1614, Novi Sad, 1965.

C. Fisković, Dalmatinske freske, Zagreb, 1965.

S. Radojčić, Staro srpsko slikarstvo, Beograd, 1966.

E. Cevc, Slovenska umetnost, Ljubljana, 1966.

Enciklopedija likovnih umjetnosti, I (1959), II (1962), III (1964), IV (1966).

N. Šumi, Arhitektura XVI stoljetja na Slovenskem, Ljubljana, 1966

A. Benac, Stećci, Beograd, 1967.

I. Redžić, Islamska umjetnost, Beograd, 1967.

P. Miljkovik-Pepek, Deloto na zografite Mihailo i Eutihij, Skopje, 1967.

I. Marasović, Dioklecijanova palača, Beograd, 1967.

D. Srejović, Lepenski Vir, Beograd, 1969.

N. Šumi, Baročna arhitektura, Ljubljana, 1969.

I. Komelj, Gotska arhitektura, Ljubljana, 1969.

M. Zadnikar, Romanska umetnost, Ljubljana, 1970.

Đ. Bošković — M. Mirković — M. Milošević i V. Popović, Sirmium, Beograd, 1971.

J. Maksimović, Srpska srednjovekovna skulptura, Novi Sad, 1971.

M. Garašanin, Đ. Mano-Zisi, Z. Vinski, S. Radojčić, M. Prelog, E. Cevc, K. Prijatelj, N. Miletić, M. Karamehmedović, F. Stelè, M. Kolarić i M. Protić, Umjetnost na tlu Jugoslavije od praistorije do danas, Beograd—Sarajevo, 1971.

A. Andrejević, Aladža džamija u Foči, Beograd, 1972.

M. Kolarić, Jugoslavija — putovanje kroz umetnost, Beograd, 1973.

V. Đurić, Vizantijske freske u Jugoslaviji, Beograd, 1974.

A. Horvat, Između gotike i baroka, Zagreb, 1975.

V. Kondić — V. Popović, Caričin grad, Beograd, 1977.

G. Tomašević, Ranovizantijski podni mozaici, Beograd, 1978.

C. Grozdanov, Ohridsko zidno slikarstvo XIV veka, Beograd, 1980.

G. Subotić, Ohridska slikarska škola XV veka, Beograd, 1980.

P. Mijović, Umjetničko blago Crne Gore, Beograd—Titograd, 1980.

D. Medaković, Srpska umetnost u XVIII veku, Beograd, 1980.

D. Medaković, Srpska umetnost u XIX veku, Beograd, 1981.

S. Radojčić, Srpska umetnost u srednjem veku, Beograd—Zagreb—Mostar, 1982.

M. Kolarić, Osvit novog doba (XIX vek), Beograd—Zagreb—Mostar, 1982.

K. Prijatelj, Dalmatinsko slikarstvo 15 i 16 stoljeća, Zagreb, 1983.

I. Petricioli, Tragom srednjovekovnih umjetnika, Zagreb, 1983.

M. Šuput, Srpska arhitektura u doba turske vlasti 1459—1690, Beograd, 1984.

A. Andrejević, Islamska monumentalna umetnost XVI veka u Jugoslaviji, Beograd, 1984.

V. Matić, Arhitektura fruškogorskih manastira, Novi Sad, 1984.

R. Ivančević — E. Cevc — A. Horvat, Gotika u Sloveniji i Hrvatskoj, Beograd—Zagreb—Mostar, 1984.

V. Marković, Zidno slikarstvo 17 i 18. stoljeća u Dalmaciji, Zagreb, 1985.

Đ. Cvitanović, Sakralna arhitektura baroknog razdoblja, knj. I, Zagreb, 1985.

R. Ivančević — K. Prijatelj — A. Horvat — N. Šumi, Renesansa u Hrvatskoj i Sloveniji, Beograd—Zagreb—Mostar, 1985.

ON THE AUTHOR

The author of this book, Dr. Lazar Trifunović, an eminent Yugoslav historian of art and art critic, was born in Belgrade in 1929. He graduated from the Faculty of Philosophy of the University of Belgrade in 1955 (History of Arts), and got his Ph. D. degree five years later, his doctoral thesis being a study of the Serbian painting of the first half of the 20th century. He became an assistant professor at the Faculty of Philosophy in Belgrade in 1957, and he was appointed professor of the History of Modern Art at the Belgrade University in 1976. Between 1962 and 1967 he was also the director of the National Museum in Belgrade.

The main field of L. Trifunović's research was the Serbian and Yugoslav art of the 20th century. In addition to a number of shorter studies, he published the following books: *Srpsko slikarstvo 1900—1950* (Serbian Painting 1900—1950), Belgrade, 1973, 534 pp.: *Stvarnost i mit u slikarstvu Milana Konjovića* (Reality and Myth in the Painting of Milan Konjović), Sombor, 1978, 217 pp.; *Od impresionizma do enformela* (From Impressionism to Enformel), Belgrade 1982: *Slikarstvo Miće Popovića* (The Painting of Mića Popović), Belgrade, 1983, 309 pp., and others. He was the leading Serbian art critic for almost three decades and he published his critical reviews in the *NIN, Umetnost, Politika* and other periodicals and dailies. He was also interested in the developments preceding the modern era of Serbian art and the studied them in several books: *Djura Jakšić, pesnik i slikar* (Djura Jakšić, Poet and Painter), Belgrade, 1984, 184 pp.; *Petar Ubavkić,* Belgrade, 1973, 239 pp.; and *Srpska crtačko-slikarska i umetničko-zanatska škola* (The Serbian School of Drawing, Painting and Applied Arts), Belgrade, 1978, 339 pp.

Dr. L. Trifunović was also interested in European art, particularly that of the present century, and he published two books on that subject: *Galerija evropskih majstora* (A Gallery of European Masters), Belgrade, 1963, 120 pp.; and *Slikarski pravci XX veka* (Trends in the 20th century Painting). He died in Paris in 1983.

PHOTOGRAPHS

Mile Đorđević
D. Manolev
M. Pavić
V. Dariš
M. Pohte-Dariš
J. Stojković
D. Srejović
A. Jovanović
Photo »Jugoslovenska Revija« (P. Batrić, J. Bešić, Bešić-Sikimić, Bevičini, K. Bilbilovski B. Boroš, B. Budimovski, Drnkov, D. Jovanović, D. Manolev, M. Pavić I. Pervan, B. Turin)
Photo »Turistička štampa« (P. Batrić, Ž. Ćirić, N. Gagović, M. Matić, G. Simonović)
Serbian Institute for the Protection of Monuments
IRO »Prosveta« OOUR Izdavačka delatnost

Front cover
Sopoćani, frescoe, St John

Back cover
Lepenski Vir, sculpture
Zgošća, stećak
Split, Diocletian's Palace, prothyron
Ohrid, The Church of St John the Divine Kaneo
Mileševa, frescoe, St Sava
Ljubljana, The Fountain of the Kranjska Rivers

Page 3
Royal door, Annunciation, XVI century, Belgrade, National Museum

Page 5
Ohrid, icon, Annunciation

Page 9
Resava

Page 53
Poreč, mosaic, Euphrasius

CONTENTS

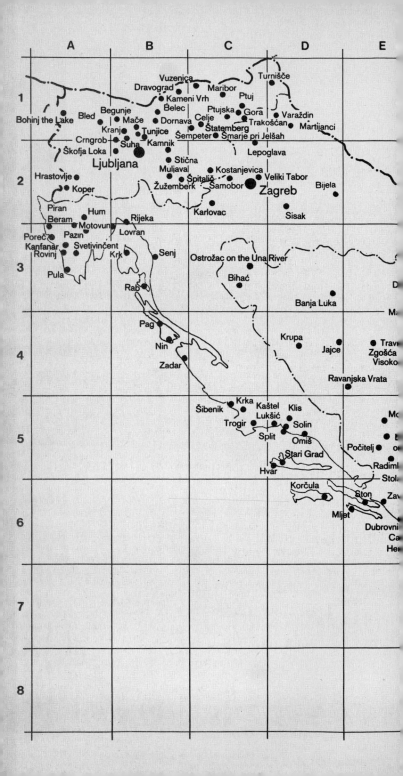